# GOD THE REAL SUPERPOWER

# GOD THE REAL SUPERPOWER

## Rethinking Our Role in Missions

*Nancy,*
*God's continued blessing!*

*12/11/12*

## J. NELSON JENNINGS

**P&R PUBLISHING**

P.O. BOX 817 • PHILLIPSBURG • NEW JERSEY 08865-0817

Printed in the United States of America

**Library of Congress Cataloging-in-Publication Data**

Jennings, J. Nelson.
God the real superpower : rethinking our role in missions / J. Nelson Jennings.
    p. cm.
Includes bibliographical references and indexes.
ISBN-13: 978-1-59638-023-3 (pbk.)
1. Missions—Theory—Biblical teaching. 2. Evangelistic work—Biblical teaching. 3. Bible. N.T. Peter—Criticism, interpretation, etc. I. Title.
BS2795.6.E82J46 2007
266—dc22
                                    2007017264

*This book is dedicated to the next generation of American church leaders.*
*May God grant them grace to suffer well.*

# Contents

CONTENTS

# Foreword

During a speaking tour through the United States in 1963, the famous German Lutheran theologian Helmut Thielicke, banned from the pulpit by state authorities in the early 1940s for his anti-Nazi sermons, courteously and eloquently opined that Americans do not know very well how to suffer. While here, he was repeatedly asked what he considered to be "the most important question of our time." Thielicke's answer was, astonishingly, that he thought the most pressing thing, at least for Americans, was to learn suffering as a way of life in a fallen world. He praised our "can-do" optimism but criticized our inclination to try to fix everything we don't like. When I first came across those remarks in his book *Between Heaven and Earth: Conversations with American Christians*,[1] I was deeply moved, sensing that he was right and that it was an important theme to come to grips with as a Christian. I still read that little piece from time to time, almost thirty years later, and it still rings too true—in my life and in these United States.

In the book you have just picked up, Dr. Nelson Jennings is calling American Christians to the same thing. He's inviting us, after the example of the apostle Peter, to take up our place as Christ's followers and suffer even as our Savior suffered. But what I hope intrigues and then engages you as you read is Professor Jennings's suggestion that the particular *form* our suffering might take as American Christians is a relinquishing of some of the power and control that our nation—with its wealth and resources, its prestige and its bravado—has mastered so well and is known

---

1. Trans. and ed. John W. Doberstein (New York: Harper and Row, 1965).

for exercising so readily throughout the world. It seems to be part of our instinct as Americans to want to jump into the driver's seat.

When I read the first draft of Nelson's book, I found myself wondering whether American readers especially would think him annoyingly preachy and condescending in his insistence that God rather than the United States is the true Superpower in the world. All serious Christians know that. But then I recalled my own history and realized that we don't always know very well in our experience what we know very well in our doctrine. As a young man I came to *learn*, by the mercy of God, that the United States is the center neither of the world nor of history; that it is not the divinely designated leader among the nations; and that Christ should be shaping me much more than the national ethos should be, however much—and rightly—I love my motherland. All of this felt, at the time, like a very dramatic revelation to me.

It was 1969–70, my first year in college and the turbulent era of the national moratorium against the war in Vietnam, Nixon's bombing of Cambodia, and the National Guard's killing of four students at Kent State University. I was on the verge of accepting an appointment to the United States Military Academy at West Point, having seen through all the left-wing silliness on campus about burning down the Establishment so that the higher-minded could take over and bring bliss. Doctrinally I was committed to the proposition that "Jesus is Lord," but practically I thought the only alternative to the gospel of the Left was another gospel, the vision and agenda of the political Right. So I threw myself into that alternative with passion at Rutgers University, a hotbed of radicalism at the time. And part of the "passion" was hating the Left because they were the enemy.

But then I was invited to a spring-break beach-ministry project in Florida. It was during that week that the Sovereign Lord of all things reached down into my life and opened my eyes to the lordship of Jesus Christ over every political polarity, over every party and national loyalty, and over my own proud and reactionary heart. How good it felt to see! It was transforming, humbling, and even exciting. In the end, I chose not to go to the Academy, that venerable institution and symbol of American military power that I had loved and visited so often growing up, and had held in awe. Instead, I transferred to a university in the Midwest and began to think seriously about pursuing some type of Christian ministry because, well, if Jesus is the real Superpower, I wanted to be learning his policies and working in his campaign.

Some readers might be bothered by the notion of God as Superpower, considering it a just-to-be-clever mixing up of categories—the political and the religious. But we would do well to remember that the cross of Christ was at the heart of just such a mixing up when the church began. Imagine for a moment how jarring it would be for us moderns to try to think of the electric chair as a religious symbol—if, for instance, members of some cult started wearing miniature electric chairs on gold chains around their necks in honor of their founder who had died strapped to one. What a mix-up of social categories we would find it! Likewise, to first-century sensibilities in the Roman Empire, the cross was anything but a symbol of religious faith and spiritual power. Crucifixion was a perverse torture that evoked shame and revulsion. The great Roman statesman Cicero, who died in 43 B.C., once said that a Roman citizen should never mention or even *think of* a cross. Yet the cross became for the early Christians the supreme symbol of their convictions, their comfort, and their hope—indeed, of their joy in the love of God.

In relative political terms, the United States *is* a superpower. During the Cold War years, the Soviet Union enjoyed the same status, and the great geopolitical drama in those days played out with these two superpowers poised in mutual mistrust and antagonism. In these days, some argue that America is the only real superpower left in the world, though others put China right up there "at the top" with us. But Professor Jennings is right to challenge us as Christians to go back and think in absolute terms, according to the Scriptures, about who is and who isn't a "superpower" because if we are always thinking in relative terms, we start forgetting that they are not absolute. Of course, people speak in relative terms all the time, as they did in Jesus' day. So the rich young ruler comes to the Lord and asks, "Good Teacher, what must I do to inherit eternal life?" (Luke 18:18). But Jesus sees the question as the opportunity for a teaching moment and decides to speak in absolute terms. He rejoins, "Why do you call me good? No one is good except God alone" (18:19). Touché. That answer had to clarify a few things for the fellow!

In absolute terms, there is no Superpower except God, and the United States is, as all nations are, "as nothing before him" (Isa. 40:17). That has to clarify a few things for us American Christians, used to taking for granted our country's remarkable military might and political clout, and usually assuming its goodwill in the world. And it seems to me that this consideration becomes even more important for Christians, not less, if the historical judgment of political conservatives, such as Charles Krauthammer, about America is true. Krauthammer, in a recent op-ed piece, wrote that "peace and prosperity" in the West "do not come with the air we breathe, but are maintained by power—once the power of the British Empire, now the power of the United States."[2]

But how can we learn to relativize our national strengths, and those things that might even be our superiorities? And how can we find our weaknesses? How can we become convinced that we have things to learn from other peoples and Christians in other nations? Dr. Jennings points us in the right direction, and I cannot endorse more strongly his plea in this book for American Christians to become more global in their connections to people. While reading, I realized how rich had been my own upbringing by simple, unsophisticated, patriotic American-Christian parents who traveled very little, yet turned their suburban home in northern New Jersey into a kind of global pension. I live now as a follower of Jesus Christ with deep impressions made on me in my youth by those who lived in our home for a time: Gary, the Canadian Bible school student; Victor, the graduate student from Ghana; Pastor Chi, a gentle man from Malaysia who knew how to cook; Chung Ha, the Buddhist high school exchange teacher from Korea who for a year slept in the bed next to mine; Evelyn, a Puerto Rican girl who just needed some love and a place to belong; Afzal and his wife, Mary, aristocratic Afghani Muslims who fled Kabul in 1979 when the Soviets invaded their country. There were political refugees from Laos, from Poland, from Bosnia, and from who knows where else. There were visits from a Dutch Christian Jewish pastor who had survived Nazi torture in a concentration camp. Some were believers

2. "Why I Love Australia," Washington Post, June 23, 2006, available online at: http://www.washingtonpost.com/wp-dyn/content/article/2006/06/22/AR2006062201468.html.

in Jesus; many were not. Many spoke English; a few didn't. But it was enormously helpful to know them all, to glimpse in them something of the glory of their own motherland and culture, and something familiarly human—something very much like me. Beyond that, the deep connection my family immediately felt with those who were believers became powerful testimony in my teenage experience to the biblical doctrine that Christians everywhere, before they are citizens of any country, representatives of any culture in this earthly, temporal order of things, are fellow citizens of the kingdom of heaven.

It gives me pleasure to write this foreword for my dear friend and colleague, for whom I have affection and great respect. Nelson was one of the first seminary students in the church we planted when I was a young (= green) pastor in the early 1980s. How delighted we were to receive him and his family back into our fellowship here in St. Louis in 1999 after a thirteen-year hiatus that had taken him to Nagoya, Japan, as a missionary; then to Edinburgh for Ph.D. work; and back to Japan again, as a professor at Tokyo Christian University. Nelson has taught me to think globally; to focus less on what is familiar and comfortable than on what is true and faithful to the gospel; to desire and pray for and strive for that Spirit-given maturity that teaches disciples of Jesus everywhere to love their country but always to keep a critical distance from its policies and prejudices, for the Lord's sake. In his consistently cheerful, gentle way he prods me and the American Christians whom he loves so to bring our presumptions and preconceptions, our star-spangled vision of things out into the open where Christ can illumine and then reform them for the sake of *his* nation, the church across the whole wide world, which he, at least, still thinks of as one, and as superior to any nation on earth—only for his grace that fills it.

Ron Lutjens
Old Orchard Church
St. Louis, Missouri

# Acknowledgments

It is no small formality to say that many dear people have helped with this book project. First are the members of the Covenant Theological Seminary board for granting me a sabbatical leave to focus on research and writing. During my absence from normal seminary duties, various members of the administration and faculty helped to cover my vacated responsibilities. I will rightly single out my world mission administrative assistant, Julie Taylor; others as well helped tremendously.

The Covenant library staff provided their usual competent assistance in acquiring several interlibrary materials. I appreciate also being able to use the library facilities of Washington University in St. Louis and the Day Missions Library at Yale Divinity School.

Marvin Padgett, Eric Anest, and others at P&R Publishing have been a pleasure to work with in getting the book to press. I owe them much for their flexibility, encouragement, and assistance.

Many friends, colleagues, and students have given significant input (often unwittingly) into the book's ideas as the work took shape over the years. I am most grateful for their passion for the gospel and for their lives as Jesus' followers.

Several friends, at my request, offered feedback on a first draft: Sayo Ajiboye, Hans Bayer, Fred Bendick, Sasha Bukovietski, Oliver Claassen, Randy Mayfield, Kelli McKie, Clark McNutt, Jessica Patterson, Lani and Rene Quimbo, Peter Reynolds, John Rollo, Ann and Bill Teachout, and my wife, Kathy. Each person's comments added significantly to the final product, and I cannot imagine producing this book without these friends' invaluable help. Thank you all so much for your time and energy!

My heartfelt thanks go as well to Ron Lutjens for his feedback, as well as for graciously writing the book's foreword. Thanks to Rick Matt and Beth Ann Brown of Covenant Seminary, who gave constructive editing suggestions for both early and late drafts of the manuscript.

I, of course, assume responsibility for the book's contents, particularly including its weak spots and flaws, both large and small.

My deepest gratitude is to our King and Leader, Jesus, for his full commitment to make his world right and for including frail people in that mission process.

# Introduction

During his life and especially his death, Jesus Christ suffered. He was misunderstood, mocked, and mistreated, and despite being completely innocent Jesus was horrifically executed as a criminal. Through it all he suffered rejection and abandonment by his heavenly Father—in order to take away the world's sin, all out of divine mercy and love. On top of everything Christ suffered willingly, without fighting back.

This same Jesus Christ who suffered also rose from the dead, reigns over the universe, lives with his people by his Holy Spirit, and is coming again as Savior and Judge. We who are his followers thus have a sure hope of salvation, not only for ourselves but for the whole created order. For now, life in this world is full of suffering and trials. Even so, in light of Christ's suffering, Christians are free to serve others and to declare God's greatness and goodness.

That, in a nutshell, is the Christ-centered message of 1 Peter. Yes, we Christians suffer, but "Christ also suffered" (2:21). I believe this message about Jesus' suffering and what it means for Christians' suffering is especially pertinent for how American Christians are to be involved in Christian missions today. Because the relationship between the message of 1 Peter, missions, and American Christians is so important and relevant, the various facets of that relationship constitute the overall subject of this book. Frankly speaking, apart from God's pointed grace we American Christians can unwittingly assume that we run the missions show. To transform that tendency, this book's ambitious goal is to sharpen our sensibilities about how God is at work in the world and how—particularly here in the early twenty-first century—we are to cooperate with him.

1

We will unpack the whole matter by considering five themes, with two chapters devoted to each. The themes first of all come out of 1 Peter. The apostle Peter was writing, in the early to mid-60s, to Christians scattered throughout the western half of present-day Turkey. Because we cannot be sure precisely when Peter wrote the letter, it is hard to tell whether Peter was specifically referencing Roman persecution under Emperor Nero in A.D. 64. In any case, the scattered Christians were dealing with unfriendly environments that were not conducive to Christian godliness. Uncertainty about their faith, social pressure to conform, and timidity as Christ's followers were among the struggles they faced, perhaps along with threats to their property and very lives. The sufferings these believers experienced were thus both internal and external.

As they endured such sufferings, Peter encouraged them to consider—and here is where the book's five themes emerge—that their "faith and hope are in God" (1:21), the One who is good and mighty. They could draw further encouragement from knowing that their sufferings were also shared by the Christian "brotherhood throughout the world" (5:9). They were therefore to live honorably "among the Gentiles" (2:12), namely, their unbelieving neighbors, not off in quarantined seclusion. Part of their collective witness among others was to be the way in which they would mutually "serve one another" (4:10). They were also to persevere "throughout the time of [their] exile" (1:17), knowing that the Christ who had exemplified godly suffering would return in triumph and with salvation for all his people.

The book's five themes have crystallized as well out of my interactions over several years with local churches, seminary students, and other Christian leaders in the United States. Those interactions have taken place against the backdrop of my having lived a major portion of my adult life outside the United States, plus traveling during recent years to nearly twenty different countries. Corresponding to the five quotations from 1 Peter, then, the book's themes are:

- God is the mission Superpower. (1:21)
- The church is international. (5:9)
- God has sent the church into the world's various contexts. (2:12)

- Christian missions should be multidirectional. (4:10)
- Christian missions are ongoing within the world's various contexts. (1:17)

I believe these themes are particularly important for U.S. Christians to work through as we consider how to build constructively on a wonderful if imperfect missions heritage. Since the early 1800s, American missionaries and missions agencies have unselfishly contributed to serving gospel causes all around the world. Countless people everywhere can point to how God has used American Christians to bring the news of Jesus Christ within their reach. Of course, none of these results are cause for pride or boasting in any human achievement. All gospel progress is by God's grace, and American missions efforts have included many mistakes that can be easily pointed out—something that many have been all too eager to do. The celebration is of God's power and goodness as we see how he has used frail human beings for his own honor and glory and for the good of millions of people in need of gospel ministry.

Now in the early twenty-first century, American missions face fresh opportunities and challenges. The church of Jesus Christ is more worldwide and interconnected than ever before. At the same time, the United States of America is more internationally powerful and active than ever before. As always, the triune God of the Bible remains actively in charge of his entire world. This book's primary concern is how we American Christians, in response to God's initiative and in cooperation with Christian citizens of other countries, can best carry out our God-given missions responsibilities in today's world—including within the United States itself.

The book is primarily aimed at an American audience, and I have written as an American to Americans. Yet others should also be able to benefit because both the book's subject and Americans' influence through Christian missions have a worldwide scope. It is important to note as well that by *Americans* I am talking about citizens of the United States of America. Others, too, lay just claim to the same designation (e.g., Brazilians and Nicaraguans). Even so, we *Americans* commonly use the term in reference only to ourselves, and many others around the world also use the term in that way. Please remember, in the name of accuracy and of sensitivity, that my use of the familiar designation *Americans* refers to "U.S. Americans."

Along the way we will encounter many subtleties and nuances that will require us to be deliberate and careful. The book will therefore be more of a study than a quick and light read, embodying the struggle and suffering to be learned from 1 Peter. I should note as well that, while arranging the material around five coherent themes, I have not been driven by a strictly logical progression. Rather, I have sought to present things in a way that will have the most personal impact, so the book's discussion proceeds according to how I anticipate readers will process the material. In general, the book will move from the level of assumption and attitude to that of application and action—although these two categories cannot be neatly separated, and thus each will appear during consideration of the other.

To facilitate processing and application of the material, at the end of each chapter there are reflection questions. Two appendices have been included to elaborate on important subjects that some readers might want to pursue further. The book is designed to be either read individually or used by a group, whether in a formal classroom, university student group, informal study setting, church leadership team, Sunday school class, or missions committee.

We are not dealing with trivial matters. Jesus' suffering, Christian missions, and how we as Americans relate to both matters deserve our utmost attention. God remains on the initiative to remake the whole world, and he desires to shape and use all his followers in that process. May he particularly help those of us who are American Christians in our service—and suffering—for the Christ who suffered for the whole world.

# THEME 1

## "Your Faith and Hope Are in God"
### (1 Peter 1:21)

# 1

# God Is the Mission Superpower

"Christ also suffered" (1 Peter 2:21). With these words Peter directs his readers' attention to Jesus. The whole Bible, in fact, points to Jesus Christ as Christians' everyday preoccupation. And as indicated by Christianity's best-known symbol, the cross, at the center of our field of vision is to be Christ's *suffering*.

Peter's original readers knew suffering all too well. These followers of Jesus were scattered throughout Asia Minor at the eastern end of the Roman Empire. They experienced the unnerving suspicion directed toward any unauthorized minority religious movement. Made scapegoats of the A.D. 64 fire in Rome, they and Christians throughout the empire suffered persecution under Emperor Nero.[1] That their suffering was unjust only compounded their discouragement.

It was into that bitter experience that Peter sent his encouraging message: no matter how unjust or painful the Christians' suffering was, they could rest assured that Jesus Christ had also suffered. Indeed, his suffering had been even more unjust than theirs, since "he committed no sin, neither was deceit found in his mouth" (2:22). Christians could be further encouraged by knowing that in suffering honorably they were following Jesus' example: "When he was reviled, he did not revile in

---

1. As noted in the introduction, we do not know exactly when Peter wrote his letter in relation to the persecution of A.D. 64.

return; when he suffered, he did not threaten, but continued entrusting himself to him who judges justly" (2:23).

Most importantly, Christ's suffering had been a substitutionary sacrifice, "the righteous for the unrighteous, that he might bring us to God" (3:18). Peter's graphic description was that "he himself bore our sins in his body on the tree, that we might die to sin and live to righteousness. By his wounds you have been healed" (2:24). With the penalty of their sin thus paid for, and as those who were undergoing the healing transformation of learning to live as God's new people, these minority Christians could thus "suffer according to God's will [and] entrust their souls to a faithful Creator while doing good" (4:19).

## Suffering as American Christians

All Christians, of any era, can relate to Christ's substitutionary death. That definitive defeat of sin's penalty and power—a victory guaranteed by Jesus' resurrection—has freed all believers to know and serve God personally. It has also broken the back of the societal curse under which "the whole creation has been groaning" (Rom. 8:22) ever since Adam and Eve's fall into sin. With respect, then, to Jesus' unique suffering as the Sacrificial Lamb of God, American Christians certainly can, must, and do relate.

There is an obvious gap, however, between the suffering that Peter's original readers faced and what we contemporary Americans experience (or do not experience). Because we do not suffer persecution and sociopolitical suspicion the way they did, we might find it hard to relate to the Christian suffering that 1 Peter addresses so prominently. How, then, should we American Christians apply that type of suffering to our lives today?

### Challenges

I believe one crucial aspect of what the suffering in 1 Peter means for us American Christians today, particularly in relation to missions, is the call to relinquish our assumed and subconscious control, rights, and privileges with respect to God and to other people. Internally we must wrestle with inherited instincts that, feeding off sinful human

8

self-centeredness, make us assume that the American way of life, along with American Christianity (at least our particular form of it), should be the world's standard and template. Externally we must wrestle with the implications of the actual economic-political-military superpower status of our country in today's world. That status on the one hand affords American Christians the financial and security resources to travel internationally as missionaries in ways that many other Christians cannot even imagine. One resulting problem is that American Christians might confuse being able to *afford to travel* abroad with a missionary *call to go* abroad (especially with regard to the recent flood of short-term missions, a subject we will pick up later). Also, much of the rest of the world has a conflicted and multifaceted resentful/admiring posture toward Americans and the United States. That widespread posture is due to the fact that individually and nationally we Americans freely exercise various forms of the control, rights, and privileges afforded us in our superpower status: our individual and corporate financial investments bring us earnings as they send material and cultural products worldwide; our military provides security for many countries while posing a threat to others; in general, our individual and national presence around the world leaves few human beings untouched by American influence, be it good, bad, or neutral.

Wrestling with these internal and external challenges is no simple matter. We must be wary on the one hand of our postmodern, multiculturalist environment. Religiously, that environment seeks to strip Jesus Christ and the Christian faith of any claims to exclusivity or uniqueness. Politically, postmodern and multiculturalist agendas can go to the extreme of criticizing any exercise of power (while using political power themselves), irrespective of that power's legitimacy. These emasculating religious and political attacks must be discerned, honestly appraised, and properly dealt with. Furthermore, we who are American Christians must not let ourselves off the hook, or at all dampen our zeal, as we play our parts in the ongoing responsibility of the worldwide church in serving Christ in his mission to save the world. Relinquishing our control, rights, and privileges within these circumstances is no small, easy, or crystal-clear task.

9

The challenge of the 1 Peter type of suffering also comes from its unfamiliarity to us. American Christians are living and serving in a new day: attitudes and actions associated with missions therefore cannot be exactly the same today as they were two hundred, one hundred, fifty, or even ten years ago. A fundamental reality that we will examine later is that, thanks be to God, the church is more worldwide than ever before. Moreover, today's post-9/11, post–Cold War, post-colonial, technologically interconnected, and ever-urbanizing world presents missions challenges unforeseeable to our predecessors. Of course, some attitudes and actions should always remain the same because God's covenantal commitment to his needy world remains the same: lost people always need to hear about Jesus, Christ's worldwide church always needs to grow and mature, and the wider aspects of God's *shalom* (peace, wholeness, and blessing) always need to be stressed throughout the world's societies. But specifically how God will use and shape his people, including American Christians, in meeting those needs will change along with how the world changes.

## Clarification

In studying 1 Peter, we will primarily focus on only one particular facet of what we might call an American "missiology of suffering." As I hope to demonstrate, relinquishing what we assume to be ours is a matter of basic and wide-ranging importance. As the book progresses, we will also delve into a related aspect of suffering as American Christians—namely, that which can come from thinking critically, listening well to others, and speaking prophetically about the prevailing U.S. sociopolitical environment (as part of our missions responsibility). Suffering associated with such ventures consists of having a humbling lack of clarity or certainty; of experiencing inner confusion about our own patriotism; and of being misunderstood or even opposed by those who see us as being overly critical. While sociopolitical themes should be unmistakable when we take them up, our study's ongoing emphasis will be that of giving up our presumed control, rights, and privileges in relation to God and others.

Other facets of suffering are pertinent to Americans and missions, including the need to co-suffer with, or to have *com-passion* for, believers and others throughout the world who live in oppressive sociopolitical contexts resembling that of 1 Peter's original readers. Another is suffering alongside the world's poor and marginalized, including orphans and widows—"religion that is pure and undefiled" (James 1:27). More space could also be given to the suffering required to see that unreached peoples hear the gospel and are gathered into the fold of God's people. The apostle Paul refers to such hardships that he endured in gospel ministry: "Now I rejoice in my sufferings for your sake, and in my flesh I am filling up what is lacking in Christ's afflictions for the sake of his body, that is, the church" (Col. 1:24). These are all crucial aspects of a "suffering missiology."

While in no way do I want to diminish the importance of these other types of suffering, suffering the loss of our assumed exclusive control, rights, and privileges cuts across the whole range of American involvements in worldwide missions. This is because it is a form of suffering that deals with a subliminal American view of the world, which all of us U.S. Christians have absorbed in our own individual ways. There are both good and bad, right and wrong, positive and negative elements in such a view. Much of this book's focus will be on exposing relevant hues and patterns embedded within certain American assumptions, as well as on inserting new colors and designs to invigorate us for twenty-first-century missions service.

This form of suffering as American Christians involves more than a one-time intellectual, emotional, and volitional acknowledgment of God's sovereign control over our lives. It is a complex process of growth in Christ that involves uncovering and dealing with deeply held assumptions and attitudes, then reforming some of our corresponding actions. Indeed, we have already entered a vital stage of the process by setting the framework of what this type of suffering means for us in the contemporary United States. By focusing here on twenty-first-century American Christians' suffering as an ongoing process of relinquishing our assumed and subconscious control, rights, and privileges with respect to God and to other people, we have identified the root from which the rest of the book's discussion can grow.

11

## Suffering in 1 Peter

Let's focus some more on connecting this understanding of our suffering with 1 Peter. In Peter's words, we American Christians are among those who

> were ransomed from the futile ways inherited from your forefathers, not with perishable things such as silver or gold, but with the precious blood of Christ, like that of a lamb without blemish or spot. He was foreknown before the foundation of the world but was made manifest in the last times for your sake, who through him are believers in God, who raised him from the dead and gave him glory, so that your faith and hope are in God. (1:18–21)

Many American Christians trace our national ancestries to northwestern Europe. Our forefathers were not all bad, but religiously speaking, the way of life we would have inherited from them was "futile." God by his grace brought (several centuries ago for most of us) the good news of Jesus' person and work into our heritages. We trust and hope in God, not in ourselves or our ancestors, because our salvation is all of his grace in Christ.

Furthermore, we are among those who are now "a chosen race, a royal priesthood, a holy nation, a people for *his* own possession, that you may proclaim the excellencies of *him* who called you out of darkness into *his* marvelous light" (2:9). Left to ourselves, we "were straying like sheep, but [by God's grace] have now returned to the Shepherd and Overseer of [our] souls" (2:25). It thus makes perfect sense for all of us who are Jesus' followers to heed Peter's instruction to "humble yourselves, therefore, under the mighty hand of God so that at the proper time he may exalt you, casting all your anxieties on him, because he cares for you" (5:6–7).

*Suffering* for American Christians thus includes learning to rest in God's work—not my, our, or any other individual's or group's efforts—of saving all his people. It also includes giving him all the credit for achieving that salvation. Put differently, for us to "die to sin and live to righteousness" (2:24) includes increasingly believing that God alone has all the control, rights, and privileges in saving all his people, across all generations and national boundaries.

## Suffering's Complexity

Yet such resting in God and giving him his due credit are not as simple or straightforward for Americans as they might appear, especially in relation to missions. To see the complexity of what we are talking about, let's examine three interrelated, ambiguous, but plausible statements that Americans might legitimately make.

1. "*We* don't suffer as *they* do." Similar to the gap we feel between our inexperience of persecution and what Peter's original readers suffered, we American Christians are not persecuted for our faith (at least in a coercive, political sense) as are Christians in some other parts of the world. In colloquial language, we've got it easy, but in countries such as China and Saudi Arabia they've got it tough. We thus thank God for the freedom we have to worship openly without fear of reprisal and persecution, and we also pray for those who do not have that same freedom.

In related fashion, Americans regularly receive reports of grinding poverty and disease throughout other parts of the world, from the Caribbean to Africa to south Asia. While domestically there are isolated exceptions to be sure, Americans enjoy a different, comfortable level of affluence and good health as a result of having the world's most powerful economy, coupled with long-term and extensive immunizations (backed by advanced medical technology).

Furthermore, American military might is second to none. On the one hand, the terrorist attacks of September 11, 2001, shattered America's immunity to the brutality that presumably occurred only elsewhere. Part of the psychospiritual trauma that Americans underwent from 9/11 was the capacity of outsiders to strike at our most symbolic sites, which had stood securely within our own borders. Even so, America's military strength has enabled our country to take the lead in waging the worldwide war on terror, including a new devotion to homeland security, in an attempt to purge the world of terrorism as well as to recover a pre-9/11 sense of domestic security against enemy attack.

All three of these conditions—freedom from religious persecution, health and prosperity, military security—are indeed to be highly valued and appreciated. The American heritage built and passed down from the sacrifices of earlier generations should be treasured and by no means taken lightly. At the same time, out of that gratitude comes the temptation to attach a normative, universal standard to our heritage. Speaking honestly, we might feel that good conditions in other countries cannot quite measure up to what we enjoy in the United States, let alone be better. And if others do happen to approach our standards, we will outcompete them. Hence the "American way of life," including our brand of socio-economic-political-religious "freedom" that is to be protected at all costs, can become the ultimate goal toward which we believe all other human societies should aspire, helped along by our not-so-subtle encouragement.

Consequently, such an assumed unique and normative status of the American way of life is problematic for American Christians in relinquishing our assumed and subconscious control, rights, and privileges with respect to God and to other people.

2. *"We* don't suffer." Along with the real and perceived quality-of-life gap between the United States and many other countries is an understanding that Americans do not suffer poverty, persecution, and related maladies. Put positively, we assume that Americans enjoy comfortable and peaceful lives, all under the just and fair administration of the rule of law. This understanding is in large measure true: the U.S. government is stable, the economy is productive, and most of us enjoy far more than the bare necessities of life.

Yet there are and have been significant exceptions. The catastrophe of Hurricane Katrina exposed ugly socio-economic-political fault lines. Past tragedies, such as the Civil War and the twentieth-century institutionalized racism confronted in the civil rights movement, are living legacies. There was persecution of religious minorities during the colonial period, during which time religious toleration was legally still being forged.

Still today thousands of Americans live under the poverty line, are homeless, have little or no health care, or are otherwise outside the mainstream prosperous lifestyle. Law enforcement can take on different qualities depending on the particular community in which it is exercised. Some of us tangibly suffer from discrimination and other forms of socioeconomic disenfranchisement. To imagine otherwise is to glorify our imperfect U.S. society.

3. "*Missions* involves suffering." In reference to missions, one widespread assumption is that American missionaries sacrifice a great deal by living and serving elsewhere. Along with the reduced incomes that all religious workers allegedly receive, U.S. missionaries leave the comforts of the American way of life that we have just been describing. Missionary children miss out on going to school in the United States, and missionary families are separated from their extended families in America. The suffering and sacrifice are filled out by having to live in societies that bear deprivation, disease, and disaster not encountered in the United States.

These assumptions are strengthened by noting the toil and sacrifice of such early American missionaries as the very first to serve abroad, Adoniram Judson (1788–1850, Burma) and the Southern Baptist stalwart Lottie Moon (1840–1912, China). Many U.S. missionaries have even suffered martyrdom, from Jim Elliot and the other "Auca Martyrs" to more recent deaths in the southern Philippines, the Middle East, and other volatile settings.[2]

People in other parts of the world often note the sacrifice that American missionaries make in leaving a higher standard of living. When asked why they would do such a thing, U.S. missionaries have a golden opportunity to give testimony to the love of God in Jesus Christ that would motivate them to share that same love with others.

Yet there is a flip side to this notion of missionary sacrifice, a flip side that counteracts a one-sided view of U.S. missionary experience as only loss and deprivation. First is the adventure of cross-cultural living. Experiencing different people, foods, customs, and societies often carries an incomparable richness that most missionaries find broadening and even exhilarating. Besides the experience of a *different* culture, the particular culture that a missionary enters has peculiar

2. Information is readily available about these and other well-known missionary figures. One convenient biographical source is Ruth A. Tucker, *From Jerusalem to Irian Jaya: A Biographical History of Christian Missions*, 2nd ed. (Grand Rapids: Zondervan, 2004).

delights and beauties that are wonderful to enjoy—festivals or social interaction, food or sports, a unique history or particular friends. Living in a different setting also brings new insights into American life, through comparison and reflection. As for children, the experience (often involving multiple languages) of growing up with American parents in a different country is usually a great privilege and benefit for the children's entire lives.

Our assumptions, then, concerning the sacrifice connected with missions cut both ways in our coming to grips, as twenty-first-century American Christians, with our assumed and subconscious control, rights, and privileges with respect to God and to other people. Hence suffering in the way we are considering it here is a complex process.

## God's *Mission* and Our *Missions*

I believe that fundamental to our being able to suffer the loss, as Christ's followers in the United States, of our assumed and subconscious control, rights, and privileges is to make a healthy distinction between *mission* and *missions*. These two terms are often used interchangeably. Some of us also use the plural form in a singular way—for example, in the grammatically challenged statement above that "*Missions* involves suffering." We speak a great deal about *missions* and seem to know what we mean—but do we? Are Christian missions and Christian mission the same thing? Churches have *missions* conferences, *mission* conferences, and *missionary* conferences. What exactly do those different terms and phrases mean?

Part of defining the terms is distinguishing between them. It is important to see the difference between God's comprehensive, singular *mission* and Christians' various *missions* activities. The latter are subsumed under the former: God's *mission* includes, but is by no means exhausted by, Christian *missions*. God has taken the initiative to act decisively in Jesus of Nazareth in his mission to remake the whole world. He carries his mission forward by bringing unbelievers to faith in Jesus Christ, maturing his people, and giving foretastes of the coming *shalom* of the heavenly city. All three of these aspects are extensively spoken of throughout the Bible, including in 1 Peter. Moreover, the Bible itself, translated as it is into different human languages, is part of God's mission initiative to speak to all people in our various mother tongues. We who are Jesus' followers respond by participating with him, at his gracious invitation and command, in our cross-cultural missions. Such missions activities include the recognition and commissioning of *missionaries*, a vast subject we will discuss as the book unfolds.

I doubt that most people would object to making this distinction between God's *mission* and Christian *missions*. Some will be aware of the history behind how these two terms have been used, and thus will already have a sense of the nuances of the terms. (I have outlined that history in Appendix A.) Those people might also be aware that the English term *mission*, which has "no direct biblical equivalent," is "derived from the Latin *mitto*, which in turn is a translation of the Greek *apostellō* (to send)." Some as well will agree that the "debate" over using *mission* or *missions* "continues and [that] consensus over this complex issue remains a goal to be reached in the future rather than a present reality."[3]

Some Christians have advocated using exclusively one term or the other, depending on their particular viewpoints (some ecumenicals and Roman Catholics use only *mission*; some evangelicals insist on speaking only of *missions*). For myself, I believe it is important and helpful to use both terms in an appropriate and self-conscious way. Doing so facilitates suffering after Christ's example as we confront our assumed and subconscious control, rights, and privileges with respect to God and to other people.

How so?

## The Importance of Both Terms

Christians have used the term *mission* in order to focus on God's initiative, not ours. That is a good motivation, and thus *mission* is a helpful word to employ. Yet eliminating the plural term *missions* can lead to losing Christian distinctives. What tends to happen is that

---

3. These quotations are taken from the beginning and end of A. Scott Moreau's article entitled "Mission and Missions," in *Evangelical Dictionary of World Missions*, ed. A. Scott Moreau, Baker Reference Library Series (Grand Rapids: Baker, 2000), 636–38.

everything—Christians' lives in the world, Christian ministries, even socio-economic-political events—gets swallowed up by God's mission, such that in the end the distinctiveness of *Christian* mission(s) just evaporates. If everything becomes mission, then nothing ends up being mission.

In order to uphold the distinctively Christian character of what Jesus' followers are to be doing throughout the world, evangelicals have focused on using the term *missions*. That term connotes the uniqueness and exclusivity of Jesus Christ as the Savior and hope of all people, the necessity of repentance and faith in Jesus for salvation, and the need for all people to hear the verbal proclamation of the news about Jesus and his death and resurrection, lest they die in their unbelief and experience a Christless eternity in hell. For fear of losing such central Christian tenets, some altogether avoid speaking of God's *mission* in the singular. (Also, as Appendix A describes, some evangelicals have wanted to avoid any association with ecumenicals and liberals and their socio-economic-political involvements.)

The problem with using only *missions*, however, is that too much emphasis can be placed on what *we do*, at the expense of our necessary attention to God and his plan, command, decisive acts in Jesus Christ, sovereign leadership, and empowerment of everything that we his followers can ever do in missions. The modern missions movement of the past two centuries—during the latter half of which Americans have had the leading role—has been action-oriented at the expense of adequate theological reflection.[4] American pragmatist philosophy, which arose in the late 1800s in association with such names as William James and John Dewey, reinforced the missions movement's focus on action and effect, and away from theoretical reflection and inquiry. A "just do it" posture has had its strengths as well as its weaknesses. One weakness is that an activist posture does not lend itself to recognizing God as the One who is orchestrating, empowering, and ultimately responsible for carrying out his *mission*.

---

4. To give my students at Covenant Theological Seminary a historical understanding of the modern missions movement and of where things stand today, I have them read Wilbert R. Shenk, *Changing Frontiers of Mission*, American Society of Missiology Series, no. 28 (Maryknoll, NY: Orbis Books, 1999). On this activist tendency of modern missions, see ibid., 33, 35, 47, 163.

Americans have been described as liking to "get to the point" and take action.[5] It is too easy for us problem-solvers to run out and try to fix the world on our own instead of consciously participating in God's initiative and commitment to restore the world to himself in Christ. We thus need the term *mission* to help us go through the suffering of relinquishing before God our control, rights, and privileges with respect to our *missions*. He is the One in charge, and we need every reminder of this truth that we can get.

## The International Status of the United States

Besides having an activist bent, we live in perhaps the most powerful economic-political-military nation the world has ever seen—and we know it. We claim to have the world's best workers, athletes, soldiers, scientists, engineers, technologies, economy, and political and legal systems, and the list goes on. If we somehow lose at something, it is because either we did not put forth our best or there was not a level playing field. We will admit that we have flaws, but in the end Americans are convinced that ours is the greatest and most powerful country on earth.

That conviction is reinforced by the constant influx of encouragements to patriotic devotion, such as singing the national anthem before sporting events, or regular holidays commemorating nationally significant people and events. Some encouragements are more subtle but at least as powerful. Recently a local high school administrator concluded his appeal to us parents to support a proposed tax increase because of the need to invest in our children, the future leaders of our "nation." He could have referred to our "community," "city," "state," "region," or "world," but instead he pulled us toward our common *national* identity, the one that demands the deepest of our loyalties. Public references to "sacred" and "hallowed" national duties or traditions also reinforce Americans' patriotic devotion.

In the midst of such a deeply patriotic and superpower-status environment, the "big stick" of U.S. military power ever looms in the

5. In order to have my students understand general American cultural traits, I also have them read Gary Althen, *American Ways: A Guide for Foreigners in the United States*, 2nd ed. (Yarmouth, ME: Intercultural Press, 2003). See in particular ibid., 58–60.

background, in case other nations disagree, get out of line, or upset the world's balance. While U.S. Christians would not, of course, call on military might to aid missions efforts, the all-encompassing reality of how the world operates in light of unmatched U.S. military firepower infiltrates, I suggest, our assumed and subconscious control, rights, and privileges with respect to instructing and guiding others. American Christians can hardly help but see the rest of the world as inferior, religiously and otherwise. Instinctively, then, *missions* should be the special prerogative of Americans, at least in terms of directing and training Christians of other nationalities.

## The American Missions Legacy

In reflecting on how Americans have contributed to missions efforts over the years, Christians have much cause for thanksgiving and celebration. The zeal and sacrifice offered, including martyrdom, have been greater than any of us will ever know. American leadership, funding, creativity, and technical expertise have greatly stimulated the recent surge in global networking, demographic tabulation, and resulting new initiatives to take the gospel to those who have never heard it before. Many other blessings have been spread throughout the world through American missions efforts, including medical relief, educational opportunities, and economic development.

Upon further reflection on the growth of American missions around the globe since the early 1800s, one can see a pattern corresponding to the expansion of the United States' international power and influence. (One can see a similar, general pattern of spreading religion together with national or imperial influence throughout the two millennia of Christian history—and indeed throughout all of religious history, for that matter—so it is not as though Americans are unique in this regard.[6])

6. Buddhism's spread throughout the Indian subcontinent, starting in the third century B.C., that resulted from the Mauryan King Asoka's edicts is a classic example of religion's spreading under imperial influence. Analyzing the early spread of Islam can be a bit more problematic, since there are conflicting interpretations of the relative importance of violence and political influence on the one hand versus trade on the other. However those complicated matters are sorted out, the consolidation of Islamic influence throughout North Africa and the Middle East unquestionably coalesced with the strength of Islamic dynasties. Clear examples in Christian history include

World War I, a time when the United States' role in international affairs increased dramatically, was when America took the mantle from Britain as the country sending out the most Christian missionaries, a distinction that the United States still comfortably maintains. Following World War II, when America became the leader of the liberal democratic world, there was a sharp upsurge in American missionary personnel and agencies. Here in the early twenty-first century, the power and reach of both the U.S. economy and its military presence have enabled the recent explosion of American short-term missions: the former provides the funding for the travel and projects that are carried out, whereas the latter provides the protection that Americans need during their international travels (whether as a warning against those who might take harmful action against American citizens or to rescue Americans out of dangerous situations that might emerge).

Similarly, American missions have tended to follow geopolitical developments. The unexpected disintegration of the Soviet Union, for decades our Cold War archenemy, led to a massive movement of American missions into eastern Europe, Russia, and central Asia in the 1990s. China's economic openness, again following decades of communist-capitalist suspicions, has spawned significant (if quiet) initiatives by American Christians going there for all sorts of reasons, including religious ones. Most recently, the 9/11 attacks of 2001 and the subsequent war on terror have been accompanied by widespread interest among American Christians in Islam. This interest has been fed by a burst in publications meant to equip Christians for interacting with Islam and Muslims, as well as by a surge in missions endeavors to Muslim peoples.

Pointing out these connections is not at all meant to accuse, malign, or discourage. Rather, seeing how American missions have, quite naturally, developed in sync with wider economic and political realities should drive us to two conclusions. First, Christians live within human history, exhibit qualities of our respective contexts, and act in ways that unavoidably have sociopolitical implications. As much as Christians might like to think that we, as well as our missions activities, flow along in a sort of

---

ways that missions efforts were facilitated by the political, military, and economic support of the Roman, Byzantine, Russian, Spanish, Portuguese, British, and (oddly enough) Japanese empires.

spiritual jet stream that is unaffected by the realities of this world, that simply is not the case. Second, the real Superpower of gospel mission, the triune God of the Bible, has afforded American Christians increasing opportunities for building on their wonderful missions heritage by serving as part of his international community of believers.

The first conclusion is a reality to be accepted, period. We are diligently to exert Spirit-enabled effort to fulfill Jesus' declaration that we are both *in* the world and *not of* it (nor any of its particular geopolitical expressions, including the United States of America). The second conclusion should give great hope and encouragement, even as it presents great challenges and largely uncharted paths ahead. Given this country's superpower status, serving Christ as citizens within today's United States of America, as well as within the rest of today's world, will demand humility and cooperation with others—the degrees of which I sense we have yet to fathom.

The reality of *God's* control, rights, and privileges with respect to his mission and indeed his whole world must thus always check our twenty-first-century American-Christian tendency to assume *our* control, rights, and privileges over carrying out what we view to be the highest of callings, Christian missions. Such a tendency, fueled by the current international economic-political-military environment, is at its root a manifestation of self-centeredness and sin. Hence, for us to "die to sin and live to righteousness" (1 Peter 2:24)—a process of suffering—includes increasingly believing that God alone has all the control, rights, and privileges in saving all his people and redeeming his world.

*God alone is the mission Superpower.* All of us who name the name of Jesus are simply his unworthy servants, blessed by his grace to know him and to suffer after his example.

## Reflection Questions

- What are some concrete possibilities of the type of suffering recommended in this chapter that my church and I currently are facing?

- What comparisons have I made to life in the United States versus visiting or perhaps even living in another country?

- Does my church have a *missions* conference, a *mission* conference, a *missionary* conference, none of these, or something else? What would I like there to be, and why?

# 2

# Four Facets of God's Mission

God is the mission Superpower. He controls his mission, including what he wants us to do in our missions efforts. As much as our instincts drive us toward assuming control, or exercising our alleged right to move ahead as we think best, God's primary call to activist American Christians is to suffer the letting go of that which we crave to be ours—but that which is rightly God's.

One important part of that ongoing suffering process is to examine how God conducts his mission. Leaving aside for now our own missions strategies (as painful as that might seem in a book about missions), in this chapter we will consider four important facets of God's work as the mission Superpower.

## God as Universal Creator-Redeemer

God made the world. He has always been concerned about all his world. He has acted in Jesus Christ to reclaim all his world. Moreover, Jesus will return and usher in the final reality of God's declaration in Revelation 21:5, "Behold, I am making all things new."

There seems to be nothing radical in these claims, but let's dissect them a bit to appreciate their full meaning. "The world" God has made includes everything in the heavens, the earth, and under the earth, to speak in biblical cosmological terms. Galaxies, beavers, spirit beings, orchids, sharks, protons, mountains, and metals have all been created by the God of the Bible. No sector of geography, biology, religion, politics, sociology, psychology, nuclear physics, medicine, history, ethics, communications, or any other conceivable branch of study can avoid dealing with something that God has made.

God cares about the entire world and has never stopped being involved with it. This is not the place to explore the philosophical intricacies of exactly how, scientifically speaking, divine involvement in his creation takes place (for example, how does God interrelate with the processes of nuclear fusion, satellite transmissions, or HIV/AIDS research?). Nor is it the place to discuss various theological understandings of exactly how God the Holy Spirit is engaged with people, Christian and non-Christian alike, throughout his world.[1] What I wish to stress here is the straightforward recognition that the God of the Bible is comprehensive in his concern for everything, everybody, everywhere, and at all times past, present, and future. That is, God is God with respect to the whole world.

We will discuss in the fourth point below what that means for the total, holistic nature of mission. For now, think of what it means: *God has always been dealing with all people, wherever and whenever they have been living.* The God of the Bible has not been confined to working with only old-covenant Israel and the new-covenant church (often subconsciously and erroneously assumed to consist of first-century Mediterranean peoples, then Europeans, and finally Americans). Be they ancient Chinese, contemporary Sudanese, or medieval English, God has been concerned about all people.

The Bible gives specific examples of God's various dealings with peoples whom we might study in school but not consider in connection with God in Jesus Christ. In Genesis 15, God covenants with Abram to multiply his descendants and to give them the land of Canaan. He adds, however, that they will spend several generations in Egypt before returning to Canaan to occupy it. God's stated reason for this delay is that the

---

1. One helpful recent study in this area that would no doubt open new vistas to most readers is Kristeen Kim, *Mission in the Spirit: The Holy Spirit in Indian Christian Theologies* (Kashmere Gate, Delhi: ISPCK, 2003).

current occupants' sin "is not yet complete" (15:16). Their judgment will have to wait 400 years more until the Israelites come and conquer them under Joshua's leadership.

This implies that God's dealings with the people of Canaan did not take place only insofar as he related to Israel. Rather, God, to whom all peoples throughout world history have been responsible as their Covenant-Creator-Master, was offended by the Canaanites' sin and rebellion against him—irrespective of his special dealings with Israel. Ultimately he would provide for the Canaanites' and all other nationalities' salvation in Israel's Messiah, the world's Savior, Jesus of Nazareth. That special work of God was interlaced with his ongoing dealings with all the peoples of his rebellious world.

The people of Nineveh also faced God's judgment until they repented when Jonah preached to them. "Their evil has come up before me," God said to Jonah (Jonah 1:2). Later God explained to the pouting Jonah, "Should not I pity Nineveh, that great city" (4:11), which he had created and cared for deeply? That universal and ongoing divine dealing with all people is why Paul could declare to the people of Lystra that God "did not leave himself without witness, for he did good by giving you rains from heaven and fruitful seasons, satisfying your hearts with food and gladness" (Acts 14:17). Similarly, Paul explained to the Athenians the divine supervision of all peoples' histories "that they should seek God, in the hope that they might feel their way toward him and find him. Yet he is actually not far from each one of us" (Acts 17:27).

We should add that God's dealings with all peoples have been in their own languages and settings. To be sure, God has brought the special message of salvation in Jesus to people through external agents, that is, cross-cultural missionaries such as Jonah and Paul. And the cross-cultural nature of that communication has often led to confusion and misunderstanding. Note, for example, the indigenous Lycaonian response in Lystra to Paul and Barnabas, when the people wanted to worship Paul as Hermes and Barnabas as Zeus after Paul had healed a crippled man (Acts 14:11–18). Even so, just as God revealed himself to the Hebrews in Hebrew and to the Greek-speaking New Testament world in Greek, so God has personally related to all of us as the one, true, living, universal Creator God who is also *our* God, not a foreign tribal deity. *All* people can say that; no particular language or nation (including English and the United States of America) can lay exclusive, privileged claim to this universal God. He has never left "himself without witness" among any people (Acts 14:17), all people's lives and deeds "come up before" him (Jonah 1:2), and he is "not far from each one of us," both individually and collectively (Acts 17:27).

God is the universal Creator-Redeemer with whom all of us in the human race—without exception—have to deal.

## God Brings Missionaries

I have a distinct memory from my childhood of trying to figure out how God could understand the prayers of people speaking to him in all sorts of different languages. I knew in my head that God must understand every language—but my actual experience was only in English. My solution for God was that somewhere in the air people's prayers were translated into English, and then they would go up to him in understandable form.

Knowing something intellectually and then knowing it by conviction and experience are not always the same. Knowing God personally—by conviction and experience—as the God who speaks all languages, as *omnilingual*, was impossible for me as a monolingual boy. It took directly relating to him in a different language (which in my case was Japanese, after my wife and I went to Japan as missionaries in 1986), apart from any English-language interference or translation, to help convince me that God really is not just a tribal, English-speaking deity, but the God of all peoples.

Understanding God in a universal, omnilingual way lets us clarify how he leads his cross-cultural emissaries throughout the world. In particular, we can say that God *brings* missionaries as well as *sends* them. There is a significant difference in perspective between those two complementary ways of putting things. This section will decipher the importance and meaning of being able to say both.

American Christians are familiar with saying that God sends missionaries to the mission field. We talk of God's calling certain people "out" (of the United States) to the foreign mission field. We speak as well of "home missions," but even there God "sends" certain people "out" to others who are different racially, linguistically, or perhaps socioeconomically.

Upcoming sections will address issues inherent in this familiar way of speaking. Here I would like to focus on American missionaries' being able to say, "Not only did God send me to this foreign place, but he *brought* me here." Is it permissible for a missionary to say that, and if it is, what all does it mean and imply?

Some would say that God is absent from places where there are only pagans and unbelievers—for example, so-called remote jungles of Africa. To suggest that God is present in dark, pagan places before Christian missionaries arrive would be a type of pluralistic liberalism that rips the uniqueness of Jesus as Savior right out of the heart of Christianity. The argument would then conclude with something like this: "God does not bring missionaries to the mission field; rather, missionaries take God there."

How does God's being the universal Creator-Redeemer fit into this line of argument? It doesn't. If God was present and dealing with people in Canaan, Nineveh, Lystra, Athens, and indeed everywhere else throughout the world he has made and always governed (which is not the same as saying that all people are followers of the God of the Bible), then God is present and working with all people now, just as he has always been. Not only is it thus *permissible* to say that God *brought* Israel to Canaan, Jonah to Nineveh, Paul to Lystra and Athens, and all other missionaries to their fields of service: it is *imperative* to say so, lest one deny God's universal dealings with the peoples of the world.

To complete the picture, it is right to say on the one hand that God *sends* missionaries. (We will consider later how it is crucial to understand how God *sends* all his people into our various areas of service, whether or not we are missionaries in an "organized" sense.) God is certainly present with missionaries' communities of origin, who send out those missionaries to serve elsewhere. It is also right to say that God *takes* missionaries from one location to another. After all, he is in control of the whole process of missionaries' traveling from their homes to their new places of service. But God's universal presence as Creator-Redeemer demands that we also believe that he *brings* his emissaries to people whom he wants to hear the particular gospel message about the crucified and risen Jesus, which they can hear only from outside their context.

There are at least *four major implications* of this discussion about how God *brings* missionaries.

## God Is God

First and foremost is the integrity of *who God is*. He is the omnilingual, universal King of all peoples and nations. He is the God of heaven and earth, whom no single house or place can contain (Acts 7:48–49). Just as Stephen's hearers wanted to confine God to a particular building and people, so do all groups have the tendency to try to domesticate God into a tribal deity. Religions often try to confine God to one language, be it Latin, Arabic, Sanskrit, or some completely esoteric and mysterious tongue. Nations often try to claim God's unique favor on their origin, prosperity, and military ventures. Yet the God of the Bible will not be limited in any of those ways. We must accordingly give him his due majesty and authority.

## People Have Histories

The second implication is the need for Christians involved in the sending aspect of cross-cultural missions to make an effort to learn the *histories* of people and areas to which people, money, or other resources are sent. It is all too easy to be ignorant of such histories, or even to sense any need to become informed. This is particularly true for us forward-looking Americans, given our relatively brief national history and reputation for lacking historical sensibilities.

When my wife and I first went to Japan as missionaries, I knew next to nothing about Japanese history, and even less about Japanese-Christian history. Worse was my unexamined assumption that I did not need to know—because I had now arrived and thus, in effect, God's history in Japan began with that incredibly significant event. I had brought God to Japan—or so I latently thought. Only when it began to dawn on me that God had been present and active there for generation upon generation did I remove my shoes, not just to be culturally acceptable upon entering a room, but to learn more of the heritage that was far older and richer than I had even begun to imagine. It should therefore come as no surprise that, besides being perhaps the greatest sign of respect that one can show to others, learning people's histories is a great privilege and fascinating adventure.

## Cultural Outsiders Are Learners

Third is the *learning posture* of missionaries when they enter a new context. Much is said about this in our day, so there is little need here to say much more. As part of their learning posture, missionaries must realize that, besides learning the indigenous language and culture for strategic purposes, they have been brought there by God to be shaped in ways they could never predict or control. God shaped Moses, born an Israelite, in Egypt and Midian. He worked on Joseph in Egypt, Daniel in Babylon, Peter in Cornelius's house, and Paul in Arabia and elsewhere. The pattern goes on throughout the Bible and Christian history.

The point is that God is the One who has brought the missionary into a new crucible of discipleship. As one insightful African analyst has put it, "They did not bring God; rather God brought them . . . ."[2]

## Missionaries Are Catalysts and Conduits

Fourth, missionaries need to realize their proper place in the *communication* process between God and the people to whom they have gone to serve. Alongside God's purpose in shaping missionaries is his purpose in using them to bring a unique message to people. God deals with those people directly, and he brings the missionary into the picture as an outside catalyst. What is crucial, therefore, is what God communicates to those people, or what they hear. What the missionary communicates is obviously important and necessary—after all, he brings the gospel message of forgiveness and salvation in Jesus Christ—but

2. Kwame Bediako, *Christianity in Africa: The Renewal of a Non-Western Religion* (Maryknoll, NY: Orbis Books, 1995), 118; cf. 226.

the cross-cultural component can often add clutter and static to what is communicated. God is fully capable of dealing with people whom he has made; in his mercy and wisdom he has chosen to bring in outsiders to help carry his message. So instead of seeing themselves in the exalted terms of being the central conduit of God's message, missionaries need to view their role as auxiliary, much like a speaker on a TV rather than the screen itself.

William Cameron Townsend came to understand this matter while he was distributing Spanish Bibles in Central America in 1917–18. Few of the people there actually knew Spanish, and finally some locals expressed their concern that God did not speak their language. It dawned on young "Cam" that there was a need for more Bible translations, and it was largely through his efforts that Wycliffe Bible Translators and its associated organizations eventually developed.[3]

For American Christians involved in missions-sending, it is quite proper to believe that God sends and takes missionaries to foreign lands outside the United States. The notion that U.S. churches *send out* missionaries indeed makes common sense. Important for our purposes here, however, is to recognize as well that the universal God of all peoples *brings* Americans to different places within his grand mission scheme of working throughout the world.

## Organized and Unorganized Missionaries

Of course, God does not send-take-bring only Americans as missionaries. There is increasing awareness that Christianity is more of a worldwide faith than ever before. In fact, the majority of Christians now live outside the West—particularly in Latin America, sub-Saharan Africa, Oceania, and various parts of Asia.[4] We will return later to this massive

---

3. You can read more about "Cam" Townsend in Ruth A. Tucker, *From Jerusalem to Irian Jaya: A Biographical History of Christian Missions*, 2nd ed. (Grand Rapids: Zondervan, 2004), 375–79.

4. On a popular level, the publication perhaps most responsible for spreading the news about this shift has been Philip Jenkins, *The Next Christendom: The Coming of Global Christianity* (New York: Oxford University Press, 2002). At the same time, Andrew Walls and other scholars have been writing about it for decades.

and surprising twentieth-century demographic shift within the Christian church. For now, we can note that thousands of non-Western missionaries—Koreans, Indians, Nigerians, Brazilians, Chinese, and others[5]—now help to make up the worldwide missionary force. (We should also note that, contrary to some popular impressions, Western missionaries, the single largest group of whom are Americans, still constitute the majority of missionaries in the organized, "official" sense. Relative economic strength and worldwide military presence no doubt have much to do with this fact.) The universal God is using all kinds of missionaries to help carry out his mission throughout the earth.

The main point of this section of our discussion, however, is to stretch our appreciation of God's mission beyond Christians' organized efforts. God's mission to restore the world is broader than missions. Missions is part of God's mission, yes. But to turn around and say that God's mission is missions limits God unbiblically.

As mentioned earlier (and explained further in Appendix A), this relationship between God's mission and our missions harks back to certain theological and missiological discussions that took place in the mid-twentieth century. Important for us here is to note how certain Christian leaders discarded the unique and necessary place of organized missions activities, wanting exclusively to emphasize God's *mission*. In doing that, they changed the traditional (at least in the West) scheme for understanding how God works in the world via the church. The assumed, traditional understanding had been that God works through the church—its preaching, sacraments, and other ministries. The new scheme that emerged in some circles was that God was at work directly in the world—particularly in socio-economic-political events—and that the church was to cooperate with God by its participation in these unfolding developments. In other words, **God → church → world** became **God → world → church**.

Enough sounds right in that new view to have made it appealing to some. After all, God is sovereignly involved in all of the world's affairs,

5. Two of the many noteworthy non-Western missions organizations and movements are the Indian "Gospel for Asia," which numerically is one of the largest missions agencies in the world (http://www.gfa.org/), and the Chinese "Back to Jerusalem" movement (http://www.back tojerusalem.com/).

and he does not confine himself to working only in and through the organized church. On a personal level, for example, my involvements in family, work, and community are as much God's work and calling for me as are my church-related tasks. If nothing else, the Reformation understanding of calling and vocation places "secular" matters on the same level of religious importance as "full-time Christian work." So what happens in societies, economies, and governments is very much a Christian concern.

The error, of course, was in throwing out the baby with the bathwater. God works directly in the world, yes, but that does not mean that he does not work directly in and through the organized church. We must not confine God to working strictly in and through one or the other; both are necessary. (Related is the idea of sphere sovereignty, in this case the respective arenas of what is civic and what is religious. There are further spheres into which the world can be divided—political, economic, philosophical, ethical, historical, physical, and so on—within each of which particular rules uniquely apply regarding how that sphere operates, all under God's providential control and design.[6])

Figure 1 illustrates this important matter of how God works in and through the church in relation to how he works in the world. Perhaps it would help to draw an additional line from God to the world that bypasses the church.

Fig. 1

**How God works in and through the church in relation
to how he works in the world.**

6. An explanation of a dialectical way of viewing the world as unified events that can also be analyzed according its component parts or spheres is in a model called "Transcendental Hermeneutics," described in Hisakazu Inagaki and J. Nelson Jennings, *Philosophical Theology and East-West Dialogue*, vol. 15 of Currents of Encounter Series (Amsterdam: Rodopi, 2000), 34ff.

There is an important ecclesiological nuance here. God works both in the world directly and in/via the organized church. But Christ's body, God's people, his church, is both an organization and an unorganized organism. God works in and through his people as we are scattered throughout the societies where he has us. When Jesus said to his disciples, "As the Father has sent me, even so I am sending you" (John 20:21), he spoke to them—and in turn to the rest of his followers—both as an organized group and as men with families and civic responsibilities. Jesus sends his people into the world as the organized church and as those scattered like salt and light throughout society. As one Filipino Christian leader has put it, "The **ecclesia visibilis** [church visible] is God's people making the presence of the Kingdom felt in all areas of life, the leaven which permeates all of human activity. It is both the **church gathered** and the **church scattered**. It is the church in academia, the church in politics, the church in the marketplace, besides being the institutional church down the street corner."[7]

This dual ecclesiology is quite evident in 1 Peter (see also Ephesians and Colossians). Because of the person and work of Jesus Christ, his followers are described as "a spiritual house" and "a chosen race, a royal priesthood, a holy nation, a people for his own possession" (1 Peter 2:5, 9). As such, we are organized, with elders who exercise oversight and gifts that we use to serve each other as well as others (4:10–11; 5:1–5). At the same time, we are to live, in an unorganized and scattered fashion, in our God-given sociopolitical, economic, and family arenas (2:11–3:7). As God's organized and unorganized people, we are "sojourners and exiles" who have received God's mercy and now live for his honor and praise (2:9–12).

To return to the diagram with the added "God → world" line that bypasses the church, we can add an enlarged, shadowed background of "church" representing the scattered people of God. This scattered church will intersect with portions of the direct "God → world" line. Those points of intersection portray the reality that God works through his people whom he has sent in scattered fashion into the world. (See fig. 2 for a version of fig. 1 incorporating the scattered people of God.)

7. Melba Padilla Maggay, *Transforming Society: Reflections on the Kingdom and Politics*, 2nd ed. (Quezon City, Philippines: Institute for Studies in Asian Church and Culture, 2004), 28 (emphasis and brackets in original).

FIG. 2

**How God works in and through his scattered people
both in the world and in the church.**

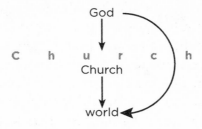

The crucial point to realize is that *God sends-takes-brings his scattered people as part of his mission force that he has sent into his world.* Along with the people intentionally set apart as missionaries, God uses people who are not missionaries in the formal, organized sense. I am not referring here just to so-called tentmakers or to people who enter "creative access" areas of the world (those not open to traditional missionaries) for missions purposes; I am putting those in the former category of set apart in the organized sense (as clandestine or loose and informal as the organization might be). The scattered people of God who make up a substantial part of God's missionary force are those followers of Jesus whom God sends-takes-brings to various places and people throughout the world as his cross-cultural emissaries without their specific intention or even awareness. That is the wide and varied group to whom I am referring.

You see them in the book of Acts as those Christians "scattered throughout the regions of Judea and Samaria" and even "as far as Phoenicia and Cyprus and Antioch" because of the persecution following Stephen's martyrdom. They "went about preaching the word" in a natural "gossiping the gospel" kind of way (Acts 8:1, 4; 11:19). Included in their vast number are the fourth-century brothers Frumentius and Edesius. These two Syrian Christians were on a trading sea voyage with their uncle and were captured upon their ship's harboring in the northeast African kingdom of Axum (presently northern Ethiopia). The brothers were eventually brought to live in the royal court, where their witness led to the growth of Christianity and its adoption as Axum's official religion. More contemporary unorganized Christian missionaries include Sudanese

Christians fleeing as refugees to various parts of the world (including the United States), Korean Christian businessmen traveling to the former Soviet Union and China for decades, Ugandan Christians living in Tokyo to buy used auto parts, and Christian African-American slaves faithfully working for their families within an oppressive and unjust system. Their numbers and types are vast and impossible to catalogue.

One fascinating account of how God's unorganized mission morphed into an organized effort concerns the planting of the first Protestant church in tropical Africa. Leading up to the American Revolution, the British promised freedom and land to certain African-American slaves in return for fighting for the British cause. Following the unanticipated "successful" rebellion, these slaves had to flee northward, to Nova Scotia. Not totally happy with their life there, the Christian African-American community developed a burden to return to West Africa for gospel ministry. With British assistance, several hundred of these African Nova Scotians sailed to the newly created Sierra Leone and began the first Protestant church in sub-Saharan Africa in modern times.[8]

To bring the point of God's unorganized mission closer to home, think of Christians of a different ethnicity or nationality whom God has brought into your local community. Many of the world's immigrants and refugees are Christians, including those who move into the areas where you and I live. I submit that these brothers and sisters in Christ are part of God's unorganized missionary force.

*Missionaries* also, of course, include those whom God sends-takes-brings in intentional and organized fashion, such as Paul and Barnabas on their church-planting missionary journey (Acts 13–14). But in the broader sense that Christians are sent into the world to live for Jesus, all of us are missionaries, particularly as we belong to the international, intercultural body of Christ (the theme we will consider in the next couple of chapters). When you include the many Christians who move around the world and across cultures because of war, economic need,

---

8. That is, the first sub-Saharan Protestant church other than in South Africa, which has its own special history of Protestant presence. For a more detailed account of this whole event, see Lamin Sanneh, *West African Christianity: The Religious Impact* (Maryknoll, NY: Orbis Books, 1983), 58–59.

or some other form of displacement, there is a great portion of God's cross-cultural mission throughout the world.

"Oh, the depth of the riches and wisdom and knowledge of God! How unsearchable are his judgments and how inscrutable his ways!" (Rom. 11:33).

## Comprehensive Character of Mission as Restoration

Here is a situation that happens in many U.S. cities: God has brought a group of Christian Liberian refugees to our community. Their stories are filled with terrible accounts of murders, narrow escapes, separated families, and other hardships. For most if not all of them, it has been totally beyond their control or even foresight that they have been resettled here. What are some of the various responses that my church and I can have to their coming?

- Shake our heads in sadness at the cruel circumstances that these poor people have endured.
- Resent their intrusion into our comfortable, stable, and homogeneous communities, and accordingly ignore them, seek to relocate them, or move ourselves farther away from them.
- Seek to ensure, personally and through appealing to others (including religious and civic organizations), that their many needs in beginning a new life are going to be met.
- Develop personal relationships with some of them through going to visit, having them into our homes, assisting them with particular tasks, or listening to their stories and collective histories.
- Listen to their observations about our communities' strengths and weaknesses.
- Learn their language that is different from ours.
- Pray for them, for Liberia and international bodies associated with it, for our communities, for God's ongoing instruction to us through these new neighbors, and for wisdom to know how we might act to help address some of the evils that caused them to have to flee their former home.

The first response is right and human—but inadequate by itself. The second response is obviously cynical and destructive—although widespread and understandable (and unacceptable). The others are constructive and necessary, together as a package, for receiving from God these cross-cultural messengers to us and our communities.

God's message through these newcomers will not simply be a strictly religious word about the afterlife. His message through these Liberian refugees will speak about international structural issues, joy and hope in Christ with or without material blessings, God's protection and faithfulness, and many other aspects. God, the universal Creator-Redeemer, is "making all things new" in Christ and is fully committed "to unite all things in him, things in heaven and things on earth" (Eph. 1:10). He sends-takes-brings his servants crisscrossing all over the world in ways that only he can understand and orchestrate. His goal is to restore the world from its present skewed state to a new heaven and new earth that will be even more glorious than was Eden. He is intent on nothing less, and as his servants we, too, should participate with him in his mission to make all things right.

That does not mean, of course, that *all* missionaries—organized or unorganized—should focus on *all* aspects of God's ongoing mission of restoration. Some of us will focus on raising children. Some will work for profit and fairness in the marketplace. Some will preach and teach. Some will tackle difficult justice issues of child trafficking. Some will have special political responsibilities. Some will focus on evangelism and church-planting. Others will deal with health issues or community development. The variety of tasks that God gives us is practically unlimited.

God's mission is a full-orbed project. Organized Christian missions will fill special niches within God's overall mission. It is only right that specifically religious tasks of missionaries should have specifically religious foci—even though it is often difficult if not impossible to disentangle religious matters from other concerns. Church-planting missionaries thus should not be about fomenting political movements or creating profit-making businesses per se. The point is not to limit our understanding of God's comprehensive mission by restricting it to organized Christian missions. God's mission is much bigger than missions by a long shot.

Christians all around the world can tend to restrict God's mission to Christian missions. This chapter is simply a plea to expand our appreciation of God's mission of restoration because of who God is as the universal Creator-Redeemer, because of how he sends-takes-brings missionaries of both organized and unorganized types, and because his mission is comprehensive in its intent and scope. God has no equal in planning and executing his commitment to the world that he made: he alone is the Superpower in mission. Hence, as 1 Peter puts it, our Christian "faith and hope are in God" (1:21).

Whereas Christians of all nationalities can be prone to limit God's mission to missions, when it comes to relating to this magnificent God, we who are American Christians face peculiar challenges to thinking both historically and concretely. We also face the challenge of holding our superpower country to its professed ideal of being a nation "under God," including his standards concerning morality and humility. Furthermore, there are particular barriers to our thinking of ourselves as belonging to worldwide communities, whether as Christians or as human beings. We will discuss these and other matters in the next two chapters. Doing so will continue our process of suffering by relinquishing our assumed and subconscious control, rights, and privileges with respect to God and to other people.

## Reflection Questions

- What is the significance of the "God → church → world" and "God → world → church" schemes and their amended versions?

- In what senses are all Christians missionaries, and in what senses are they not?

- Do missionaries take God to foreign peoples? If not, what or whom do they take? What or whom do they bring?

- What are some more examples of "unorganized" missionaries?

# THEME 2

## "Your Brotherhood throughout the World"
### (1 Peter 5:9)

# 3

# Who Are We Concretely?

The previous chapter considered four "big picture" facets of God's mission. We stepped back and surveyed how God deals with the world as a whole. These next two chapters will also have the whole world in view, specifically the church "throughout the world" to which we American Christians belong. The international identity that all Christians have is an extremely important trait for us to work through on a personal level.

Peter, after being specially taken by Jesus to the Gentile house of Cornelius (Acts 10), had finally come to recognize how important this trait was for all Christians. That is why, toward the end of his letter that we know as 1 Peter, he drew his suffering readers' attention to the wider, international church. Peter was encouraging Jesus' followers scattered throughout the western half of present-day Turkey to stand firm in resisting the devil. For them to remember that others "throughout the world" were undergoing "the same kinds of suffering" (1 Peter 5:9) would strengthen them to endure until "the God of all grace, who has called you to his eternal glory in Christ, will himself restore, confirm, strengthen, and establish you. To him be the dominion forever and ever. Amen" (5:10–11).

As we consider our international Christian identity today, we must not allow the magnitude of the matter to keep it safely away at arm's length. God in his mission intends on working in our lives in such a way that we, as part of the Christian "brotherhood throughout the world," grow in our personal experience of suffering after Christ's example. As we have already repeatedly said, basic to our experience of suffering is learning to relinquish our assumed and subconscious control, rights, and privileges with respect to God and to other people. That experience includes dealing in focused ways with specific and concrete aspects of our personal identities.

There are, of course, many facets of who we are as human beings: religious, social, ethnic, and national, to name just a few. The main purpose of this chapter is to allow Jesus to interact with what can be an unassailable aspect of American Christians' personal identity, namely, our patriotism-nationalism.[1] We will need to think as concretely as possible about this part of our identity. Also and necessarily, we will need to keep in the back of our minds our international identity in Christ, so as to help us better identify our particular American identity.

After focusing in this chapter on our patriotism-nationalism, in the next chapter we will consider more explicitly how our international Christian identity relates to this as well as other aspects of our multifaceted personal identities.

## American and Christian

Most Americans feel no deeper stirring of the heart than love of their country. When major tragedies occur, the American flag is displayed to give courage. Flyovers and "The Star-Spangled Banner" inspire sports fans to greater heights of excitement. Arguably since 9/11 and the invasion of

---

1. Given the following distinction between patriotism and nationalism, I would argue that Americans—especially as viewed by the rest of the world—exhibit obvious nationalist sentiments:

"Nationalism is more than patriotism, which is a sentiment or loyalty to the nation to which one belongs, because it includes the belief that one's own nation has a higher calling and greater value than other nations, and that the nation is the only legitimate source of power. Nationalism supports the belief that perceived threats or enemies to the nation need to be eliminated, destroyed or defeated—be they internal oppressors, agents of foreign domination or merely other, rival nations—in order to raise the worldly status or rank and increase the glory and the prestige of the nation." Timothy Baycroft, *Nationalism in Europe: 1789–1945*, Cambridge Perspectives in History Series (Cambridge: Cambridge University Press, 1998), 4.

Iraq there has been a "reassertion of nationalism via schools" initiated by all levels of government.[2] Moreover, American patriotism can have a religious feel to it: "God Bless America" and "Amazing Grace" have become alternative national anthems, especially in times of grief and challenge. Even with the continuing advance of secularism throughout U.S. society, Americans are still a deeply religious people—and the phrase "civil religion" best characterizes what that religious faith is for many of us.[3]

At the same time, we U.S. evangelicals seem to be growing in number. U.S.-evangelical "organized" missionaries are skyrocketing, particularly with the virtual explosion of short-term missions trips. Furthermore, conservative Christians' political influence in the United States has dramatically increased in recent years. One can only conclude that U.S. evangelicals hold strong and clear beliefs about their faith, including salvation and missions, together with strong and clear beliefs about U.S. citizenship.

Yet I would like to suggest that for U.S. evangelicals (and U.S. Christians as a whole), the connection between our religious experience of salvation and missions on the one hand, and our patriotism-nationalism on the other, is somewhat disjointed and awkward. It's as though the heartstrings for each are strummed in mutually dissonant chords and rhythms. The mutual coexistence of those two areas is comfortable and settled for many. But hold them up simultaneously and try to bring them together, and you will find a pair of topics that, like oil and water, are difficult to mix.

Why is that the case, and what are we to do about it? Considering this pair of questions is where we are headed.

## Jesus the *Kurios* Saves Real People

We noted in the previous chapter the comprehensive character of God's mission to restore and even re-create the world. God's remaking of *people* is at the forefront of this redemptive mission. God's salvation

---

2. Michael L. Budde, "Selling America, Restricting the Church," in *Anxious about Empire: Theological Essays on the New Global Realities*, ed. Wes Avram (Grand Rapids: Brazos Press, 2004), 83.

3. Martin Marty and Robert Bellah are two of the best-known analysts of U.S. civil religion.

of real, live people is more concrete and integrated than a narrowly spiritualized understanding that carries the central message, "God saves souls." In such a defective mind-set, evangelism and missions become merely the fervent effort to populate heaven with as many disembodied spirit-substances as possible. For its particular part, *missions* is reduced to the work of "saving souls" in the "uttermost part of the earth."[4]

Most if not all readers of this book will be well aware of the inadequacies of such a narrow notion of salvation. We realize that the view is too small and individualistic for God's grand mission to remake the world. But we as U.S. evangelicals often struggle with having an integrated notion of salvation that allows God's gospel to work itself into all areas of life. Such an integrated view recognizes that Jesus shoulders his way into every aspect of people's individual lives, as well as into each society's public life.[5]

Such an integrated view will also be able to recognize that the early church's confession of Jesus as *Kurios* may have been appropriately translated into English as "Lord" centuries ago—when *lord* was a socially active designation of "the owner and head of a feudal estate"[6]—but a more explosive and faithfully equivalent designation is needed for contemporary Americans. *Kurios* was by no means a confining, strictly religious title for first-century Christians in the Roman Empire. It rather posed a religio-socio-economic-political threat to the reigning powers. Hence, whereas Caesar expected full and final allegiance by claiming the title *Kurios*, Christians countered by confessing the risen Galilean carpenter Jesus as *Kurios*, not only of their own lives but over all competing authorities as well, Rome or otherwise. This confession was thus also a

---

4. We are getting ahead of ourselves in delineating how U.S.-American Christians (in particular, Caucasian evangelicals) often instinctively understand the "uttermost part of the earth," in the manner of Acts 1:8 (KJV). Suffice it for now to note that on the one hand a political, modern nation-state framework dictates that those regions are anywhere outside the United States. An ethnic-racial framework that often accompanies this view casts non-Caucasians (e.g., Native Americans) as belonging to the outermost regions, even if they actually reside within the borders of the United States. One of the central purposes of this chapter is to hold up these latent but powerful frameworks for fresh consideration.

5. I am indebted to Dr. Kwame Bediako of Ghana for this image of Jesus' "shouldering his way" into settings.

6. This is the second definition listed in Victoria Neufeldt, ed., *Webster's New World College Dictionary*, 3rd ed. (New York: Macmillan, 1997), 798.

constraining call to radical obedience for Jesus' followers. We need, and Jesus demands, similar terminology in our settings today.[7]

Take, for example, the title "Commander in Chief." Americans today, of course, know that designation to be uniquely reserved for our president. Here is a question to consider: what prevents those of us who are Christians from confessing Jesus as our Commander in Chief, thereby breaking through the subtle but powerful bracketing of him out of our socio-political-patriotic-military life? Not thus acknowledging Jesus could amount to confining him to a nonthreatening, domesticated, and strictly religious arena. Actually confessing Jesus as our Commander in Chief might raise uncomfortable questions and concerns. Even so, wouldn't those odd feelings that would no doubt accompany singing in church the American political-military song "Hail to the Chief," the actual tune of which we hear only when the U.S. president makes an appearance, be at least in part our wrestling with Jesus as he insists on being Christians' God in every arena of life?

> Hail to the Chief we have chosen for the nation,
> Hail to the Chief! We salute him, one and all.
> Hail to the Chief, as we pledge cooperation
> In proud fulfillment of a great, noble call.
>
> Yours is the aim to make this grand country grander,
> This you will do, That's our strong, firm belief.
> Hail to the one we selected as commander,
> Hail to the President! Hail to the Chief![8]

What about confessing Jesus to be our "President"? We could change a couple of phrases in "Hail to the Chief," as well as mentally adjust the

---

7. I have explored this theme more fully in my chapter entitled "Christ-Centered Missions," in Robert A. Peterson and Sean Michael Lucas, eds., *All for Jesus: A Celebration of the 50th Anniversary of Covenant Theological Seminary* (Geanies House, Great Britain: Christian Focus Publications, 2006), 255–58.

8. This song was composed in Scotland and England, first performed in the United States in 1812, first played for a U.S. president in 1828, and officially established by the Department of Defense as a musical tribute to the U.S. president in 1954. "History of 'Hail to the Chief,'" "'The President's Own'—United States Marine Band," available online at http://www.marineband.usmc.mil/learning_tools/library_and_archives/resources_and_references/hail_to_the_chief.htm.

referent of "nation" and "country" to Christ's international kingdom, and sing the following as a hymn of praise and worship to Jesus:

> Hail to the Chief God has given to the nation,
> Hail to the Chief! We salute him, one and all.
> Hail to the Chief, as we pledge cooperation
> In proud fulfillment of a great, noble call.

> Yours is the aim to make this grand country grander,
> This you will do, That's our strong, firm belief.
> Hail to the one we agree is our commander,
> Hail to the President! Hail to the Chief![9]

Worshiping Jesus in these terms would not mean that American Christians were therefore declaring the U.S. president and commander in chief to be invalid and in need of replacement by Jesus. Nor would it imply that the American separation of church and state (variously interpreted as that is) should be obliterated.[10] Rather, American Christians' singing to Jesus as our President and Commander in Chief would faithfully appropriate the biblical, Christian tradition of acknowledging that he has our ultimate allegiance, as well as that no area of individual and sociopolitical life is off limits to his reign.[11]

Such an example points to how Jesus our Commander in Chief, President, Sole Owner, Master, Boss, CEO, King, and Hero thus comprehensively and concretely saves *real, live people*. He is not simply a religious "Lord" who provides only for the current and eternal well-being of our mystical, religious inner selves. Nor is he simply an abstract doctrine to which only intellectual assent must be given. He is the actual first-

---

9. The two phrases I have changed reflect the necessary adjustment from an American confession of the sovereign right of the citizenry to choose our political-military leaders to the Christian acknowledgment that God has sovereignly made Jesus our ultimate leader. Thus in stanza 1, "*we have chosen for* the nation" has become "*God has given to* the nation"; and in stanza 2, "we *selected as* commander" has become "we *agree is our* commander."

10. See my brief comments about interpreting Jesus' "render to Caesar and to God" remarks in "Christ-Centered Missions," in Peterson and Lucas, *All for Jesus*, 268.

11. A quick survey of Christian hymns ("Come, Thou Almighty King," "All Hail the Power of Jesus' Name," "Lead On, O King Eternal," etc.) shows the political-military feel of both the words and the music we readily employ from our European heritages.

century Jewish carpenter from Nazareth who overcame death and lives forevermore.[12] This formerly distant foreigner, this Suffering Servant and slain Lamb of God, is now the universal *Kurios* who reigns over the whole world. All aspects of my concrete being, as well as of U.S. (and every other) society, are taken up by this dangerous and kind Jesus. His mission and work are comprehensive; so must be the effect in my redeemed life and in the societies in which we his people live. I am his in all parts of my concrete reality, bar none.

The point is simple yet profound: God does not save only inner religious souls. He saves real and particular people who work, play, and love their families and countries.

## Nationality and Ethnicity

The point just made is nothing controversial. What is difficult is bringing together, or integrating, who we are as Jesus' followers and who we are as patriotic U.S. citizens in concrete, countless, and detailed ways (e.g., how we might use "Hail to the Chief" as contemporary Christian praise and worship music). As one insightful analyst has put it, "We don't leave our citizen roles and our patriotic affections at the door when we enter the church building for worship. . . . But seductive patriotic symbols and nationalistic boastings have no proper place in Christian worship."[13] Both of our commitments, as Jesus' disciples and as citizens who love our country, run very, very deep within us: do they overlap, clash, or what?

Jesus himself, the One who invades our contemporary settings with fresh zeal and vigor, is the path toward solving our dilemma of not-fully-integrated spirituality and patriotism. On the one hand, a domesticated religious Jesus will not help: such a false personal-peace-giving idol only perpetuates the distinction. Nor will a national-ideal-promoting Jesus

---

12. Lamin Sanneh has described in an enlightening way how his boyhood appreciation for Muhammad the man, gained from his Muslim upbringing, has carried over to heighten his adult Christian appreciation for the Man Jesus. Lamin Sanneh, *Piety & Power: Muslims and Christians in West Africa*, Faith Meets Faith Series (Maryknoll, NY: Orbis Books, 1996), 29–51.

13. Richard J. Mouw, "The Danger of Alien Loyalties: Civic Symbols Present a Real Challenge to the Faithfulness of the Church's Worship," in *Reformed Worship* 5, no. 15 (March 1990), available online at http://www.reformedworship.org/magazine/article.cfm?article_id=264.

break the stalemate: he would simply assure us that our "American way of life" is right, no matter what light the Bible might shed on the matter. Jesus in his full reality, our Exemplar of suffering, that Man who rose from the dead and now "commands all people everywhere to repent," intends to turn our entire world upside down, just as he did in and through the apostle Paul (Acts 17:6, 30).

Simply believing in a gospel that comforts and delights my heart thus will not do. The full expanse of God's good news in Christ must be uncorked and have its fragrance permeate the air we breathe. The breadth of the *evangelion* ("gospel") is indicated by its political overtones in the Roman Empire, insofar as the *gospel* was the proclamation of a new emperor's enthronement.[14] God's work in Jesus has its gospel-effect "far as the curse is found."[15] Curses such as death, racial discrimination, injustice, loneliness, and poverty of all sorts will one day be alleviated in Christ. The gospel, the good news, is that Jesus has overcome and is dealing concretely with all these enemies.

For you and me personally, that means that all aspects of our lives are thereby affected. It means that we see the Creator and Providential Ruler of societies and governments, as well as of our families, our work, our bodies, our nationalities, and our recreation, as the same God who aims in his salvation and mission to conform all those areas of the world and of our lives to what he wants them to be.

The apostle Paul was always conscious of how national, cultural, and ethnic realities interfaced with Jesus' salvation and mission. Earlier than Peter, the Apostle to the Gentiles had worked through how Christ unifies different sorts of people without obliterating their ethnic-national, socioeconomic, and gender distinctions. Paul at one point actually had to rebuke publicly Peter for refusing to eat with non-Jewish believers. The overriding truth of the gospel was that Christians' primary identity in Christ overshadowed their secondary identities, to the point that by

14. Paul Marshall, *God and Constitution: Christianity and American Politics* (Lanham, MD: Rowman & Littlefield Publishers, 2002), x, 44, 50–52. Note a similar observation in Mark Lewis Taylor, *Religion, Politics, and the Christian Right: Post-9/11 Powers and American Empire* (Minneapolis: Fortress Press, 2005), 159.

15. For a fresh, clear consideration of God's full covenantal dealings with his world, see my Covenant Theological Seminary colleague Michael D. Williams's recent work, *Far as the Curse Is Found: The Covenant Story of Redemption* (Phillipsburg, NJ: P&R Publishing, 2005).

comparison, "there is neither Jew nor Greek, there is neither slave nor free, there is neither male nor female, for you are all one in Christ Jesus" (Gal. 3:28; cf. 2:11–16, 3:26–29).

Paul's letters thus repeatedly stress the need not to "pass judgment on one another," as well as "never to put a stumbling block or hindrance in the way of a brother," with regard to religio-cultural preferences concerning eating (Rom. 14:13ff.). Paul "made [himself] a servant to all"— Jews, those under the law, those outside the law, the weak—"that by all [cultural] means [he] might save some . . . for the sake of the gospel" (1 Cor. 9:19–23). Paul had his new ministry partner Timothy circumcised so that his parents' mixed marriage would give no unnecessary cultural and ethnic offense to Jews (Acts 16:1–3). Paul knew that God aims to reshape all these areas into a new mosaic in his salvation and mission.

Our nationalities and ethnicities, then, are included in what God desires to reshape in his salvation and mission. He will not simply leave them alone. Nor will he simply baptize them with his unqualified stamp of approval and allow us to use our nationalities and ethnicities however we please or to our own advantage. The dangerous and kind *Kurios*, the Jesus who lives and reigns over the whole world, the One in whom you, I, and all of God's people find forgiveness and justification and adoption through his death and resurrection, intends to save all of you, me, and the rest of his children to serve him in his comprehensive mission to make the world right again.

This means that Christians living in slums and in upscale communities throughout the world's cities—Havana, Peking, Cincinnati, Milan, Tehran, Buenos Aires, Auckland, Cairo—are living each day as Christ's servants. Christians in tribal communities of Tanzania, towns of South Carolina, and villages of Paraguay are in their concrete, daily activities following the living Nazarene carpenter who now reigns on high. Christian salvation and mission involve particular and concrete people for whom Jesus has died and risen and whom he has sent into his world as his servants. Christians are real people who have real religious, social, ethnic, and national identities.

How to fit these identities together—particularly including our national identity—is what we are wrestling with here, and it is a challenge we all face in our own peculiar situations.

## Pluses and Minuses

We who are Americans have things going both for and against us in working through the whole matter of integrating religious and patriotic aspects of life. On the positive side of the ledger, ever since the early 1800s Christian missionaries have been going from the United States to serve in other parts of the world. Over these past two centuries, many mistakes have been made and many lessons learned. This long experience has helped to mature an American-Christian understanding of Christian missions throughout the world.

Another positive is that the Christian gospel has been at work for generations in many of our various heritages, whether African-American, European-American, Asian-American, Latin-American, or otherwise. Together these long Christian heritages have helped shape the public and structural life of the United States.[16] This extensive experience is another plus in developing an integrated, Christian view of religious and national life.

At the same time, the particular type of American-Christian experience (varied as it is) just outlined works against formulating an integrated view of life. The same pluses we have mentioned are minuses as well. Through the generations-old U.S. missions experience, many crucial lessons about finances, organizational structure, cultural sensitivity, missionary selection and training, strategy, teamwork and partnerships, language learning, and a host of other important missions-related topics have been learned.[17] The multigenerational, foundational assumption that salvation and missions primarily mean populating heaven with souls

16. We should note, however, that the extent and the manner of Christianity's input into both the founding and ongoing development of the United States is an ongoing and complicated discussion. Without taking the time to enter directly into that volatile conversation, suffice it to say that within the unique historical milieu of the North American colonies and the United States of America, Christianity has without question been a major player in defining basic U.S.-American sociopolitical characteristics. In my judgment, there have been numerous other major players as well—for example, European Enlightenment ideals, various African traditions, injustices toward Native Americans, urbanization (especially from the late nineteenth century), and racism. How these, Christianity, and other factors have interrelated within U.S. history is the essence of the discussion. I would distance myself from any exclusive claim for Christianity, or any other single factor, to have been *the* foundation of what is, and always has been, unquestionably a pluralistic United States of America.

17. Many of these topics will be addressed later in the book.

has reinforced the lack of integration by effectively prohibiting reexamining the meaning of salvation and missions, particularly in relation to American sociopolitical ideals.[18] The modern missions movement has largely been an activist enterprise devoid of penetrating self-reflection,[19] so preexisting, basic notions have for the most part been strengthened, not called into question.

Self-awareness of long-standing Christian heritages can also reinforce status quo notions—in this case, the lack of integration between religion and nationality. "If the Christian gospel has been at work in our heritage for generations, then the basic structure of what we have today must be right," the subliminal reasoning goes. Layer on top of that reasoning what for many Americans is the "article of faith" of the separation of church and state.[20] The resulting "wall" between government and religion (whatever that "wall" means) makes it nearly impossible to consider how to integrate our patriotism and religious faith.

Our whole problem is compounded by the relatively insular existence (paradoxical in light of the extensive U.S. international influence) of many U.S. Christians vis-à-vis international affairs and people. Criticisms that might come against the United States and Americans are often met with bewilderment (due to obviously altruistic motives behind U.S. actions) or dismissal (since irrational anti-Americanism obviously is not worthy of our attention). As politically varied as the different U.S. media outlets are, a basic American worldview that assumes the primacy of U.S. interests encompasses them all. Add to the mix the monolingual (English) capacity of the vast majority of Americans (notwithstanding the developed multilingual capacities of missionaries, diplomats, and others, along with the extensive presence of non-English-speaking immigrants), and the

18. Appendix A traces the mid-twentieth-century development of the *missio Dei* ("mission of God") concept within ecumenical mission circles. This most definitely called into question the relationship between Christian mission and the United States—but evangelicals separated from the circles within which such discussions have taken place.

19. Wilbert R. Shenk, *Changing Frontiers of Mission*, American Society of Missiology Series, no. 28 (Maryknoll, NY: Orbis Books, 1999), 34–47.

20. Andrew F. Walls, *The Missionary Movement in Christian History: Studies in the Transmission of Faith* (Maryknoll, NY: Orbis Books, 1996), 232. While there are various nuanced understandings of what U.S. church-state separation means, essentially it is the result of a historical progression from colonial government support of monopolies of single religious institutions to federal government recognition of a plurality of religious institutions in the United States.

capacity of even hearing, much less seriously entertaining, suggestions or criticisms that others might make becomes all the more limited. As the well-known sociologist Robert Bellah has put it, "We remain a profoundly provincial, monolingual nation. Most Americans are not interested in the rest of the world and certainly don't know much about it. Foreign news has been in decline as a proportion not only of television news, but even of newspaper reporting for decades. Our degree of national pride is unmatched in the world."[21]

The net effect is an isolated American-Christian environment deeply assured of itself as the apex of Christian development. We know that America does not always live up to its ideals, but do we not unquestioningly believe in the universal standard of the U.S. Constitution's particular articulation of the ideals of "liberty and justice for all"? Are we able, or willing, to examine critically America's basic sociopolitical values, such as those regarding human rights or our political system? Can we meaningfully interact with the claim that, viewed both historically and internationally, the U.S. Constitution itself is "Americentric," reflecting the "moral limitation of nation-states" that have arisen in the modern world?[22] In raising such questions I have no particular political agenda in mind. I am simply attempting to bring, on both a theoretical and a personal level, our American patriotic-nationalistic assumptions under the scrutiny of Jesus and his Word.

Adding to our problematic self-assurance is what scholars have long termed "American exceptionalism—the messianic conceit that allows America to believe itself exempt from the clichés of geopolitics."[23] In other words, we need to be able to see the international dealings of the United States through the lenses of self-interest and power and not just

---

21. Robert N. Bellah, "The New American Empire: The Likely Consequences of the 'Bush Doctrine,'" in Avram, *Anxious about Empire*, 24.

22. Allen R. Hilton, "Who Are We? Being Christian in an Age of Americanism," in Avram, *Anxious about Empire*, 153.

23. Peter Scowen, *Rogue Nation: The America the Rest of the World Knows*, trans. of *Le livre noir des États-Unis* (Toronto, ON: McClellan & Stewart, 2003), 7. Cf. as well the following telling comments from Taylor, *Religion, Politics, and the Christian Right*, 5: "For a long time U.S. citizens have had a strong sense of national identity, a sense of vocation that scholars have named 'American exceptionalism'. After 9/11 . . . that exceptionalist sense—of being, for example, a special city on a hill, a light to the nations—was used in an almost desperate, self-congratulatory sense, letting loose what Anatol Lieven has called 'the demons of radical nationalism.'"

altruistic motives. Furthermore, we are heirs to the colonial conviction of being an exemplary "city set on a hill" for the rest of the world. We also retain the late-nineteenth-century "white man's burden" for the world's people of color. At that time the United States had defeated Spain and thus acquired the Philippines, thrusting America forward into its twentieth-century growth into a global empire.

All these assumptions help to shape our *American* vocational sense of obligation to share our unique blessings with the rest of the world. Within this environment, it is no small task critically and constructively to integrate views of salvation and missions on the one hand with an almost all-powerful and unquestionable patriotic-nationalistic fervor on the other. Paradoxically, for many U.S. evangelicals those two areas of life seem to coexist both in a comfortable, settled manner and in two separate compartments. Such a paradoxical outlook resembles that of Charles Briggs, who served as an American missionary in the Philippines in the early 1900s:

> The complete roster of missionary forces in the Philippines working for the speedy evangelization must include the American Government itself. Even though it be not ostensibly engaged in a missionary enterprise, the underlying motive that has constrained the American Government to occupy the Islands and administer them, is a missionary motive in essence, and a humanitarian motive by open declaration.[24]

Apparently Briggs was comfortable enough in keeping his patriotic and religious fervor on separate, parallel tracks, while overlapping them in their missionary effects. That paradoxical lack of integration is at the heart of what we are discussing here.

How to integrate constructively our lives as Jesus' followers remains our difficult challenge. In terms of applying the message of 1 Peter, suffering the loss, or at least a readjustment, of our assumed and subconscious American-Christian control, rights, and privileges with respect to God and to other people is deeply intertwined with this challenge.

24. Charles W. Briggs, *The Progressing Philippines* (Philadelphia: Griffith & Rowland Press, 1913), 136.

## Jesus Our Guiding Light

Evangelicals can look to recent leading sociopolitical thinkers for help in meeting this challenge. Carl Henry, Abraham Kuyper, Francis Schaeffer, and John Howard Yoder, for example, represent a spectrum of attempts at guiding Christian political thought and action "in the public square."[25] Within their respective evangelical traditions, these men thought, spoke, and wrote much that is instructive about political philosophy. For our purposes here, however, they do not aid us much in terms of how to understand and posture ourselves as Americans within an international situation. Their thought exemplifies Western evangelical thought in general—and Western political thought in particular—in how they failed to incorporate the worldwide input that the Christian church has to offer. Perhaps it was due to being people of their day, but they (as well as their subsequent Western analysts) confined themselves to their own Western traditions.

This is one of those situations into which Jesus seems to shine the brightest. He shines forth in his greatness, creativity, and power as the *international Kurios*. He shines to expose fault lines and dark corners, as well as to affirm what is good and right. Through it all Jesus sheds guiding light for the future, even as he uses light shed in the past as well as in other parts of the world.

Let's inch forward, conscious of needing Jesus' help, by asking ourselves some questions:

How can I more seamlessly integrate my thinking about God's world mission in Jesus and the U.S.-led international war on terror? One mistaken extreme is to keep those two realms totally distinct: "One is religious, one is political, and I will think about each of them in those totally unrelated ways." Another mistaken extreme is to conflate the two so that they become indistinguishable in my mind: "The U.S. military is God's force of good in this world, and their mission is God's way of dealing with the world's forces of evil, namely, terrorists." We can do better than either of those extremes.

25. These four "formative voices" are examined in a recent perceptive analysis by J. Budziszewski, with responses by David L. Weeks et al., *Evangelicals in the Public Square: Four Formative Voices on Political Thought and Action* (Grand Rapids: Baker Academic, 2006).

How does "freedom" in Christ relate to "freedom" in the United States? One extreme answer is to see one as spiritual and one as socio-economic-political, totally unrelated to each other. Another extreme is to see these two freedoms as one and the same, wherein I am free to pursue whatever I want, as guided by Christ. Again, we must do better than either of these two options. (Keep reading for further thoughts on how we can do better regarding both of these areas.)

How do non-Americans see American missionaries, in terms of religious affiliation, nationality, and ethnicity? This is a different type of question that I believe will help us move forward. While it is, of course, impossible to say what people all around the world think about anything, it is safe to suggest that non-Americans view American missionaries as concrete people, as bundles of traits that cannot be unraveled—with the "American" trait as paramount. How, then, did people in Japan view me while I was there? While I saw myself primarily as a religious emissary, they saw a Caucasian middle-class American (and non-Japanese) Christian family man, and—depending on the particular relationship—teacher, softball teammate, or neighbor. "White-foreigner-American" was the foremost label that overshadowed all others.

The main point here is that various aspects of an American missionary identity, as seen by others, are intertwined with each other—but the "white American" trait trumps all others.[26] Everything else associated with that trait inseparably comes along with it as well, from the 1861–65 U.S. Civil War to current economic-military power to the confusing array of morality and culture embodied in U.S.-produced movies.

In terms of how to approach the earlier questions in this section, then, it behooves us to keep in mind the categories of nationality and ethnicity as key links between the religious and political realms. (There are, of course, many other aspects than what we can discuss here of a Christian view of the relationship between religion and politics, some of which are discussed in Appendix B.) What is the relationship between God's mission and the war on terror? We know that a central part of

26. This is not to suggest that all U.S. Christian missionaries are white. Most are and have been, but black American missionaries have been and are active as well. See, for example, the April 2000 issue of *Mission Frontiers*, entitled "The African American & Missions: The Past, the Present, the Possibilities," available online at http://www.missionfrontiers.org/2000/02/200002.htm.

God's mission in Jesus, indeed of the Christian gospel itself, is that different nationalities and ethnicities are brought together in Christ. We also know that God saves us as nationally and ethnically identifiable people, not just as spirit-substance souls. Real, concrete people are involved in salvation and in God's mission to make the world right again.

So it is with respect to terrorism and war. Real, concrete people are involved. The causes of terrorism are neither straightforward nor reducible to a single category, be it economic, religious, ethnic, national, historical, or something else. Even defining terrorism is not as easy as one might think: Was Samson, for example, a religious terrorist (at least from the Philistines' perspective), similar to contemporary suicide bombers?[27] If you think that question is ridiculous and even sacrilegious or treasonous, why do you think so? Is your reaction due to religious or political instincts? How can you tell?

A key is for Jesus to step in and help us to think—*including through discussion with others whose nationality is different and who think differently* (chapter 4 is coming)—coolly and honestly about who we are and what war and terrorism are all about. Pat, defensive answers will not do for us as we seek to integrate our thinking in constructive and fair ways.

What about "freedom"? Jesus' words "the truth will set you free" (John 8:32) are as misquoted as any in public conversation today. Jesus, of course, points to himself as "the truth" (John 14:6), as well as "the way" and "the life," the One in whom we know and follow God. That central qualification of "the truth" as the particular person Jesus tends to be omitted too frequently. Simply knowing the state of affairs accurately is not what Jesus means: knowing him personally is the main thrust of being freed by the truth.

---

27. Naim Ateek, "Suicide Bombers: What Is Theologically and Morally Wrong with Suicide Bombings? A Palestinian Christian Perspective," *Cornerstone* 25 (Summer 2002): 2, available online at http://www.sabeel.org/old/news/cstone25/suicidebombers.htm. Interestingly enough, an astute analysis of Islamic fundamentalism, written very much from a U.S.-evangelical viewpoint, has this as one of its chapter titles: " 'Let Me Die with the Philistines!' Martyrdom and Suicide Missions"—but with no exploration (except a notation to the Scripture reference) of why this connection with Samson has been made or of the implications of making the connection. David Zeidan, *Sword of Allah: Islamic Fundamentalism from an Evangelical Perspective* (Waynesboro, GA: Gabriel Publishing, 2003), 99.

That is especially important when we realize that the context of Jesus' conversation with the Jewish religious leaders of his day concerned their ethnicity. They had come to equate their ethnic heritage with religious standing before God. Their confidence of belonging to God was directly tied to their being ethnic Israelites. Jesus confronted their false, settled notion by asserting, "If you abide in my word, you are truly my disciples, and you will know the truth, and the truth will set you free" (John 8:31b–32). He then speaks of their needing to be freed from their enslavement to sin (8:34–36). Believing and following *him*, not just relying on mere ethnic identity, was central to the Jewish leaders' being freed to know and serve God.

That notion of freedom affects how I might understand freedom in a U.S-political sense. The "freedom" of which Jesus speaks is not simply a libertarian environment wherein I can pursue my socio-economic-political dreams independently from the state. Arguably, such a notion is a central tenet of the current "American dominant ideology."[28] Instead, true "freedom" is the capacity to know and serve God and others, to live as I was created to live. It is that freedom to which Peter refers in the midst of his words on sociopolitical involvement: "Live as people who are free, not using your freedom as a cover-up for evil, but living as servants of God" (1 Peter 2:16). That capacity does not come by inalienable right that is due to ethnic identity, even though as a Caucasian U.S.-American I may have inherited socio-economic-political privileges that others don't have. While such privileges may actually enable me to serve God and others, freedom in Christ fundamentally comes to me and others regardless of ethnic or national identity.

The freedom to know and serve God enables me to realize that others see me in my ethnicity and nationality—and that such identities affect my capacity as an American missionary, for example. A close Japanese friend once asked me, "Why are all of you American missionaries white?" By that question my friend was not intending to castigate black

---

28. Joseph B. Tamney, "American Views of Islam, Post 9/11," *Islamic Studies* 43, no. 4 (Winter 2004): 604–8. Stanley Hauerwas is another author who has provocatively written about the interrelationship between biblical teaching and U.S. values, for example in his *Unleashing the Scripture: Freeing the Bible from Captivity to America* (Nashville: Abingdon Press, 1993).

American Christians for not sending missionaries to Japan. Rather, he was genuinely puzzled why missionaries from the racial majority were the only ones representing what he knew to be a racially pluralistic society. It was a good question, illustrating the light that Jesus often shines through others on our own situations that might need fresh evaluation. How our international Christian identity comes into play on such matters is the subject of our next chapter.

And so we walk forward, behind Jesus' sure guidance. The answers to how everything fits together are not neat and ready-made. We follow Jesus in our particular situations, as particular people, within particular histories, with ongoing questions. Moreover, we do so as real, concrete people, who are integrated wholes composed of various facets of our existence.

We as American Christians are real, live people whom God saves and uses for his purposes. It is the same for Christians of other nationalities and ethnicities. God's salvation and mission are comprehensive, not simplistic, as well as concrete, not abstract. The shining Jesus leads us step by step, each day, within our concrete and particular situations. He skillfully strums our heartstrings, and by his Word and Spirit he graciously directs our hearts to beat in sync with his. A central component in how Jesus does that is the input of our international Christian connections, the cultivation of which we will be considering in ensuing chapters. (See Appendix B for examples of how he has given guidance through Christians of earlier generations as well.)

If these last couple of summary paragraphs ring true with you, this chapter's central message has come through. That means as well that Jesus—our President and Commander in Chief, the international *Kurios*, the Suffering Servant and slain Lamb of God—is leading us through the path of suffering the loss of assumed and subconscious American control, rights, and privileges with respect to God and to other people, particularly others in our "brotherhood throughout the world." It is to our identity within that worldwide family that we will turn next.

## Reflection Questions

- Why is it important to relate to Jesus as a particular person, not just a doctrine?

- How might my ethnic and national identities enter into my interactions with God during my personal devotions, as well as during my experience of corporate worship?

- How is my patriotism the same as, and different from, nationalism? How do, and how should, my patriotic-nationalistic feelings interrelate with my feelings toward Jesus?

# 4

# Who Are We Collectively?

All aspects of our lives and of this world, including patriotic devotion, nationhood, and ethnicity, are within the scope of Jesus' reshaping work as *Kurios*. The central question of this chapter concerns identifying who *we* are with respect to Jesus *our* Master, President, Exemplar of suffering, Friend, and Commander in Chief. Jesus has sent *us* into the world, he lives with *us* by his Holy Spirit, and he is reshaping *us* his people. Our focus here: *Who are "we"?*

## Corporate Mentality

The answer to that question can, of course, be formulated at any number of levels. The preceding chapter discussed the *concreteness* of who "we" are as American Christians, particularly with regard to our *national* and *ethnic* identities. A *theological* answer would certainly be appropriate as well; for example, "we" are Christ's body, his people, and Jesus' followers. *Sociological* descriptions could also help explain "our" identity: "we," as those whom Jesus has sent into his world on his mission, are poor, middle class, and rich; we speak all sorts of languages; we live in cities and the countryside; we are young and old; we are male and female.

Before exploring specific ways of describing ourselves, however, we must first consider the necessity—and the challenge—simply of having an ingrained *corporate*-identity instinct. In practical terms, we need to know in our gut that there *is* a *group* before we start describing who it is. Furthermore, we need to add quickly that having such a gut-level awareness of one's own group's existence—where I think of my group when I think of myself—comes neither naturally nor easily to most American Christians.

One of the causes of a narrow evangelical understanding of missions as ultimately being only for the salvation of individual souls was the rise of Western individualism. Mention of "Western" individualism need not imply that individualism exists only in "the West," because in fact individuals and individualism exist all over the world. Nor does the implication have to be a negative one, as if an appreciation of people as individuals were somehow wrong or detrimental to how one views human beings. The Bible affirms the worth of individuals in many ways—for example, in how people bear responsibility before God for their own actions (e.g., Ezek. 18).

At the same time, the notion of individualism has developed in the modern West in striking and unique ways. Moreover, modern Western individualism—particularly in the United States—has taken extreme forms, as manifest for example in the degree of cultural uprootedness that so many people experience, and in the individual "Lone Ranger" type of superheroes about whom movies are continually made.[1] Much of the explanation of the extreme nature of individualism in the United States comes from the social dynamics of the twentieth century associated with urbanization and industrialization. One can also point to earlier European developments of individual political and economic rights, which were then carried forward in the more newly formed United States. But the single most distinguishable mark of how a specifically Western individualism emerged was in its philosophical crystallization by René Descartes (1596–1650): *cogito, ergo sum.* To make this claim ("I think, therefore I am") is to base everything from the most basic beliefs to my very existence on the foundation of my solitary thinking process. That fountainhead of modern Western philosophy is as solitary and *individual* as is imaginable.

1. One popular and perceptive analysis of the loss of "social capital" in the United States is Robert D. Putnam, *Bowling Alone: The Collapse and Revival of American Community* (New York: Simon & Schuster, 2000).

The carryover effect for all of us who have this philosophical and socio-economic-political heritage is potent and far-reaching. To cut to the chase of this discussion, at the level of instinct we are nomadic individuals whose connections with the outside world radiate out from "me" as the center. Insofar as I am a part of a group, it is "I" who am a part of "my" group (family, school, company, etc.); it is not the case that first the "group is," then therefore I am. Crucial also is the way in which we instinctively read the Bible as if it had been written exclusively to "me"; and we tend to assume that "the gospel" means that Jesus died exclusively for "me" (and for other individuals who believe).

Are those instincts patently wrong? No. Are they extreme? Yes.

Balance and correction can come from many other cultural settings. For example, African self-identity has been described this way: "I am because we are, and because we are therefore I am." The community's life is paramount, and a member-individual's well-being is inextricably bound up in that community. A Japanese self-introduction commonly starts with the group label (place, company, school, etc.) and ends with the individual's name. While Japan may very well exhibit individualism's opposite extreme of communalism, nevertheless it serves as yet another instructive counterbalance.

Even more powerfully than from other cultural experiences is how balance and correction come from the Bible's corporate emphases. God's covenantal initiative at the heart of his salvation and mission is the corporate "I will be their God, and they shall be my people" (Jer. 31:33). Interesting is the corresponding individualized covenantal formula in, for example, Revelation 21:7: "The one who conquers will have this heritage, and I will be his God and he will be my son." Biblical salvation and mission is not a one-sided communalism that obliterates individualism, but instead is a more balanced communitarianism.

When asked by his disciples to teach them to pray, Jesus instructed them to do so out of a corporate framework, "Our Father."[2] Not only

---

2. I explore this theme at great length in a three-sermon series, "God's World Mission and the Lord's Prayer," 2000 World Mission Week Lectures (St. Louis: Covenant Theological Seminary AV Services, February 2000), available online at http://www.covenantseminary. edu/resource/Jennings_WM2000_OurFatherInHeaven.mp3, http://www.covenantseminary. edu/resource/Jennings_WM2000_HallowedBeYourName.mp3, and http://www.covenant seminary.edu/resource/Jennings_WM2000_ForgiveUsOurDebts.mp3.

Peter's letters but also most of Paul's are written to Christian communities and thus use, in the main, plural *you*s, or *y'all*s. The entire Bible is given to the corporate people of God, not just to nomadic individuals. Through his death and resurrection Jesus the second Adam dealt with the world's sin and the resulting creationwide curse, in addition to my sins and those of other individuals (Rom. 5:12–19).

These balanced collective emphases in God's Word should infiltrate and shape our deepest notions about who we are as human beings. As Americans, we have had those deepest notions shaped by numerous individualistic influences, some healthy and some unhealthy. Our instinct should be that we as the human race have a corporate interconnectedness of responsibility before God and for the rest of creation. As the people of God—including those who have gone before us, those still alive, and those yet to come—we are the firstfruits of God's re-creation of his world. The corporate notions that *we* (again, whoever "we" are) are a central part of God's salvation and mission should be at the very core of our being.

## Public Awareness

Related to our need as American Christians to develop an ingrained corporate-identity instinct is the importance of a *public* mind-set with regard to salvation and mission. God's work in Jesus Christ was not a private affair or a backstage maneuver. Rather, Jesus was "seen by angels" (1 Tim. 3:16); he put Satan and his hosts "to open shame" (Col. 2:15); God now openly and tauntingly declares "to the rulers and authorities in the heavenly places" (Eph. 3:10) his wisdom of reuniting estranged peoples, beginning with Jews and Gentiles. Over the centuries, as people have been coming to Christ they have been transferred from one public kingdom, that of darkness, to the other public kingdom of Jesus (Col. 1:13). Even if many people are currently unaware of these heavenly, spiritual realities, one day everyone will bow and openly acknowledge "that Jesus Christ is Lord, to the [public] glory of God the Father" (Phil. 2:11).

Because that day is still to come, we must wait for the ultimate public display of Jesus' kingdom reality. But even though that day is still in the future, God's salvation and mission are already public in the political realm as well. God is the Sovereign Ruler of all those in authority, since they all "have been instituted by God" (Rom. 13:1). God laughs at monarchs' grandiloquence (Ps. 2:4), striking them down in judgment when necessary (e.g., Herod in Acts 12:20–23). Jesus submitted himself to public execution, then repeatedly demonstrated his power over military strength by freeing not only himself but also his followers from their guard-watch (himself in Matthew 27:62–28:4, Peter in Acts 12:6–11, Paul and Silas in Acts 16:25–34). God uses political authorities for his own special purposes (e.g., Cyrus ruler of Persia in Isaiah 44:28), and Jesus' followers are to maneuver skillfully within their understanding of proper political authority (e.g., Paul in Acts 16:35–40). All these examples help us to realize that the very centerpiece of the most basic Christian confession of faith, "Jesus is *Kurios*," speaks directly to the public, political, and sovereign reign of God's Son, our Savior, Jesus the Nazarene. The full display of Jesus' public reign has yet to come; Jesus' followers often live as persecuted minorities, for example, the original readers of 1 Peter. Oddly enough, however, Peter encourages Christians to "be subject for the Lord's sake to every human institution, whether it be to the emperor as supreme, or to governors" (1 Peter 2:13–14); yet the Bible's declaration is that we honor political authorities "for the Lord's sake" and because we "fear God" (1 Peter 2:17). Jesus alone is the ultimate Ruler.

The Christian gospel also has public socioeconomic aspects. The city of Ephesus broke out into a rioting protest over the "disturbance concerning the Way" (Acts 19:21–41). Famine relief (Acts 11:27–30), employment and work (Eph. 4:28; 6:5–9), attitudes toward the judicial system (1 Cor. 6:1–8), and myriad other areas of public life are inexorably connected to God's work of salvation and mission in Jesus. Furthermore, these areas range in scope from the global political economy to particular local settings. God's mission is concerned, for example, with loans and interest rates between nation-states (as Jubilee Debt Campaigns have helped to point out[3]) as well as between individual parties.

The church stands at the center of Jesus' public mission. In the future new heaven and new earth, the Holy City, the New Jerusalem, is the "bride

---

3. Information about one Jubilee Debt Campaign—concerned with forgiving the international debt of the world's poorest countries—is available online at http://www.jubileedebt campaign.org.uk/?lid=282.

adorned for her husband" (Rev. 21:2). This organic, public civic-church is the collective body of Christ sent into society, the workplace, and families to serve in these civic spheres (Eph. 5:22–6:9; Col. 3:18–4:1; 1 Peter 2:13–3:7). God's taunting of the satanic powers is his public, spiritual declaration "through the church [of his] manifold wisdom" (Eph. 3:10). At the heart of God's public mission is how we as God's people live in the midst of angels, demons, and the social-public square.

On the one hand, mixing religious faith and public matters is familiar to Americans and even institutionalized in contemporary U.S. society. Certain officials, most notably the president, swear on the Bible upon inauguration. Biblical language is often used in political discourse.[4] "God" is openly invoked to "bless America." Religious chaplains are employed by the government. Additionally, select religious-political issues regularly make the mainstream news—for example, the place of prayer in schools, the public display of the Ten Commandments, abortion, sexuality, and marriage. Furthermore, Americans (if we are listening) regularly hear of religion's active role in other countries as well. Recently the Malaysian prime minister publicly requested citizens to pray for rain to relieve Kuala Lumpur and surrounding areas from a debilitating smog. "When something like this happens, we have to ask for God's help," he explained.[5]

American Christians, however, face stiff challenges to cultivating a public mentality about salvation and mission. By common consent in U.S. society, religion is considered to be a private affair. Not only, therefore, is each individual free to believe whatever he or she chooses, but politeness and postmodern political correctness prohibit public discussion of religious subjects beyond those embraced by a civil-religious consensus. (Compare the situation in many other countries, where politics and

---

4. Stephen B. Chapman strongly warns against the dangers of such language—most especially "the application of Christ language to America," for example, George W. Bush's reference to America's being the light shining in the darkness ("and the darkness will not overcome it"); his refrain that "There's power, wonder-working power, in the goodness and idealism and faith of the American people"; and his comparison of America to the Good Samaritan. Stephen B. Chapman, "Imperial Exegesis: When Caesar Interprets Scripture," in *Anxious about Empire: Theological Essays on the New Global Realities*, ed. Wes Avram (Grand Rapids: Brazos Press, 2004), 91–96.

5. "Malaysians Told to Pray for Rain," BBC News, August 12, 2005, UK ed., available online at http://news.bbc.co.uk/2/hi/asia-pacific/4144242.stm.

religion are not taboo subjects.) Judiciaries wrestle with how religion fits in public institutions, for example, schools. Moreover, not only does U.S. society have conflicting understandings of what church-state separation means, but there are also shifting demographics of ethical-religious convictions.

What is clear biblical teaching for American Christians is that we must buck the trend toward strict religious privacy and develop the instinct that following Jesus in his mission is very much a public affair. God's mission takes place in a very public arena, whether that be heavenly and unseen, socio-economic-politically, or interpersonally.

## We Are International

We have seen that Paul writes, "Through the church the manifold wisdom of God [is] made known to the rulers and authorities in the heavenly places" (Eph. 3:10). The "*manifold* wisdom" that God puts on public display stands out as God's plan of bringing together different kinds of people. The original Greek term translated *manifold* means something like "many-varied." The central emphasis is on plurality and variety. Paul has employed a striking term to emphasize that point.

This is where we can become more specific and concrete in answering this chapter's main question, "Who are we collectively?" To this point this chapter's discussion has stressed the preliminary need to develop the instinct that a corporate, public "we" is central in God's mission and salvation. The importance of this preliminary framework cannot be overemphasized. In fact, I encourage you to stop reading for a moment or two and reflect on the extent to which the type of corporate-public instinct we have been discussing has developed in your own heart and mind.

As we noted at the top of this chapter, there are any number of levels at which we could describe who "we" are as God's people. For our purposes here, in light of the book's overall thrust of examining ourselves as Americans in relation to God and to others, we need to focus on the biblical and demographically accurate description of us as *international*. Coming to grips with this international character of the community of Jesus' followers is absolutely vital to our overarching purpose of constructively suffering the loss of assumed control, rights, and privileges.

## Biblically

*International* as used here has both political and ethnic meanings. Jesus is Head over a people with representatives from every member-state of the United Nations. And insofar as *the nations* in the Bible refers to "peoples" (*ethne*),[6] various ethnic groups as well make up the church. *International* thus means both "between nation states" and "between ethnic groups."

Perhaps the biblical passage cited most often to demonstrate this central trait of God's people is John's description of "a great multitude that no one could number, from every nation, from all tribes and peoples and languages, standing before the throne and before the Lamb" in worship (Rev. 7:9). This coming reality is based on Jesus the Lamb's work on the cross: "You were slain, and by your blood you ransomed people for God from every tribe and language and people and nation" (5:9). The everlasting people of God will be made up of all kinds of people because Christ purchased them by his own blood.

This future international church is a fulfillment of God's promise to Abraham to bless "all the families of the earth" (Gen. 12:3). God's covenantal initiative through Abraham and his offspring was a particular way of fulfilling God's original creation plan for his international people to "be fruitful and multiply and fill the earth and subdue it" (1:28). Through the prophet Jeremiah, God promised to "gather the remnant of my flock out of all the countries where I have driven them, and I will bring them back to their fold, and they shall be fruitful and multiply" (Jer. 23:3). While the immediate fulfillment of that promise was the restoration of old-covenant Israel to their old-covenant real estate, the

6. This is a point particularly stressed in many recent expositions of Matthew 28:19, where Jesus commands his disciples to "make disciples of all nations." Some commentators are concerned to stress the *religious* connotations of "the nations" in the Bible versus the more recent *sociological* stress on people groups. Cf., e.g., Richard De Ridder, *Discipling the Nations* (Grand Rapids: Baker, 1971), 189. Thankfully, in my judgment, we do not face an exclusive either/or choice between these two options.

primary and ultimate fulfillment is the salvation of all sorts of people from among the nations to inhabit the world and follow Jesus in his worldwide mission.

Jesus poured out his Holy Spirit at Pentecost as a living demonstration that he was *Kurios* and Christ, as well as that his people were to be composed of all language speakers "from every nation under heaven" (Acts 2:5–11, 33–36). Jesus continued working on Peter to convince him that he could not "stand in God's way" of incorporating all nations, Jew and Gentile alike, into Christ's international church (Acts 11:17). Paul recognized Jesus' gift of the Holy Spirit to all sorts of people as "the blessing of Abraham . . . to the Gentiles [*ethne*], so that we might receive the promised Spirit through faith" (Gal. 3:14). Paul's international identity in Christ the international *Kurios* repeatedly shows through his writings: he regularly stressed that "there is no distinction between Jew and Greek; the same Lord is Lord of all" (Rom. 10:12).

In sum, at the heart of the entire biblical story line is God's mission to save an international people through the person and work of Jesus Christ.

## Demographically

The church has realized this international focus of the Christian faith better at certain times than at others. Judaizers in the New Testament were slow to believe that the omnilingual, universal God and Father of Jesus the *Kurios* is fully determined to have an omnilingual, universal people, not just a monolingual tribe. In recent centuries the Latinized church of Europe, as well as those of us who constitute its North American stepchild, have been slow to believe that the omnilingual, universal God really wants an omnilingual, universal people. Yet what has happened over the past few generations is compelling and undeniable testimony to the worldwide, international scope of God's salvation and mission in Christ.

Figure 3 shows the relative percentage makeup by continent of the worldwide Christian church throughout the twentieth century. As indicated, in 1900 the great majority (70.6 percent) of the world's professing Christians lived in Europe, with sizable portions in North America (11.4 percent) and Latin America (11.5 percent) as well. Together those three

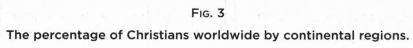

FIG. 3

**The percentage of Christians worldwide by continental regions.**

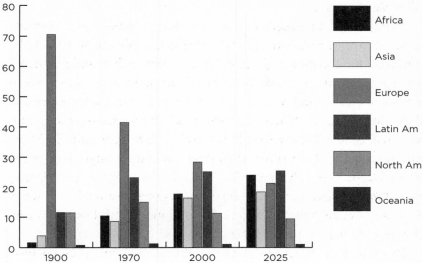

areas accounted for 93.5 percent of the world's Christians, and Africa (1.7 percent), Asia (4.0 percent), and Oceania (0.8 percent) made up the remaining 6.5 percent. But by 1970 one can see major demographic changes. Europe's portion had significantly decreased (to 41.5 percent, which is a generous figure by some standards), whereas large increases are evident in Africa (to 10.4 percent) and Latin America (to 23.3 percent). By 2000 these trends have continued, and the Christian world will look even more different by 2025.[7] Whatever one makes of such statistical information, these numbers are too definitive to be disregarded.

Many Americans who have traveled abroad have encountered the vibrancy of faith and life in other sectors of the worldwide church. The church in Korea has been zealous in prayer and international missions work. Much of the church in Africa and Latin America suffers in poverty

7. David B. Barrett, George T. Kurian, and Todd M. Johnson, *World Christian Encyclopedia: A Comparative Study of Churches and Religions in the Modern World*, 2nd ed., vol. 1, *The World by Countries: Religionists, Churches, Ministries* (Oxford: Oxford University Press, 2001), 12, table 1-3. I explore this theme more fully in "Christianity in a New World-Historical Situation," World Mission Article Archive (St. Louis: Covenant Theological Seminary AV Services, 2005), available online at http://www.covenantseminary.edu/resource/Jennings_ChristianityInNewWorldSituation.pdf.

and deprivation, yet does so joyfully and passionately. Churches in politically oppressive contexts know the special presence of their heavenly Master and Protector, the One who suffered as their example. Minority churches experience daily their weakness as well as the power of God. We must not romanticize other situations, but we must not neglect them, either.

The basic point for this discussion is that "we" who are Jesus' public community of followers are in actuality more worldwide and international than ever before. We are sent by our omnilingual, universal *Kurios* into, and we are scattered among, the political-ethnic nations of the world. No one political-ethnic sector of the church is Christian headquarters: Jesus himself is the Director and Sustainer of his worldwide mission.

## Coming to Terms as American Evangelicals with the International Church

Intellectually acknowledging the worldwide character of the church may not be too difficult, but emotionally and instinctively coming to terms with it is another matter. That's because we American Christians are accustomed to operating as if the church in the United States were the center of the Christian world. (While this may not be a peculiarly American problem, the current superpower status of the United States, as well as this particular book's focus, make it a peculiar problem for us here.) We instinctively assume that theology, missions, and sociopolitical values have their standards set in the West in general, and in the United States in particular. The "city set on a hill" and "white man's burden" aspects of our American heritage push us to show and tell others how to live; they do not help us to live cooperatively with others throughout the world.

*Barriers.* Perhaps most powerful of all the root causes of this complex instinct that says American Christianity is the center of worldwide Christianity is the slowly dying, and centuries-old, background of European Christendom. That territorial notion, which says that "our land" is Christian (and only Christian), crossed the Atlantic to North America with early European migration. While assuming that its own territory is fully Christian, the all-encompassing Christendom notion assumes that everyone and everything outside itself is unenlightened heathendom. The carryover to this day is clear in the instinct that U.S. Christianity is the center of worldwide Christianity. That instinct is an assumed privilege that must be exposed and examined.

An unquestioning patriotism-nationalism builds on this inherited, territorial Christendom worldview to help produce an America-based U.S.-evangelical Christian reflex in relation to the rest of the world. I once saw this posture displayed while the world's flags were being carried into a U.S. church's sanctuary during a missions conference. The American flag was carried in first, and then all the other flags were dipped in deference to the U.S. flag when they passed it. The reflex to exalt the United States in such a religious manner has been cultivated by two generations of American evangelicals growing up in an environment of U.S. global hegemony since World War II, which has now turned unilateralist since the end of the Cold War and especially since 9/11.[8] I would argue as well

8. David Skidmore's summary arguments at the end of his stimulating article are quoted in full here:

"The U.S. has never pursued a genuinely multilateralist foreign policy. Rather, U.S. strategy in the post–World War II period is best characterized as hegemonic. While the U.S. embraced the creation of international institutions as an effective means for exercising U.S. power and maintaining international order, the rules and procedures of these institutions bound other states far more than the U.S. itself.

"The growing conflicts between the U.S. and its major allies in recent years are the result of two shifts: the waning willingness of the U.S. to invest in strong international institutions and the growing insistence by other states that the U.S. conform to the same international rules as the rest of the international community. These dual challenges to the two principal pillars of U.S. hegemony have resulted in an increasingly unilateralist American foreign policy, one that rests more upon the raw application of power and less upon the willingness of other states to follow the U.S. as a legitimate international leader.

"This move from hegemony to unilateralism in U.S. foreign policy can be traced to the end of the Cold War. The demise of the Soviet Union removed an important constraint on U.S. power while reducing the dependence of allied states on U.S. protection. At home, the removal of the Soviet threat weakened the authority of the president to pursue broad national interests while empowering parochial interests that generally oppose multilateral commitments.

"The foreign policy differences between Bill Clinton and George W. Bush are not as stark as many have perceived. The preferences, ideology, and rhetoric of the two presidents are quite different. But structural forces at home and abroad have played more important roles in driving presidents (Clinton reluctantly and Bush enthusiastically) toward a pattern of unilateralist behavior in U.S. relations with the world. The appropriate contrast is . . . between two unilateralisms that differ not in kind but more in tone, emphasis, and degree. . . ." David Skidmore, "Understanding the Unilateralist Turn in U.S. Foreign Policy," *Foreign Policy Analysis* 1, no. 2 (July 2005): 224.

that both the national government and the U.S. media (U.S. evangelicals' often negative view of the media as "liberal" notwithstanding) exclusively propagate an America-centered worldview, in which the world's events are conveyed in terms of their relationship to the United States. For example, an acquaintance visiting from England remarked, upon hearing the news of the July 7, 2005, London bombings, how difficult it was to get adequate reports of what had happened, since the media here were so quick to explore the bombings' implications for America. Within such an America-centered environment, for American Christians it is next to impossible to escape the same viewpoint.

Subconscious racism—such strong language is necessary to expose what is actually the case here, I believe—has also perpetuated the crippling, latent territorial notion that the United States is Christendom and the rest of the world is heathendom. Noting the presence of racism helps to explain the unspoken, operative notion that only Western-language-speaking Caucasians can produce genuine Christian theology. Hence Western seminaries, especially including U.S.-evangelical ones, for the most part exclusively use Western-language-speaking, Caucasian theologians' materials; and one prominent missionary agenda is the translation of Western theologians' material into non-Western languages—all despite a massive amount of available indigenous non-Western theology. (There are other reasons as well for these phenomena—ready access to Western publishers, for example—but the power and place of racism must not therefore be skirted.) Racism also helps to explain the framework that gospel ministry among nearby Caucasians is *evangelism*, while ministry to other types of people is *missions*.[9] Saying that God's mission, and missions, take place among Caucasian Americans is offensive to the racist assumption that our kind of people don't need the kind of effort that others do.

Racial issues are undoubtedly woven deeply into the fabric of U.S. social and national life, and quite naturally the U.S. context in part determines how we as American Christians live our lives and view our world. Not all these issues are clear, and Christians disagree over their nature and solutions (as well we should, so long as we can discuss the issues

9. We will come back to this particular distinction later.

constructively). Even so, the response to Hurricane Katrina exposed at least some measure of racial problems in New Orleans. The lack of U.S. media specifically reporting on (and my lack of concern about) Iraqi, Pakistani, and Afghani deaths during the first few years of U.S. military activities there was, arguably, due at least in part to racist notions (along with cultural and national ones) of whose lives are important and whose are not. How my fellow church members, my family, and I respond to changing ethnic dynamics in particular neighborhoods, restaurants, schools, and churches in our cities—leave or avoid, engage and participate, be primarily concerned for my property values, or whatever—can reveal racially based foundations with serious cracks desperately in need of repair or even replacement.

*Solutions.* The challenge for U.S. Christians is to deal, by God's grace, with these deeply rooted national and racial instincts through his Word and Holy Spirit working in us as we interact with Christian brothers and sisters who are of different nationalities and ethnicities. God shows us our nationalistic small-mindedness and racial pride as we interface with Christians (and others) from different parts of the world. Through international Christian fellowship, we can experience how "the ties that bind Christians throughout the world run counter to the claims that nationalism would make on our primary loyalties."[10] As our sin is brought to light, we can respond not out of guilt, but out of a heartfelt desire to grow and out of "a good conscience, [assured] through the resurrection of Jesus Christ" (1 Peter 3:21).

One common feature of our thinking, for example, that can be exposed is the almost magical character of the outline of the 48 continental United States. When we expand our limits for future possibilities of work or ministry, we commonly think of being willing to go "anywhere in the country." The question has to be asked: why does "the country" define our world's limits? To take the matter a step further, what is it about my political-national citizenship that seems to trump other crucial aspects of my identity?[11]

---

10. Wes Avram, "Introduction," in Avram, *Anxious about Empire*, 13.

11. Interesting in this regard are the following observations about some early North American colonial views of supposed "continental" expansiveness of Atlantic seaboard colonies:

Behind the exposure of such assumptions is Jesus' passion to transform my life, as part of his mission to transform the world. He comes, through other brothers and sisters in Christ, to my part of the world to help me "die to sin and live to righteousness" (1 Peter 2:24). As an American Christian in particular, by following Christ's example of suffering I can relinquish my assumed rights and privileges of belonging to an assumed uniquely Christian nation. In so doing I can allow my international Christian identity to trump my political-national identity.

With respect to America's role in global politics, the parameters of an American political discussion normally stretch from nationalist-unilateralist to internationalist-multilateralist.[12] That is, the scale moves from a stress on American interests and America's right to take international initiatives, including military ones, to emphasizing global interests and America's responsibility to act in accord with the wishes of the international community. I believe that American Christians can—and should—disagree about politics, even while we honestly and respectfully engage each other and others about such matters. I also believe that, as American Christians working through these complicated but crucial issues, we must not uncritically confine ourselves either to strictly political considerations or to strictly American input. We need to take intertwined multiple factors (religious, economic, historical, etc.) into collective consideration, and—of particular relevance here—we need to incorporate the input of fellow Christians around the world.

---

"Europeans' and colonial Americans' ignorance of northwestern North America meant that they were unfamiliar with the Rocky Mountains north of New Mexico, or the general aridity of the west. . . . Unaware of natural boundaries that would form obstacles to westward expansion, and influenced by Enlightenment thought regarding the relationship between political borders and nature, many saw potential for politically homogenous, expansive polities that stretched across the continent. The charters of Virginia and Massachusetts granted lands between set latitudes that extended from 'sea to sea.' . . . The colonies as described in charters might stretch from sea to sea, but colonists did not."

This is yet another thread woven into the strong tapestry of the "continental" 48 states, the outline of which so powerfully influences U.S.-American self-identity. James D. Drake, "Appropriating a Continent: Geographical Categories, Scientific Metaphors, and the Construction of Nationalism in British North America and Mexico," *Journal of World History* 15, no. 3 (September 2004): 329–30.

12. One helpful and nuanced study (compiled just prior to September 2001) of the complicated nature of U.S. unilateralism versus its "ambivalent multilateralism" is Steward Patrick and Shepard Forman, eds., *Multilateralism and U.S. Foreign Policy: Ambivalent Engagement*, Studies in Multilateralism Series, Center on International Cooperation (Boulder, CO: Lynne Rienner Publishers, 2002).

Incorporating that input is particularly important given America's superpower status. When you function only "within the strongest nation you don't realize you're strong. . . . Empires seldom feel like empires from the inside out. . . . For this reason, there has never been a better time for Christians to consider the fact that we are truly an international church. There has never been a better time to remind ourselves that Christianity is not a state religion." This provocative description of our present situation continues: "As the American empire grows, the church in America can remind people that Jesus' death and resurrection marked the end of a chosen people with a single zip code." This prophetic posture comes from our international networks, since "contact with congregations around the world can provide the insight we miss from the inside."[13]

Allowing our Christian international identity to affect our political viewpoints does not mean that we as American Christians throw healthy patriotism out the window. God has placed all his people as citizens in our respective countries, and we are gladly to "honor everyone," including godly and ungodly leaders alike (1 Peter 2:17). As Americans, we are to be grateful for much, including our Christian heritage. Sociopolitical freedoms that are deeply woven into the fabric of this nation are to be treasured, as are the crucial roles that the United States played especially in World War II in defeating militaristic and tyrannical empires bent on ruling wide areas of the world.

Nor does taking seriously my Christian international identity mean that I simply disregard what I honestly think simply because my view may be unpopular on a worldwide scale. Suffering by relinquishing my assumed rights and privileges before others does not mean that I stop being honest. It does mean, though, that our fundamental identity as the international people of God should deeply inform how we as American evangelicals think about, work through, and act with regard to global political matters.[14] Christians in America and in Japan have much to

---

13. Lillian Daniel, "Empire's Sleepy Embrace: The View from the Pew," in Avram, *Anxious about Empire*, 183–84.

14. I agree with Charles Marsh when he notes how leading American evangelical preachers, in the run-up to the 2003 U.S. invasion of Iraq, argued for the justness of the coming American military action in disregard of wider, including global, Christian viewpoints. "Wayward Christian Soldiers," *New York Times*, January 20, 2006, available online at http://www.nytimes.com/2006/01/20/opinion/20marsh.html?ex=1295413200&en=9611bfdb755d0d6d&ei=5090&partner=rssuserland&emc=rss.

learn from each other, for example, regarding how to think about nuclear armaments; our children, raised in Japan, tell us of the value in being able to sympathize with very different viewpoints on that issue. American Christians and Palestinian Christians have many mutually instructive perspectives to share with each other about the Middle East, for example. And the list goes on. Whether I will take a more "nationalist-unilateralist," "internationalist-multilateralist," or some other creatively crafted position on certain issues will hinge on what I decide in dependence on God, others, and a host of other factors.

My own example shows how ethnocentric, monolingual, and nationalistic small-mindedness can, by God's grace, at least begin to be constructively dealt with. I grew up seeing the world through a southern United States lens, which was not necessarily bad but which definitely was a limited view. Slowly but surely, God began to stretch the boundaries of his world as I saw it. The woman I married is not from the South. We moved to what to me at the time was the big, dirty, "Yankee" city of St. Louis, Missouri. We then, of all places, moved to Japan—and went through the revolutionary experience of learning the Japanese language and adjusting to Japanese culture. Next it was postgraduate work in Scotland. Among the many challenging experiences there was my studying with black Africans who were more intelligent than I—and God gently exposed my latent but real racism I had imbibed from my upbringing. The refining, suffering process in my life continues to this day, as God grants the privilege of interacting with various kinds of people whose histories and lives challenge the smallness of my vision of how God works throughout his vast and fascinating world.

"We" are Christ's international people—therefore, I am. Of all the ways of defining ourselves, the fact that we in Christ are composed of all sorts of people is as biblically foundational as any. This international trait needs to color all other ways in which we see ourselves. This includes how we live in the public arena, both in the heavenly-spiritual realm and in various macro/micro sociopolitical realms. We are Jesus' public, international community sent throughout his world. Therefore, "evangelical Christians, of all people, should be those who think *biblically* and *globally*."[15]

God has acted in Jesus to save us, and he has sent us into his world to live for his kingdom. After a brief checkup, we will explore more concretely what that life-mission means.

## Reflection Questions

- What are some specific evidences of having an "ingrained corporate-identity instinct"?

- How do spiritual-heavenly-unseen authorities and socio-economic-political authorities interrelate?

- How do racist and nationalistic assumptions inhibit the kind of international self-identity advocated in this chapter?

- What are some specific examples whereby the "international trait" we have as God's people can "color all other ways in which we see ourselves"?

15. Christopher Catherwood, *Christians, Muslims, and Islamic Rage: What Is Going On and Why It Happened* (Grand Rapids: Zondervan, 2003), 235. Catherwood's book is an excellent exploration of how an international Christian self-understanding relates to crucial contemporary issues, in this case extremist Islam.

# Checkup

We have reached an appropriate spot to pause for some brief summarizing and reflection, as well as consideration of a few particularly significant points. The book's overall focus is to hear and apply afresh, as part of the entire biblical revelation, 1 Peter's message of suffering after Christ's example. For us as twenty-first-century American Christians in relation to missions, that suffering most pointedly involves relinquishing our assumed and subconscious control, rights, and privileges with respect to God and to other people. What that process involves is the main thread running through the entire book.

Our discussion took us first to resting and trusting in God as the One in charge of his mission. We looked at four facets of God's mission, namely, that God is the universal Creator-Redeemer, how God brings missionaries as well as sends them, how cross-cultural missionaries come and go in both unorganized and organized fashion, and how restoration is a comprehensive framework for understanding the character of God's mission. We concluded, in special reference to our American tendency to assume too much to ourselves, that God alone is the Superpower in his mission to restore and re-create his world.

Next we considered certain aspects of our identity as Jesus' community. We discussed the concreteness of who we are as real, live people who have particular nationalities and ethnicities. We looked specifically at what that means for understanding ourselves as U.S. Christians. We then explored the basic importance of instinctively sensing our corporate and public identities as Christ's church, especially in terms of the biblical and demographic realities of being Jesus' international people.

In short, as American Christians we, together with other sectors of Christ's worldwide church, are to participate with God in his worldwide mission.

## Missions

It is vital to reflect on how we talk about *missions*. We have already noted that, with respect to God's mission, missions are organized Christian activities, particularly cross-cultural activities. Conceptually, God's mission is all-comprehensive; Christian missions are part of that greater whole.

We will be exploring practical implications of this understanding of missions as we continue through the rest of the book. Here we must point out that the most commonly assumed evangelical meaning of the term *missions* must be checked and clarified. As always, we must be careful about making generalizations, but the term's use is so pervasive that generalizing here will not take us away from standing on safe ground.

U.S. evangelicals commonly assume the term *missions* to mean something like "Caucasian-American Christians' going to minister the gospel to non-Caucasians, as well as to Europeans now that they have turned secular. While this may involve staying within the United States to minister to Native Americans and immigrants, normally it means going to different parts of the world as ambassadors for Christ." The understanding is never expressly stated quite that way, but I contend that it is, more or less, most American evangelicals' operative definition of *missions*.[1] Key concepts include race and national citizenship, "going," and gospel ministry.

Please forgive the stark language I have just used, but I believe it serves to make the point that such an assumed understanding needs significant adjustment. Building on the themes we have already discussed, we will proactively and constructively be looking at such necessary improvements.

---

1. To state the matter even more crassly, I often tell my students that the operative definition for many American Christians involved in missions is basically "white people telling others about Jesus."

For now, allow me to suggest that the importance of reexamining the common, operative understanding of *missions* cannot be overemphasized. The goal is not simply to criticize hallowed territory. Rather, it is to participate most constructively with God in his mission, including suffering the loss of some of our assumed American control, rights, and privileges.

## The Gospel

Another crucial area that I believe can be expanded in order to take in more fully what the Bible teaches is our evangelical understanding of *the gospel*. Like the term *missions*, the phrase *the gospel* is frequently used in a commonly assumed way. Personally, I venture to say that, since moving back to the United States several years ago, I have found these two terms to be as pervasive as any others I have heard in evangelical circles with respect to their assured, assumed, but almost always implicit meanings.

To try again to express what that common assumption is, it seems to me that *the gospel* is understood as "God's forgiveness of my sin, and embracing me as his child, due solely to his love and grace worked out in the substitutionary death and resurrection of Jesus Christ. I need not—indeed, I cannot—earn this divine love and favor by anything I could ever do. It is all because of God's gracious initiative to bring me into a secure and loving relationship with him." Key concepts here include God's love and grace, as well as each Christian's individual, personal relationship with God.

What we have already discussed should indicate that we want to expand this individualistic and otherwise limited notion of what constitutes God's "good news" in Christ. Of course, we want only to echo the emphasis on God's gracious and loving initiative. Where wider understanding is needed relates on the one hand to our corporate, international self-identity as God's people. It is indeed very good news that we all, as one people, are brought to Christ as his new community. We also desire a wider understanding of the gospel, beyond its religious and spiritual dimensions, to include as well its comprehensive aspects connected with the good news that God is remaking the world. How this concretely plays out has sometimes been a contentious matter within the worldwide Christian movement, but I believe that the Bible teaches us of such breadth and depth in the very gospel that Jesus and his earliest followers embodied and taught.

## The Great Commission

One more fundamentally important phrase and concept for missions is Jesus' *Great Commission*. Matthew's recorded version is the one most often quoted: "All authority in heaven and on earth has been given to me. Go therefore and make disciples of all nations, baptizing them in the name of the Father and of the Son and of the Holy Spirit, teaching them to observe all that I have commanded you. And behold, I am with you always, to the end of the age" (Matt. 28:18–20). No other single passage of Scripture carries the weight that this one does for evangelicals with regard to "fulfilling the task" of missions.

We will look at various aspects of this passage later, at a more appropriate juncture in our discussion. For now I would like to point out the dynamic, life-encompassing aspect of these words of Jesus, recorded as part of the entire gospel of Matthew. Much like 1 Peter's original readers, the Christian community that first received Matthew's gospel was a struggling, suffering, minority religious group that needed the encouragement of Jesus' power and presence. Jesus' words to his disciples—that they were to bring to bear on those around them the influence of his life and teaching—pointed to an ongoing covenant-commitment and process, "as you are going through life." As we will see later, the participle *as you are going* also has an imperative sense of "go," so the picture is not as simple as we might want it to be. Even so, more than strictly describing a specific task to be accomplished, Matthew 28:18–20 points to Jesus as the One assuring his weak followers, whom he will use for his own purposes, that he has the control, rights, and privileges over restoring his world as its rightful Covenant-*Kurios*.

So much for our brief checkup. It is now time to pick up on the previous chapter's conclusion about more of the practical implications of God's sending us, his international and public people, into his world as part of his mission.

## Reflection Questions

- Is the stark definition given above of the assumed U.S.-American evangelical understanding of *missions* accurate? Why or why not?

- What is *the gospel*?

- How does *the Great Commission* relate to your church's life? To your individual life?

# THEME 3

# "Keep Your Conduct among the Gentiles Honorable"
## (1 Peter 2:12)

# 5

# Living as an Interdependent Worldwide Church

> So when they had come together, they asked him, "Lord, will you at this time restore the kingdom to Israel?" He said to them, "It is not for you to know times or seasons that the Father has fixed by his own authority. But you will receive power when the Holy Spirit has come upon you, and you will be my witnesses in Jerusalem and in all Judea and Samaria, and to the end of the earth." (Acts 1:6–8)

You have probably heard, or perhaps even preached or taught, messages from this passage during a missions emphasis in your church. The ever-widening concentric-circle paradigm taken from Jesus' words in the latter part of verse 8 pervades American (and broader) evangelical missions assumptions. As a paradigm, the prescriptive scheme takes on slightly varying applications, basically ranging from *geographic areas* (Jerusalem = our community; Judea = our state; Samaria = our country or region of the world, in Americans' case the United States or North America; the end of the earth = the rest of the world, or all that is outside the United States or North America) to *cultural groupings* (Jerusalem = our kind of people; Judea = people similar to us; Samaria = people somewhat different from us, e.g., Spanish speakers; the end of the earth = everyone else). We pray for and challenge each other to do our part (pray, send, or go) in seeing the Christian gospel preached from our own backyard to people who are the furthest away from us (again, whether geographically, culturally, or both).

The question I want to raise is this: did Jesus speak Acts 1:8b prescriptively to twenty-first-century Americans, or did he speak predictively to his immediate disciples?

The way I have phrased the question is a bit unfair, since (besides restricting the groups that could apply his command) it forces an exclusive either/or choice. One could argue that Jesus was both commanding his followers throughout the ages to reach ever outward and foretelling how that process would historically unfold. And in fact, the original Greek could go either way in terms of grammatical form: technically speaking, the verbs *you will receive* and *you will be* (each one word in the Greek) could be taken as either imperative or indicative.[1]

Even so, I still want to raise the question at least with regard to the thrust of what Jesus meant—as well as the thrust of how his words are taken today. As already suggested, and as I am anticipating that your experience will bear out, evangelicals instinctively hear Jesus prescribing a Jerusalem-Judea-Samaria-end of the earth concentric-circle paradigm for conducting missions activities. And as you have probably already guessed, I want to suggest that Jesus spoke in a more predictive, historical way.[2]

More than simply making an esoteric exegetical point, I am trying to point us toward something extremely practical and concrete: how my church and I understand Jesus here relates directly to how my church and I interact with others. That is, who has control over the interac-

---

1. The future middle indicative is the preferred option; cf. Nathan E. Han, comp., *A Parsing Guide to the Greek New Testament* (Scottdale, PA: Herald Press, 1971), 229. But as my Covenant Seminary colleague Greg Perry pointed out to me, the imperative force of Acts 1:8 can come from Luke's connecting record of Jesus' command to the disciples to "stay in the city" (Luke 24:49), or "not to depart from Jerusalem" (Acts 1:4), until the Holy Spirit was poured out.

2. Generally, commentaries first point out how the "Jerusalem-Judea and Samaria-the end of the earth" framework outlines the rest of Acts. They then (while discussing whether the immediate view of "the end of the earth" was Rome or Spain) usually note, in general terms, how Jesus' progression foretells how Christianity will expand. I will be suggesting here that Jesus' prediction can—and for the sake of having a healthy perspective should—also be taken in more concrete and specific terms vis-à-vis where and when the gospel will be proclaimed, be believed, and have its effects.

tion, and who exercises rights and privileges in relation to the other people involved? Furthermore, how my church and I understand Jesus here relates directly to the activities we implement—how we plan them and actually carry them out. Once again, who is in control, and who is authorized and privileged to do what?

Those are practical and concrete matters. They are the engine driving this chapter, in which we will explore what it means to be *inter*national Christians who are *inter*dependent on each other.

## Examples

A close friend and East African Christian leader once told me that he struggled for years with receiving American student missions groups. These groups, my friend explained, would dictate the type of ministries (evangelism and discipleship) they wanted to conduct during their summer excursions to East Africa. They would plan and train in the United States and then come over to evangelize and disciple new believers in Christ.

My friend's problem was not at all that he was opposed to evangelism and discipleship; in fact, he is about as zealous in these areas as anyone I know. Neither was my friend unaware or unappreciative of the U.S. students' need and desire to grow in their prescribed areas of ministry. What was troublesome, of course, was the manner in which the U.S. group unilaterally decided what their agenda was going to be on the East Africans' turf. What the East African Christians thought regarding what might be helpful was apparently not a consideration.

In other words, Jerusalem—in this case, the U.S. Christians— decided what was best for the end of the earth, or East Africa.

My friend finally decided to tell the U.S. leadership to stop sending groups until they were seriously willing to consult with the East Africans about the nature and manner of the whole enterprise. The Americans had to suffer a loss of assumed control, rights, and privileges.

In the early twentieth century, an Australian missionary went to serve in Vella Lavella, part of the western Solomon Islands in the South Pacific. The islanders among whom the missionary served were head-hunting savages. After several years of ministry, the islanders' society had undergone great changes through the missionary's ministry. Per the missionary's description, "The Night of Savagery" had given way to "The Dawn of a New Day." These changes, with their descriptions, were documented in a circa 1920 film produced by the missionary entitled *The Transformed Isle: Barbarism to Christianity—A Genuine Portrayal of Yesterday and Today. The Story of Fifteen Years among the Head Hunters of Vella Lavella.*[3] Head-hunting—the past evils of which were reenacted for the film—had ceased, while regular Christian worship, school attendance, English clothing, and more advanced agricultural methods had begun. One unforgettable scene in the movie shows the men of Vella Lavella appropriately dressed and playing cricket, like "true English gentlemen."

Clearly, there was a mixture of importing unnecessary cultural elements into a setting foreign to the missionary who had "gone out" from a cultural-spiritual Jerusalem to barbaric savages who lived at earth's end. The missionary assumed control and the right to determine all sorts of things, including what were obviously secondary, relative concerns. (Perhaps as well, in ways that the missionary could not understand, much less control, the recipients were simply imitating the new Christian subculture that was being offered to them.)

One can see a similar dynamic in the New Testament. For example, the ascended Jesus seemingly worked extra hard on Peter to help him see that "God shows no partiality, but in every nation anyone who fears him and does what is right is acceptable to him" (Acts 10:34–35). One also senses a begrudging acquiescence in the Jerusalem church leaders' reaction to the transformed Peter's description of how the Holy Spirit fell on the Gentile "end-of-the-earth" house of Cornelius: "When they heard these things they fell silent. And they [reluctantly?] glorified God, saying [my guess is with a resounding lack of enthusiasm], 'Then to the Gentiles also God has granted repentance that leads to life'" (Acts 11:18). The first-century Jerusalem Christians had to be forced by compelling

---

3. Allan Davidson of St. John's College, University of Auckland, Auckland, New Zealand, showed the film on the evening of July 7, 2005, to those of us attending the "Yale-Edinburgh Group on the History of the Missionary Movement and Non-Western Christianity" at Yale Divinity School, New Haven, Connecticut.

visions and life-threatening persecutions to see the unthinkable: that those who were in different cultural and geographic settings could be full members of God's people through faith alone in Jesus alone. As such, Paul argued with all his might, believers in Christ were not to have secondary religio-cultural customs of diet and dates imposed on them by those coming "out" to them from Jerusalem (e.g., Gal. 2:4–5, 11–14; Col. 2:16). Instead, the good news was that different sorts of people could eat together, dress in their own particular ways, understand God in their own languages, and observe their own particular customs—because through faith in Christ, and not by anything else, people are acceptable to God.

Even after Jesus rose from the dead, his disciples were shackled by kingdom parochialism. They were confining God to Israel and its traditions, history, socioreligious practices, prescribed formulae, and institutions. To use the language we have noted earlier, the disciples were making God into a tribal deity. (To be sure, the disciples were also wrestling with the abrogation of old-covenant regulations for converts, part of the "guardian" no longer needed "now that faith has come," as Paul taught [Gal. 3:25].) They thus asked Jesus about when he was going to restore God's rule to its former glory—within their own national heritage. Jesus countered by describing God's universal, worldwide concern. This one God, Paul later pointed out to the coexisting Jewish and Gentile Christians in Rome, is both one and the God of all peoples (Rom. 3:29–30). That is why Paul addressed, in his theologically rich letter to them, the mundane yet always crucial matter of being able to eat together (Rom. 14).

The New Testament's emphasis on being nonjudgmental and flexible regarding diet runs counter to many religious impulses that make standards of eating ultimate. For our present purposes, we can extrapolate from food matters to wider concerns of lifestyle, relationships, and ministry strategies. Put differently, we must be careful to avoid the parochial tendency to make ultimate and universal what might be appropriate in our own local "Jerusalems." Thus my standards of housing, clothing, children's education, vacationing, spending and investing money, voting, conversation topics, expression of familial love, and all sorts of other areas come under scrutiny upon living among people who are not like me (as well as when different people enter my neighborhood

and community). Relationally, all these lifestyle areas are up for nego-
tiation when interacting with people who are different. The prospect
arises of unforeseen, beautiful new understandings and practices upon
genuinely interacting with others who also belong to *Kurios* Jesus (Rom.
14:4–9)—and our both changing into new, culturally hybrid people as
a result. In carrying out ministry activities, my church and I must be
careful to listen to others—be they Christian or not—in planning and
carrying out service activities that might otherwise seem obviously right
to us if we consult only ourselves.

Present-day parochialism,[4] with its adverse implications for lifestyles, cross-cultural relationships, and ministry strategies, needs a regular
dose of the gospel's message that believers of varying nationality, social
rank, and gender "are all one in Christ Jesus" (Gal. 3:28). That gospel
shapes how my church and I relate to various types of people, as well
as how we carry out ministries, particularly cross-cultural *missions*. We
must take the path of relinquishing our assumed control, rights, and
privileges in relation to people who are different from us.

## The Importance of History/Histories

As recorded in Acts 1:6–8, Jesus' disciples asked him whether he
was going to rebuild their nation's former prestige. Jesus replied with
a historical overview of how the Christian gospel was going to be proclaimed all over the world.

In other words, Jesus checked the disciples' well-meaning but self-
serving provincial and nationalistic enthusiasm with a broader view of
history.

One of the clearest implications of a Christian understanding of
God and the gospel as universal, not tribal and parochial, is how a person views history. Again, this is a very practical and concrete matter. As
I have already mentioned briefly, my own personal example illustrates
well how an ever-inwardly-spiraling provincialism restricts God's work

---

4. Jesus in Acts 1:7–8 is confronting two errors: "eschatological inquisitiveness and . . . paro-
chialism. . . . Twenty centuries later these two errors are still seen in the church." Ajith Fernando,
*The NIV Application Commentary—From Biblical Text . . . to Contemporary Life: Acts*, NIV
Commentary Series (Grand Rapids: Zondervan, 1998), 56.

in history to me and my people, and not to the person and people in front of me with whom I am dealing.

When we first went to Japan as missionaries, about all I knew about Japanese history was that there had been an ugly, brutal war during the 1940s that the Japanese obviously had started "out of the blue" at Pearl Harbor. I also knew that a long time ago there had been sword-wielding samurai that lopped off heads at the drop of a hat. More recently, both the Summer and Winter Olympics had taken place in Japan. That was about the extent of my historical knowledge of Japan.

I knew even less about Japanese-Christian history, or more generally about Japanese religious history. I knew of some of our own postwar missionary forerunners. That was about it.

But for me, that was all okay. That's because *I* was in Japan now, and Japan was about to come to Christ because of *my* presence.

In other words, Japanese history—in particular Japanese-Christian history—began with my gracious arrival in their midst.[5] All I had to do was to learn to speak Japanese (admittedly a daunting task) so that people there could hear the truth (obviously, so I thought, a simple process).

Compounding the problem of my blissful ignorance was that, on top of being largely unaware of how uninformed I was, I was unaware of how desperately my smug state of ignorance needed correction. As far as I was concerned, I was taking God, who had worked in my life and my people's history (Jerusalem to Europe to the United States), to Japan. The poor Japanese living in total darkness, intelligent and hardworking as they were, were finally going to be confronted with the love of the God of the Bible—through meeting up with the God of Europe and the United States in the person of yours truly.

It came as quite a shock to begin to realize not only that God had sent our family to Japan to proclaim the Christian gospel, but also that

---

5. A similarly ridiculous view of history is in the intentionally humorous compilation of "all the History that you can remember . . . the result of years of research in golf-clubs, gun-rooms, green-rooms, etc.," regarding the history of India: "It was in the 18th Century that Indian History started. Indian History is a great number of wars in which the English fought victoriously. . . ." Walter Carruthers Sellar and Robert Julian Yeatman, compulsory preface to *1066 and All That: A Memorable History of England Comprising All the Parts You Can Remember Including One Hundred and Three Good Things, Five Bad Kings, and Two Genuine Dates* (repr., New York: Barnes & Noble, 1993), 85.

he had *brought* us to Japan to teach and shape us. Speaking historically, God was already there and had been at work for generations. That was true with respect to our next-door neighbors and their ancestries, the cities and regions in which we lived, the varied Christian church(es) there, as well as Japan as an ever-changing nation. When all of that began to dawn on me, the path of suffering the loss of my assumed, privileged Christian-American place of dispensing God to "the Japanese" began to open up.

## Interpersonal Costs and Benefits

Realizing that God has been present and at work in people, prior to and totally independently of my (and my church's) contact with them, frees and even compels one to learn about others' histories. As mentioned earlier, I believe that people can be paid no greater respect than to have someone else be genuinely interested in their history and background. The purpose of that interest, of course, should not be to manipulate or control people (a subtle, or perhaps not so subtle, form of which can be to see how they can most readily be converted). Rather, wanting to know people's histories comes from care and concern for them, as well as from a desire to learn from them, all fueled by a wonder of how God has been at work as we relinquish our assumed, subconscious right of controlling him and others.

We should always be interested in others' histories, but it is particularly important in relating to people cross-culturally. Concretely, that means that my church and I must check our parochial instinct simply to take "out" from our Jerusalem what "those other people" need "out there" in the dark void of heathendom. Rather, from information and relationships that God gives us,[6] we work to know (and

6. As for information, the Joshua Project, begun in the 1990s as part of the AD2000 Movement, has documented people groups all throughout the world. Regularly updated data is available online at http://www.joshuaproject.net/. Another massive source of information, available in Bible-college and seminary libraries and one that I recommend for church libraries, is the aforementioned David B. Barrett, George T. Kurian, and Todd M. Johnson, *World Christian Encyclopedia: A Comparative Study of Churches and Religions in the Modern World*, 2nd ed. (Oxford: Oxford University Press, 2001). Relationships can arise in any number of ways, through international students to business travel to tourism to immigrants and refugees.

to grow through knowing) people and their backgrounds, interests, hopes, needs, customs, arts, and other qualities. These people may be individuals, or they may be groups. They may live next door, or they may live halfway around the world. They may look, act, talk, and smell in similar fashion as others in my church and I do, or they may be very, very different. In any case, our privilege as Christians who are interested in knowing God's world better, in growing as his people, and in serving others is to make the effort to know people's histories and backgrounds. In so doing, God inserts my church and me into others' histories—and vice versa.

Again, special care and effort is needed in relating to people who live in (or come from, in the case of recent arrivals to the United States) a different part of the world from my church's and mine. Together with Christians who are members of that different group or nationality, or perhaps together with Christians who are not members of that group but have a mutual interest in them, we can prayerfully consider how God might want to use and shape us together in ministry. Personal meetings, joint Christian worship, digital communication, having fun or crying together, or whatever other means are available must be part of the process of considering how God might lead, shape, and use us. U.S. groups interested in East Africa, for example, must be in close, mutual consultation with Christians and others there to see how, where, and when God might lead, shape, and use everyone involved.

All these efforts and attitudes toward knowing each other's histories facilitate deeper and more meaningful interpersonal relationships. Learning the complex and varied nature of people's histories can also help avoid damaging relational faux pas. For example, it is parochially natural for American Christians to assume, and thus casually or more formally (in sermons, journal articles, etc.) remark accordingly, that most Christian movements around the world trace their origins to the United States—for example, worldwide Pentecostalism. The complex and varied nature of Christian history, however, manifestly demonstrates that Pentecostal and charismatic churches around the world (by far the fastest-growing Christian movements) should not automatically be "causally linked to North American initiatives." In fact, there were "unique origins of other previous but equally significant or even simultaneous Pentecostal outpourings [experiences] around the world."[7] Beyond Pentecostal and charismatic circles, even for the many (but certainly not all) non-Western Christian churches that have had Western links, many of those connections have been European, not American. More importantly, all churches have their own indigenous traditions, leaders, crises, and victories. Not to recognize the integrity of those histories in their own right undermines the benefits that come from mutually respectful and beneficial cross-cultural Christian relationships.

## Integrating Engrafted Histories

In terms of understanding Jesus' words in Acts 1:8, what should be evident at this point is that adopting a strictly prescriptive paradigm, whereby I place my church and myself in Jerusalem and everyone else in Judea-Samaria and the end of the earth, runs the risk of neglecting how God has been dealing with "everyone else" (except, perhaps, for his preparing them for my church and me to make contact with them). It also runs the risk of reinforcing our assumed American right to control, from the alleged world Christian headquarters in the United States, how the gospel is at work through our privileged role of communicating it to others around the world.

It should go without saying as well that such a prescriptive paradigm runs into problems with the demographic reality that there are now countless "Jerusalems" all around the world. The Christian church is more worldwide than ever before, and numerous Asian, Latin American, African, and Oceanic churches and organizations, in addition to European and North American ones, are carrying out missions activities in their own regions and around the world. Within a concentric-circle paradigm, pretty much wherever you are is simultaneously Jerusalem, Judea-Samaria, and the end of the earth.

7. Note as well this accompanying clarifying comment: "In the documentation of the history of Pentecostalism, the origins of the movement in different contexts across the world should be distinguished from the efforts of its American versions to globalize knowledge of it." J. Kwabena Asamoah-Gyadu, *African Charismatics: Current Developments within Independent Indigenous Pentecostalism in Ghana*, vol. 27 of Studies of Religion in Africa Series (Leiden, Netherlands: Brill, 2005), 10–11.

These problems should not, I believe, cause us to reject what the prescriptive paradigm has to teach us. Thinking of the world in terms of ever-widening concentric circles helps us to focus on all areas, including those close to home as well as those far away. One can also think of the image as a target, with the primary goal of hitting the central bull's-eye without neglecting the outlying areas. Realizing that other "Jerusalems" are also actively reaching out in missions activities can help us coordinate our cross-cultural ministry efforts.

*Advantages.* At the same time, there are several advantages in hearing Jesus' words in Acts 1:8 historically and predictively. First, we can have our instinctively narrow, linear view of Christian history expanded to a more accurate worldwide understanding. As alluded to earlier, an inherited tendency is to see Christian history aligned with Western history, wherein the Christian church is understood to have spread exclusively from Jerusalem to the Roman Empire to Europe to North America.[8] By extension, in recent generations Western missionaries have created "missions history" by taking Christianity throughout much of the rest of the world. Truer to reality, however, is the multidirectional picture that Jesus suggests. What actually happened is that the Christian faith spread very early to northeast Africa, west Asia (i.e., other parts of it), and south Asia as well as around the Mediterranean and into Europe.[9] And while the incredibly influential modern missions movement sprang particularly out of the West, God as the universal God of all peoples has been at work for centuries bringing the gospel of Jesus Christ to all sorts of people (with whom he has always been at work), and doing so through all sorts of Christians.

8. Most study-Bible maps showing early Christianity don't help here, exclusively focusing on Paul's missionary journeys around the northeast Mediterranean world. We need more maps showing the Indian, Chinese, Parthian, and northeast African as well as the Roman imperial areas in order to see the full arena where early Christianity grew.

9. Thankfully, some recent accounts of Christian history are taking a more worldwide approach than simply a Western one. One analysis that constructively attempts to provide the intellectual apparatus needed to incorporate multiple Christian trajectories within an overall Christian history is Dale T. Irvin, *Christian Histories, Christian Traditioning: Rendering Accounts* (Maryknoll, NY: Orbis Books, 1998).

Related to this fuller, worldwide Christian historical understanding is the awareness of the need to know Christian history in settings other than one's own. There is simply no excuse for charging into an area, with well-intentioned but ill-informed missionary zeal, without at least attempting to know the history of the Christian faith there. In every region of the world (unreached peoples notwithstanding, a topic we will address later), Christianity already has a presence, usually one that is lengthy and significant. I do not doubt the sincerity of obeying a missions "call" to go somewhere internationally to proclaim the gospel. But I do question the viability of assuming that international settings are de facto sub-, non-, or even anti-Christian (i.e., outside "Jerusalem") and that U.S.-American Christians therefore are simply to "go" somewhere "out there" to preach the gospel and thus "do missions."

A further and particularly crucial aspect of hearing Jesus historically is to understand that, as American Christians (along with most other Christians around the world), it is both healthier and more accurate for us to see ourselves as living at "the end of the earth" rather than in "Jerusalem" or even "Judea-Samaria." After all, at the time about two millennia ago when Jesus told his disciples that they would be his witnesses throughout the world, where were your and my ancestors? As far as I can tell, mine were in northwest Europe. In relation to Jesus and his disciples, that was most definitely part of "the end of the earth." Geographically northwest Europe was far away, culturally and linguistically it was very much separate from Israel-Palestine, religiously it was very different, and historically the Christian gospel took centuries (certain apostolic traditions notwithstanding) to reach there. Historically and otherwise, then, my (and probably your) ancestors were very much at the end of the earth, as far as Jesus' intended meaning and the disciples' understanding were concerned.

*Implications.* That historical understanding has at least three significant implications for how my church and I concretely relate to various people. First, it demonstrates that God is committed to bringing his gospel to all kinds of people. If he brought the gospel even to my kind of people, he can and will bring the gospel to unreached peoples today and until Jesus returns. Besides giving hope to us, this determined commitment of God evokes humility and gratitude in us before him and before others. U.S. Christians are among those whom 1 Peter addresses when it references the prophet Hosea: "Once you were not a people, but now you are God's people; once you had not received mercy, but now you have received mercy" (2:10). We who together are now "a chosen race, a royal priesthood, a holy nation, a people for [God's] own possession" (2:9) come from all sorts of ethnicities and nationalities who stand before God and each other by grace and grace alone.

Second, understanding that my people and I were at the end of the earth helps me to see that our own indigenous (and ever-changing) traditions and values were, and still are, skewed and sin-scarred, just as are any other people's traditions and values. To be sure, the gospel has had profound effects on Americans' backgrounds. As we have already described (in chapter 3), however, there are pluses and minuses in consciously possessing such a heritage. Moreover, the gospel's work in any setting is always particular and mixed. There is an ongoing need to hear the gospel afresh in ever-changing contexts, including my own American one. Furthermore, there is always the need to interact respectfully with different cultural contexts, since my own context is necessarily polluted, mixed, and peculiar in its manifestations of Christian faith and life. As my church and I relate to people from necessarily polluted, mixed, and peculiar settings different from our own, together we can more fully discover God's goodness and grace in our collective midst.

Third, because my ancestry and cultural-national heritage (fluctuating and mixed as they have been) have been so foreign to those of the Bible, there is the continual need to consider how my people's background and the Bible interface. More than just comparing relatively insignificant, surface-level customs (eating with hands or utensils, dress, architecture, technology, etc.) or even institutions (family, government, education, social groupings, etc.), how my church's cultural-national setting matches up with such biblical values as personal identity, sexuality, interethnic relations, economic decision-making, war and peace, "freedom," and "justice" must be continually reexamined. How the Bible actually speaks into my church's ever-changing context—through the use of new translations, yes, but more profoundly through fresh considerations of what the Bible's translated words (e.g., the English translation(s) of *Kurios*) actually *mean* to us here and now—requires intentional openness to the Spirit's teaching through the insights of other cultural branches of Christ's church. Along with these other branches, my church and I have been "grafted into" the culturally complex history of the people of God, to borrow Paul's imagery in Romans 11. Instead of assuming a straightforward historical-cultural connection with the peoples in the Bible, my church and I must be constantly hearing afresh, in some sort of integrated fashion together with other parts of the worldwide church (through small-group studies comprising people of different nationalities, shared commentaries produced in different settings, joint conferences, e-mail interaction, etc.), how God is speaking in the Bible to us today.

## Toward Interdependency

The sort of mutuality described above is part of *inter*dependent, cross-cultural relationships. Those involved in such relationships know both the richness and the necessity of living as the international-intercultural people of God. While there are, no doubt, hassles and difficulties in dealing with each other across linguistic, cultural, and other often very difficult barriers,[10] international Christian relationships are necessary because, as John Stott notes in his comments on Acts 1:8, "Christ's kingdom, while not incompatible with patriotism, tolerates no narrow nationalisms. He rules over an international community in which race, nation, rank and sex are no barriers to fellowship."[11] The triune God is universal and omnilingual, and we his people are to reflect his character and design for who we are.

10. Some of the most difficult barriers I have observed and personally experienced involve different historical perspectives, for example, the U.S. decision to drop the atomic bombs on Hiroshima and Nagasaki. I have yet to meet a Japanese Christian who sees any justification whatsoever for that decision. On the other hand, I know many U.S.-American Christians—particularly those who were alive at the time—who believe that it was the wisest choice available. I have always found it a challenge to get each side at least to understand how Christians on the other side could think the way they do—and be no less sincere and devoted in their Christian faith because of it.

11. John R. W. Stott, *The Message of Acts: The Spirit, the Church & the World*, The Bible Speaks Today Series (Downers Grove, IL: InterVarsity Press, 1990), 43.

We have discussed earlier how this notion of being the *international* people of God must be basic to understanding who we are as Christians. As Stott's words indicate and as we have already considered, there is an inward-directed, centripetal, self-serving, competitive tendency in all human groups to reify, make normative, and universalize ourselves as the ultimate standard for other groups. For those of us who are Americans, this threat of an unhealthy nationalism is ever-present at our doorsteps. After all, we have baseball's "*World* Series," and we are ever mindful of being the *world*'s lone superpower. It is easy to believe, even if we would never admit it, that we don't really need others, even as Christians. They might need us, but (so the thought process goes) we have the resources to sustain ourselves and everybody else, if need be.

International and cross-cultural *inter*dependency is thus difficult even to picture, and even harder to achieve. Part of our difficulty as Americans is having to suffer the loss of control, rights, and privileges associated with feeling sufficiently independent of others. Another challenge is the presence of timeworn concepts, including the so-called three-*self* formula of church-planting, that mitigate against interdependency between Christians across cultural and national boundaries.

## The Three-Self Formula

One of the most widely assumed and used goals of all church-planting endeavors, especially international ones, is the creation of self-governing, self-propagating, and self-supporting churches. This "three-*self*" formula was articulated in the mid-nineteenth century by missionary leaders Henry Venn of England and Rufus Anderson of the United States. Later it was more fully developed and implemented in Korea by the American John Nevius. Venn had come up with the idea in search of funding, while coffers were empty, for Anglican ministers serving in far-flung locations throughout the British empire.[12] Whatever the formula's exact origins, new churches that are no longer dependent on outside resources is the assumed goal of many outreach efforts.

12. Wilbert R. Shenk, *Changing Frontiers of Mission*, American Society of Missiology Series, no. 28 (Maryknoll, NY: Orbis Books, 1999), 182.

Interestingly, this formula has undergone fairly intense discussion of late. One point that many have wanted to make is that a fourth *self*—namely, "self-theologizing"—should be added. This issue has come forth in light of the whole topic of "contextualization" (something we will consider further) that has arisen since the early 1970s. The important point made is that newer churches should mature to the point of producing their own theological expressions, such as confessional statements, instead of simply repeating what Western counterparts have dictated to them.

More germane to our current discussion is the question of *inter*dependency, which some say is hindered by the three-*self* formula. Those who raise this matter (I include myself here, as well as among those making the former point) suggest that the goal of producing independent (or nondependent) churches can unwittingly run counter to the need to live as the pilgrim people of God who are always, by nature, beyond and foreign to any particular setting. Yes, we are to be "at home" wherever we are, but at the same time we are to be pilgrims and strangers—international, with respect to national settings. If we seek to create nondependent churches that mirror ourselves (as allegedly nondependent churches, which need no other part of the body of Christ), both we and they can fall prey to the quicksand of each setting's enveloping power that will inevitably render our life and witness ineffective, parochial, and ultimately self-serving.

Fair enough in theory, the retort will come, but when you talk about such concrete matters as leadership and money, you must avoid creating dependency, or those whom Mahatma Gandhi called "rice Christians" because of their basic goal of materialistic gain.[13] Nineteenth- and twentieth-century colonial missions established churches and institutions that were run by expatriate missionaries and funded by Western money. Such unfortunate results must increasingly be owned by national, indigenous Christians who are self-reliant, the response will continue.[14] If there is any funding of

13. Anto Akkara, "India's Christians Face Continued Threats," *Christianity Today* (February 1, 2001), available online at http://www.christianitytoday.com/ct/2001/107/45.0.html.
14. Along with Robertson McQuilkin, Glenn Schwartz has been one of the leading advocates

projects, it must be done along a clearly and rapidly decreasing scale to avoid dependency.

Contrary to this pro-self-reliance position, others strongly advocate a missions strategy of financial support for "nationals," since they are already culturally adjusted, cheaper than Western missionaries, and the most effective way to see world evangelization progress.[15]

Right now I am not interested in debating the effectiveness of missions strategy, which is the arena where the pro-self-reliance (against dependency) versus support-nationals discussion in large part lies. Our current topic is the need to live as the international body of Christ in ways that express our genuine need for each other, our *inter*dependency. What strikes me as the root issue for Americans at this point is whether or not we believe that we actually need other types of Christians to live faithfully as God's people. Are we willing and able to suffer the loss of an allegedly rightfully inherited, privileged, self-reliant relational status? After all, if what you need is the "three *self*s" of trained leadership, adequate funds, and the capacity to propagate the Christian gospel without outside assistance (as well as a fourth self-theologizing ability), then it would appear that American churches by and large do not need other churches around the world.

Certainly, however, *all* branches and expressions of the Christian church need other parts of Christ's people to enable effective, prophetic living within our own particular contexts. This still-unredeemed world will swallow us up if we try to go it alone in our own settings. For many American evangelicals, this means that such issues as racism and nationalism, wealth and self-comfort, and privatized and individualized religion desperately require others' input in order to help us in our blindness and weakness to deal constructively with such monsters.

First is our need for *inter*dependency. Then come actual expressions of it.

---

of this position against dependency. Cf. Schwartz's articles on the World Mission Associates Web site at http://www.wmausa.org/.

15. Mission Link International is one such organization. Information is available online at http://www.missionlink.org/.

## The Barriers of Money and Military

One twin set of realities to recognize in the challenge to actualize interdependent international relationships is the disparate levels of financial resources and military power that Americans have in comparison to many others. One must not think that everyone outside the United States (and Europe) is poor and that militarily the United States can overwhelm any other country at will. Clearly, neither of those overly simplistic ideas is at all tenable. There is, in fact, fantastic wealth (particularly oil-based wealth) in various parts of the world, and there are significant military capabilities elsewhere around the globe as well. Nevertheless, in comparison to many places in the world with which American-Christian churches have missions-related dealings, and in comparison to many settings from which refugees, immigrants, and other recent arrivals have left to come to the United States, most Americans are inordinately wealthy and militarily protected.

Simply put, those disparities present major challenges to developing interdependent international relationships of genuine trust. On a local U.S. level, it is extremely difficult—even with the Spirit of God working and with dedicated intentionality on the part of American Christians—to experience full trust between recently arrived refugees who have next to nothing and those of us who are comfortably settled with spacious homes, shiny automobiles, advanced schools, retirement accounts, and adequate health insurance.[16] Outside the United States, add the component of U.S. military might, which will intervene in many volatile situations to protect, and evacuate if need be, U.S. citizens (including missionaries). Whether one agrees with others' views or not, the truth of the matter is that many people around the world do not have a favorable opinion of U.S. military unilateralism, including its worldwide war on terrorism. Americans living abroad thus face serious obstacles "when the chips are down," either personally or on a more structural international level, to trusting others and to being trusted.

Thankfully, there are many examples of the Spirit of God working through American Christians exercising dedicated intentionality toward

---

16. If this phraseology sounds critical, please know that yours truly would fall right into the target group.

becoming interdependent with others. In local U.S. situations, some have focused on knowing, learning from, suffering together with, and working sacrificially to meet immediate material, spiritual, and psychological needs of recently arrived refugees. Abroad, some have chosen to remain and suffer along with that area's permanent residents and citizens, at least for as long as possible, in situations of war, disease, and disaster. Some who live abroad, whether as missionaries, as nongovernmental organization (NGO) staff, as educators, or in other capacities, decide to take a reduced salary or otherwise live, as much as possible, among that area's permanent residents and citizens. "Going native" is usually not the most constructive approach to take, since expatriates are in fact, as well as by others' perception, expatriates. Even so, learning from, being changed by, serving and being served by, laboring together with, and otherwise taking the risk of changing unpredictably into a cultural hybrid by living among those into whose setting you have entered is a healthy posture to take toward forging interdependent relationships.

On an organizational level (for example, a local U.S. church or missions organization relating to a church or ministry in a less affluent part of the world), the posture of desiring interdependency is similar, but the issues are more complex. How plans are formulated and decisions are made are important matters, of course. This is especially true when money is involved (and it usually is). How much do you put in writing—for example, should you draw up some sort of contractual agreement involving time frames and decision-making authority? To what extent (e.g., receipting), and for whose benefit (governments, donors, boards, etc.), do you account for fund expenditures? How do you handle different cultural expectations about "honesty," "transparency," and "accounting"?

Who travels where (e.g., U.S. donors and supervising board members to "the field," "national"[17] workers to the United States), how often, and for what purposes?[18] How do all these practical, financial, and

---

17. I have placed these commonly used missions-related terms in quotation marks because *all* Christians, regardless of location or nationality, are serving on "the field" as "nationals."

18. Daniel Rickett, among others, has written extensively on this whole matter of international "partnerships." *Building Strategic Relationships: A Practical Guide to Partnering with Non-Western Missions* (San Jose, CA: Partners International, 2003) is one of his numerous publications.

procedural concerns mesh with Paul's clear teaching of international interdependency in 2 Corinthians 8 and 9, along with Peter's encouragement to keep in mind the suffering "brotherhood throughout the world" (1 Peter 5:9)? The complexity of these questions should not discourage or intimidate U.S. churches or missions organizations, but they point to the need to consider how assumed control, rights, and privileges—especially those associated with money—must be managed well in close, trusting partnerships.

As for American missionaries serving in other parts of the world, there have been shifts in many missions organizations from conducting "front-line" ministry to "equipping" and "training" indigenous "nationals." Discussions about this shift are usually strategic in nature: "nationals" can sometimes minister where Americans cannot; "nationals" are more cost-effective; Americans can multiply their effectiveness by training others with our vast resources. We are raising questions throughout the book about where "front lines" are and who "nationals" are. Here, however, in talking about interdependency, the issue concerns how much this shift in missions strategy represents a recognition of genuine need (beyond missions strategy) for each other, and not just another disguised form of condescension. We will come back later to the matter of resources: who has what kinds and how we can share them. For now, we want to stress the importance of cultivating interdependent international relationships, on both personal and structural levels, that involve suffering the loss of assumed control, rights, and privileges.

Again, here I am not too concerned with strategy per se. Much of the current evangelical discussion about how American Christians can partner with Christians elsewhere focuses on the issue of choosing either developing self-reliance over dependency (which should persuade us not to give financial support) or supporting "national" workers because they are both cost- and ministry-effective. On that issue, at least on an across-the-board basis, it seems to me that we do not face an exclusive either/or choice. The more fundamental issue, and the issue out of which we can decide how to structure financial support and other organizational matters in particular situations, concerns the extent to which we know, trust, and need each other across all sorts of cultural and national barriers—because together "we are the Lord's" (Rom. 14:8).

As the Head of his church, Jesus Christ has brought all sorts of people together to serve him. "For in one Spirit we were all baptized into one body—Jews or Greeks, slaves or free—and all were made to drink of one Spirit" (1 Cor. 12:13). Because this one international body to which we belong has many different types of parts, we are to capitalize on our interdependency, for "God arranged the members in the body, each one of them, as he chose" (1 Cor. 12:18). In particular, "the parts of the body that seem to be weaker are indispensable. . . . God has so composed the body, giving greater honor to the part that lacked it, that there may be no division in the body, but that the members may have the same care for one another" (1 Cor. 12:22–25). God has thus given gifts to us his people, both on a global scale and in our local expressions of Christ's universal church. Whether in Ephesians, 1 Corinthians, or elsewhere in his writings, "Paul's concept is that the whole defines the identity of the parts, and is more than the sum of the parts."[19] That's because Jesus, even as he works in and through individual Christians and our local congregations, fundamentally has in mind his entire, universal church that he will one day "present . . . to himself in splendor, . . . holy and without blemish" (Eph. 5:27). With that same worldwide vision, through the "excellent way" of love (1 Cor. 12:31bff.) we can pursue, in the power and blessing of the Holy Spirit, walking and serving together as an interdependent, worldwide church.

Just as Jesus said would happen, Christian people have been and continue to be his witnesses "in Jerusalem and in all Judea and Samaria, and to the end of the earth"—including even to my kind of people (Acts 1:8). "Therefore, my beloved brothers, be steadfast, immovable, always abounding in the work of the Lord, knowing that in the Lord your labor is not in vain" (1 Cor. 15:58).

## Reflection Questions

- What are some other examples (besides those mentioned in the text) of exporting cultural particularities to other settings?

19. Charles Van Engen, *Mission on the Way: Issues in Mission Theology* (Grand Rapids: Baker, 1996), 108.

- How have you and your church benefited from learning about Christian traditions that are culturally-nationally different from your own? How have you blocked such benefits by not pursuing such historical knowledge?

- Where are your church and you situated within the progression that Jesus described as Jerusalem-Judea-Samaria-the end of the earth? What difference does your answer make?

- What are some specific examples of interdependent international relationships with which you are familiar?

# 6

## Living Locally as an Interdependent Worldwide Church

*I'm zooming the video in on my daughter Suzy during her solo in the grade-school musical. This tsunami disaster is mind-boggling in its devastation all around the Indian Ocean. My mother's bypass surgery is tomorrow, and I have all sorts of cooking and other preparations to take care of—even as I carry my prayerful concern for Mom. It sure would be nice if the G-8 leaders could make some sort of headway this week on alleviating world poverty. If I can make a B on tomorrow's math test, I'll be home free.*

We are constantly expanding and contracting our attention on macro and micro issues. That same type of vacillation is what is involved in living locally—or "glocally," as some have put it, in an attempt to combine "local" and "global" mind-sets—as part of the interdependent global church. We instinctively think glocally when we apply as local churches Jesus' crucial directives and promises to his first disciples: "As the Father has sent me, even so I am sending you. . . . Receive the Holy Spirit" (John 20:21–22). "I am with you always" (Matt. 28:20). The importance of these words stretches across generations and around the world. Jesus has sent all his people into our respective corners of the world to participate with him in his grand mission to build his good and just kingdom.

## Macro History and Our Local Situations

In the previous chapter we considered some practical implications of Jesus' macro-historical assurance that his Spirit-empowered followers would be his witnesses throughout the world. The backdrop of that ongoing drama is your and my heavenly Father's universal and omnilingual dealings with the human race ever since Adam and Eve. The God with whom I fellowship in my quiet times, and with whom my local church interacts in corporate worship each Lord's Day, is the same Creator-Redeemer who rules over all things and who has acted in Jesus of Nazareth to save the world.

It is the worldwide, macro-historical process of God the Covenant-Creator-Master-Redeemer dealing with concrete local people such as you, me, and others across the globe that Jeremiah's prophecies (as mentioned earlier) ultimately have in view: "Behold, I will gather them from all the countries to which I drove them in my anger and my wrath and in great indignation. I will bring them back to this place, and I will make them dwell in safety. And they shall be my people, and I will be their God" (Jer. 32:37–38; cf. 16:14–15; 23:3, 8). The immediate reference of Jeremiah's prophecies was the restoration of the kingdom of Judah that had been exiled into Babylon and beyond. Similarly, the immediate references of God's promises to Jacob (Gen. 28:15) and to Joseph (Gen. 48:21) were to return them and their descendants to the land he had promised earlier to their ancestor Abraham. The ultimate and overarching reference of these promises to *return* people to land from which they had to leave for a season is God's worldwide covenant to restore his people and his creation in Christ to the glorious state in which he had made everything—and then some. In this sin-shackled world, the entire human race lives as "all the countries to which [God] drove [us] in [his] anger and [his] wrath and in great indignation." But God restored Jesus from death—to which God the Father drove Jesus the Son in his anger, wrath, and great indignation against our sin—to life and enthroned him on high. And just as Jesus thus enabled and then predicted, God is in the process of lovingly gathering us—people such as you, me, and others across the globe—from among the world's nations to restore us into his people.[1]

1. I fully realize that I am following a covenantal theological hermeneutic and not a dispensational view that attributes an ultimate fulfillment of God's promise to Abraham

The same global scope of fulfillment comes into view as well within a present-day, new-covenant consideration of the oft-cited words of 2 Chronicles 7:14: "If my people who are called by my name humble themselves, and pray and seek my face and turn from their wicked ways, then I will hear from heaven and will forgive their sin and heal their land." Here God is speaking in a night vision to Solomon after he had dedicated with great fanfare the recently completed magnificent temple. The temple thus became God's special dwelling with his people. That building in the midst of Judah-Israel of old was a shadow-picture of the coming temple, Jesus of Nazareth, who declared about himself to the leaders of his day, "Destroy this temple, and in three days I will raise it up" (John 2:19). The risen and exalted Jesus is now assembling and crafting together the living stones of his people (1 Peter 2:4–5) into a holy temple, into which all sorts of people are brought together as his international house (Eph. 2:14–22). The "land" of "my people" should therefore not be restricted to that of a single modern nation-state, such as the United States of America. Taking that kind of nationalistic tack, as sensible, right, and patriotic as it might seem, would unjustifiably be taking a step backward in terms of God's forward-looking and ever-expanding redemptive history. It would also be reinforcing an assumed place, in relation to God and to others, of right and privilege for the United States of America. God is renewing and healing the whole world as he continues his mission toward a new heaven and a new earth that we his worldwide people will inhabit. That full, global scope is to inform how my church and I pray, live, and work as we participate with Jesus in his ongoing mission.

## Matthew 28:18–20

Please keep in mind that same worldwide, macro-historical process of God the Covenant-Creator-Master-Redeemer dealing with concrete local people such as you, me, and others across the globe as we consider

---

and his biological descendants as restoring them to Palestine in its current real-estate form (at least more or less).

the practical outworking of the most oft-used form of Jesus' Great Commission: "And Jesus came and said to them, 'All authority in heaven and on earth has been given to me. Go therefore and make disciples of all nations, baptizing them in the name of the Father and of the Son and of the Holy Spirit, teaching them to observe all that I have commanded you. And behold, I am with you always, to the end of the age' " (Matt. 28:18–20).

With these important words of Jesus in mind, let me go ahead and give you the main punch line for our current discussion: *Jesus has us who are his followers living among the world's peoples and nations. Wherever we live and whatever we do, we are Jesus' servants among the nations; all places and people (e.g., my suburban U.S. community) are part of "the nations." This is true whether the nation where a particular Christian is living and serving is that person's "home" (e.g., a U.S. setting for an American) or someplace "foreign." As Jesus' servants among the nations, we are to work toward realizing his kingdom by helping people come to faith in Jesus, Jesus' church to mature, and Jesus' kingdom values to be realized in our societies. We do this through both organized and unorganized activities.*

That complex statement draws on much of our discussion up to this point. The purpose of this chapter is to build on this punch line and further examine what Jesus' Great Commission means for my local church and me.

Perhaps your initial instinct when you hear Matthew 28:18–20 is to focus on the little but potent word *go*. One line in a sermon I heard years ago still rings in my ears: "The King said 'Go,' so *go!*" That declaration is a compelling and oft-used appeal for cross-cultural missionary service.

The qualifiers usually quickly follow: "Even if you can't go, you can send (especially give money) and pray." In addition, most of us have heard how the main imperative in these verses is Jesus' command to "make disciples." That is, "going," "baptizing," and "teaching" are actually participles augmenting the central task of "discipling the nations."

What I am concerned with here is the framework within which this Great Commission is understood and used. The "send-go-pray to disciple the nations" paradigm is normally coupled with the common prescriptive, concentric-circle understanding of Acts 1:8 that we examined in the previous chapter. Hence for us Americans, we send-go-pray *from* the United

States (Jerusalem) *out to* the mission field, which consists of "the nations" or countries outside the 48 continental United States.[2] Even if we interpret *nations* as "people groups" (*ethne*) and think in terms of sociological ethnic groups instead of geopolitical nation-states, a combined racist instinct (cf. chapter 4) and majority-status blindness still keep "the nations" at arm's length "out there" by defining them as "foreign" and "ethnic" people. Those non-Caucasian and non-U.S. people are "the nations" that "we" are to disciple. (Again, I cringe at using such strong language—which nevertheless is true, if I am honest, about me and, if I am not mistaken, about others in my sociological-ecclesiastical circles.[3]) Racism and nationalism are subtle, nasty monsters that do not die easily.

As nonintuitive as it might feel, I'd like us to break through that underlying framework and consider the "punch line" formulation expressed above. As we seek to do that, please rest assured that there is no question here about whether or not "We've a Story to Tell to the Nations," as the old hymn goes. At the same time, how does the worldwide, international character of who "we" are relate to "the nations" among whom "we" are citizens and insider-members? What was Jesus saying to his disciples in Matthew 28:18–20, and what, therefore, does that mean practically and concretely for us today?

### Jesus Empowers an Overmatched Group

It is helpful first to note that this passage that we have come to call Jesus' "Great Commission" has not always had the place of central importance for Christians that it has for the past two centuries, namely, since William Carey's 1792 tract *An Enquiry into the Obligations of Christians*

2. The name of my denomination's international missions organization, "Mission to the World," reflects our historical background and continuing instincts about who "the nations" are. While logistically there are good reasons for distinguishing between "foreign" and "domestic" missions programs (the latter of which our church calls "Mission to North America"), biblically and theologically those reasons are hard to find, much less justify. One is left to wonder to what extent distinguishing ourselves in North America from "the world" "to" which we go in missions influenced the choice of our missions organization's name.

3. Pertinent to note here is that the General Assembly of my church (the Presbyterian Church in America) has wrestled with racial matters since soon after its inception in the early 1970s. See, for example, our 2002 adoption of an acknowledgment of complicity with racist attitudes and practices, available online at http://www.pcahistory.org/pca/race.html.

*to Use Means for the Conversion of the Heathen.* The eminent South African missiologist David Bosch has argued that during Christianity's early centuries (patristic period), the understanding of mission was succinctly expressed in John 3:16; for medieval Roman Catholic missions, Luke 14:23 ("compel people to come in") was particularly influential; during the Protestant Reformation, Martin Luther's foundational experience established Romans 1:16 and following and its teaching of justification by faith as the main missionary text. With Carey, and then with others throughout the 1800s who were combating the encroachment of rationalism, secularism, humanism, and relativism, the irrefutable appeal to obey Christ's final command took center stage.[4]

Noting this progression of understandings is helpful not because we can see how Christians finally "got it right." Rather, we can catch a glimpse of how our contexts cause us to highlight the importance of certain Bible passages. Being aware of that dynamic ought to foster our humility, in light of our situational finitude. It should also help us both to anticipate how future Christians will look back on our limited understandings of Scripture and to seek the input of other Christians today who live in different contexts. The result should be a fuller understanding of the Bible's scope, in this case about what mission is.

It is also helpful to realize that Jesus' words recorded in Matthew 28:18–20 were not delivered at a missions conference or special seminar per se. He spoke them to his disciples as a continuation of his previous teachings. Related is the fact that Matthew wrote these words in connection with the rest of his gospel account. He thus drew together many of the emphases he made throughout the entire gospel, such as worship, doubt, authority, and discipleship.[5] To be sure, the fact that here in Matthew, as in other equivalent gospel accounts, Jesus' Great Commission comes at the *end* of his earthly ministry should carry its due weight of particular importance. Still, we must not rip these

4. David J. Bosch, *Transforming Mission: Paradigm Shifts in Theology of Mission* (Maryknoll, NY: Orbis Books, 1991), 339–41.

5. My Covenant Theological Seminary colleague David W. Chapman makes these and other connections in his lucid and careful article "The Great Commission as the Conclusion of Matthew's Gospel," in *All for Jesus: A Celebration of the 50th Anniversary of Covenant Theological Seminary*, ed. Robert A. Peterson and Sean Michael Lucas (Geanies House, Great Britain: Christian Focus Publications, 2006), 85–101.

words away from the rest of Jesus' life and ministry and place them into a special, unrelated "missions" category.

Important as well is the consideration of the people for whom Matthew composed his gospel. We evangelicals believe in the divine origin of all of Scripture, coupled with the particular contexts within which God used the Bible's human authors. In Matthew's case, he was writing for a new, struggling, minority Christian community, probably situated in Syria. Matthew wanted this community to be assured that Jesus was indeed the One promised for generations as well as the One who, even though they themselves might have felt powerless in the midst of the unbelief surrounding them, would sustain and use them out of his unrelenting power and commitment.[6]

Jesus thus invited the weak and weary to "come to me . . . and I will give you rest. Take my yoke upon you. . . . For my yoke is easy, and my burden is light" (Matt. 11:28–30). He is the risen One to whom "all authority in heaven and on earth has been given." He promised to be "with you always, to the end of the age" (Matt. 28:18, 20). Those words surely encouraged Jesus' disciples, as well as the original recipients of Matthew's gospel account and indeed all who have subsequently had access to this portion of God's Word. We may be weak and overmatched, but Jesus lives and is committed to completing his mission. Moreover, he will do so throughout the world as he leads us, his global church, into the particular settings where he sends us to serve.

## Jesus Sends Us His People into Our Various Settings

One of the other equivalent gospel accounts of Jesus' Great Commission is John 20:21. There Jesus said to his disciples, "Peace be with you. As the Father has sent me, even so I am sending you." John continues in verse 22: "And when he had said this, he breathed on them and said to them, 'Receive the Holy Spirit.' "[7] We cannot help but be reminded at

---

6. Bosch, *Transforming Mission*, 56–83.

7. Several contemporary missiologists stress John 20:21–22 as a helpful text on which to base thinking about Christian mission. Cf. Ajith Fernando, "Jesus: The Message and Model of Mission," in *Global Missiology for the 21st Century: The Iguassu Dialogue*, ed. William D. Taylor (Grand Rapids: Baker Academic, 2000), 209; Samuel Escobar, *The New Global Mission: The Gospel from Everywhere to Everyone*, Christian Doctrine in Global

this point of Luke's progression from the end of his gospel account into the beginning of Acts, his second volume: "Thus it is written, that the Christ should suffer and on the third day rise from the dead, and that repentance and forgiveness of sins should be proclaimed in his name to all nations, beginning from Jerusalem. You are witnesses of these things. And behold, I am sending the promise of my Father upon you. But stay in the city until you are clothed with power from on high" (Luke 24:46–49). That promise was, of course, initially fulfilled at Pentecost, as recorded in Acts 2.

It is particularly important for you, me, and others across the globe to realize that just as Jesus was sent into the world, and just as he then sent his first disciples into the world, so, too, does he send us into the world—wherever our parts of the world might be. I don't just happen to live and work where I do by chance. God has sent me here. I am here by his calling and assignment. So are others of his followers, including my own particular church as well as other particular congregations and conglomerate parts of his overall, worldwide church. Jesus as our Leader and King has assigned us to serve him in the world, and wherever he sends us is part of his mission field that he aims to redeem and make right again. In that sense our very lives are a continuous missions trip, whether we stay in one locale or move around here and there.

The *go* in Matthew 28:19 thus takes on a fascinating significance. Much has been made of the grammatical fact that the original Greek word is a participle that modifies the main imperative verb *make disciples*. Some have therefore concluded that Jesus' intended meaning was: "As you live, as you go through your various stations in life, make disciples. . . ." Most commentators, however, point out that in tandem with the imperative *make disciples* the participle *as you go* also—actually, primarily—takes on an imperative thrust: "Go!"[8] That thrust is grounded in the fact that Jesus sends us to live and serve among all people, whether it be as organized missionaries or in more typical, unorganized ways. It could be that

Perspective Series (Downers Grove, IL: InterVarsity Press, 2003), 25, 88, 108 (Escobar quotes Stott twice).

8. Representative of commentators who carefully examine the participle's possible meanings is D. A. Carson, *Matthew: Chapters 13 through 28*, The Expositor's Bible Commentary with the New International Version, ed. Frank E. Gaebelein (Grand Rapids: Zondervan, 1995), 595.

Jesus will direct us to move to a different place or situation from where we are now. It could be that he will continue to direct us to stay where he already has us. However and wherever he directs us, he is the One who sends us into the world. He has sent his global people, my church, and me onto the mission field of his still-unredeemed world.

Many kind, well-meaning people have asked me since we moved to the United States from Japan, "What is it like since you left the mission field?" As we will note shortly, their question makes perfect organizational sense. But in the sense that we have been discussing here, it is impossible for any of us to leave the mission field of this world until either we die or Jesus returns. His comprehensive mission to make the world right again continues throughout his world—and he sends us into the harvest field as his servants.

## Unorganized and Organized Missions Activities

So all Christians are missionaries, right? We have discussed this matter earlier (in chapter 2), but we need to pursue it further here in our discussion of the Great Commission, particularly Matthew 28:18–20. Jesus said to his first disciples and to all subsequent Christians that, as we are going into the world into which he sends us, we are to make disciples of all nations, baptizing them and teaching them. In the sense we have just been exploring, yes, all Christians are missionaries. All Christians have been sent into their communities, families, jobs, schools, and other networks where he inserts us. As those who have been sent by God on his mission to help restore the world, we are all his missionaries.

This is exactly the framework of 1 Peter, as the apostle encourages the suffering Christians to "keep your conduct among the Gentiles honorable" (2:12). God had made them into a special people, living among "the Gentiles" or unbelieving people, "that you may proclaim the excellencies of him who called you out of darkness into his marvelous light" (2:9). They were God's envoys sent into their particular sociopolitical settings (2:13–17), work environments (2:18ff.), and families (3:1–7). As Jesus' followers engaged with those around them, those first-century believers—and all others since, including us who have been sent into our own settings today—thus have Peter's further encouragement to "in your hearts regard Christ the Lord as holy, always being prepared to make a defense to anyone who asks you for a reason for the hope that is in you" (3:15).

## Disciple All Nations

Important in this regard of "unorganized" Christian mission is to pay careful attention to how Jesus has told us to make disciples "of all nations." As we have already stressed, all Christians are members of nations, or peoples. It is not as though the nation or people of which I am a member were not itself a nation or people. *All* nations must be discipled, not just those "out there." (Relevant here is the fact that *panta ta ethne* ["all nations"] refers to "the whole world of humanity,"[9] not just Gentiles apart from Jewish people.) This is an extremely important point, and we will come back to it later when we discuss the importance of ongoing missions among all peoples and situations.

Relatedly, Jesus said to make disciples of all "nations," not just individuals within nations. The phrase in Matthew's account has a corporate thrust, whether we view "nations" sociologically (as ethnic groups), sociopolitically (as countries), or theologically (as unbelieving peoples). To be exegetically fair and balanced, we must note that Jesus' words also have individuals in view, since the nations are to be "baptized," something that only individuals undergo. We have discussed earlier the penchant of evangelicals for individualism, and thus we tend to hear Jesus' words about discipleship primarily along individual lines. Accordingly, in our discipleship relationships a leader trains a believer younger in the faith. One person learns from another believer how to follow Jesus, and disciples are thus made. Student ministries give a special emphasis to this discipleship process, and countless adult believers today have benefited greatly.

But again, Jesus said to make disciples of all "nations," which are corporate entities. In former centuries, "Christian nations" thus took it

9. John Nolland, *The Gospel of Matthew: A Commentary on the Greek Text*, The New International Greek Testament Commentary, ed. I. Howard Marshall and Donald A. Hagner (Grand Rapids: Eerdmans, 2005), 1265–66.

upon themselves to make non-Christian nations into Christian ones. The Spanish did that in Latin America and the Philippines, the British attempted the same throughout their massive empire, and even more recently the United States (after the late-nineteenth-century Spanish-American War) sought to Christianize the Philippines (in a way that was understood to be better than the Spanish had attempted). Is that what Jesus meant?

## One Contemporary Approach

Such a position is obviously untenable today.[10] One recent evangelical approach that takes seriously Jesus' command to disciple "nations," while avoiding an out-of-date territorial Christendom approach, is to focus on saturating a nation-state with church growth. The goal in mind is that of "Discipling a Whole Nation." All groups of about 500 to 1,000 people are to have an indigenous church, all individuals in those people groups will then have an optimum and a reasonable opportunity to respond to Christ, and all believers will then be in situations of being trained in discipleship. A further way of putting this approach is that Jesus Christ is to "become incarnate in all his beauty, compassion, power and message in the midst of every small group of people . . . in a country on a long-term basis." The process is to be indigenous to each nation-state as well as to all people groups comprised in it.[11]

This approach has much to commend it, particularly in the way it seeks to hear the corporate meaning of Jesus' Great Commission. Its desire for evangelism and church growth, and the accompanying honor given to Jesus and his impact throughout the earth, is only to be encouraged and supported. One possible downside of the program's emphases is an almost exclusive focus on organized programmatic progression—although to be fair, this movement would no doubt welcome and encourage what we are calling God's "unorganized" mission. Another point of discussion is whether the goal of a nation's being discipled

10. At the same time, pondering what the difference is between Christianizing and civilizing the Philippines at the beginning of the twentieth century and democratizing Iraq at the beginning of the twenty-first is at least a meaningful consideration.

11. All this information and more is available at the DAWN Ministries Web site at http://www.dawnministries.org/.

is really achievable. The eschatological import of this goal is central, whereby "this gospel of the kingdom will be proclaimed throughout the whole world as a testimony to all nations, and then the end will come" (Matt. 24:14). Besides the dubious manner in which Matthew 24:14 is used in some circles almost to predict when Jesus will return, and while no doubt observable church growth and its accompanying social impact has occurred and does occur, can we say that any nation or people will ever be fully discipled before Jesus' return?

## Shared Distinctives

Along those lines, we can also say that part of what Jesus meant and has in mind for us today regarding "discipling the nations" is that "national distinctives, the things that mark out each nation, the shared consciousness and shared traditions, and shared mental processes and patterns of relationship, are within the scope of discipleship."[12] As another commentator has put it (perhaps in extreme fashion to make the point), "The Great Commission is in fact about the conversion of cultures. . . . Evangelisation and conversion mean turning to Christ all that He finds when He meets us, and asking that He cleanse, purify and sanctify us and all that we are, eliminating what He considers incompatible with Him."[13] In other words, various collective habits and practices that "everybody does" need redemptive attention. In the midst of our ever-changing and unredeemed contexts, such patterns and processes will always need addressing. Christian communities are to be alternative examples of beauty, care, and Christlikeness.

All of us as Christians, insofar as we live in this world, know of these matters that regularly arise simply as we "go" into this world and are thus given the opportunities to "disciple" our particular groups. It is common practice, for example, to lie about the actual sale price of a privately purchased car so as to reduce the amount of sales tax the buyer then owes. To act honestly as a Christian is a wonderful God-given

12. Andrew F. Walls, *The Missionary Movement in Christian History: Studies in the Transmission of Faith* (Maryknoll, NY: Orbis Books, 1996), 27.

13. Kwame Bediako, "Facing the Challenge: Africa in World Christianity in the 21st Century—A Vision of the African Christian Future," *Journal of African Christian Thought* 1, no. 1 (June 1998): 53.

opportunity to disciple one's society regarding how that practice should be carried out. Another accepted and common social pattern is how the use of the designation *ethnic* is restricted to minorities. That, too, presents a golden opportunity to note that all of us are ethnic, meaning that we all have particular traits, habits, and so on. (Is there such a thing as a nonethnic restaurant, e.g., McDonald's, or church, e.g., yours?) All sorts of shared assumptions and casual discourse about sexuality, criteria for financial investments, competition, "luck," "success," "Mother Nature," and countless other areas are ways that Christians can live distinctively and speak up for Jesus' sake in participating in his mission.

To press the matter further, not all American values (manifold as they are), even when expressed in their ideal forms, are necessarily universal, normative, or the perfect model for all people, given their particular and mixed forms. Take this expressed view, for instance: "The desire for freedom is not the property of one culture. It is the universal hope of human beings in every culture." One analyst has termed this view an "evangelical Enlightenment or enlightened evangelicalism." That view "combines the Enlightenment heritage of optimistic humanism with the evangelical fervor of an altar call"—on the basis of a peculiar "American version of the Enlightenment—which was shaped by Lockean empiricism and the rationality of the market."[14] American "freedom" thus has its own peculiar features. Even given those values that represent the best of "our [U.S.] way of life," Americans are not lacking in the need to learn from other societies, including those considered fundamentally different or even hostile—for example, Islamic ones.[15]

14. Stephen H. Webb, "On the True Globalism and the False, or Why Christians Should Not Worry So Much about American Imperialism," in *Anxious about Empire: Theological Essays on the New Global Realities*, ed. Wes Avram (Grand Rapids: Brazos Press, 2004), 120.

15. I realize that this paragraph is saying a mouthful and needs further explanation—which time and space will not allow. Suffice it to note here that even such cherished and basic values as "democracy" and "freedom" are understood and practiced in particular settings as well as carry their own nuanced meanings, depending on who is using the terms. With particular reference to comparing U.S. and Islamic societies, Joseph Tamney insightfully notes on the one hand that both have a religious right with potent political presences. Additionally, Tamney suggests that there could be value in at least an assessment of "how Islam in some ways might be superior to Western civilization or of how Westerners might benefit from learning about Islamic societies." Joseph B. Tamney, "American Views of Islam, Post 9/11," *Islamic Studies* 43, no. 4 (Winter 2004): 617–19, 629. U.S. Christians can appreciate, for example, the lack of brazen sexual displays in Islamic societies, in sharp contrast to the bombardment that one experiences in America.

As Christians in the United States, as is the case with the rest of us in Christ spread throughout the other nations of the world, we are confronted in our national context with fundamental challenges to faithful Christian living. Even so, we can act with humble confidence and hope with respect to our particular U.S. contexts, since Jesus is the One with all authority, the One who suffered for us, and the One who is always with us as we live and suffer in this still-unredeemed and imperfect world.

## Organized Efforts

As the situations to which we have just alluded exemplify, so much of our participation in Jesus' mission takes place in unorganized fashion. At the same time, our organized and structured efforts are important as well. Besides witnessing about Jesus to individuals as God gives unexpected opportunities, we as churches are to be intentional and organized about evangelistic services, sermons, Bible studies, and training programs. As is the case in communities all around the world where we as Christ's church live, my church has been sent into our area as Jesus' witnesses to see people come to faith. And because there are peoples in the world who do not have an adequate witness—perhaps they don't yet have the Bible translated into their language, for example—we as Christians (including we who are American Christians) can move, in humble cooperation with others, to see that such a witness takes place.

We as Christ's church, in all parts of the world, need to mature. That includes the need to grow numerically by seeing more people come to faith and brought into the people of God. We must, as Scripture enjoins us over and over, grow into the maturity of the "new man" in Christ of Ephesians 2:15 and 4:13, 24. We thus have regular preaching and teaching, training of leaders, growth in families, small groups, and other organized activities. So that some leaders can get the insight gained from leaving their cultural contexts and learning the Christian faith elsewhere in a different community, many students leave their homes and go to seminary for a period. At the same time, some leaders need to stay where they are and have education and training brought to them; hence, extension training takes place in various forms. So that pastor-scholars can grow in their perspectives of the fullness of God's

Word given to his worldwide church, there is the desperate need for the exchange of international perspectives through books, conferences, and other means of interaction.[16] There are myriad ways for the church to push toward maturity in organized ways, under Christ's mission to grow us up as his body.

We also, by organized and structured means, can follow Jesus in his comprehensive mission to bring kingdom values to bear in our societies. As touched on earlier, this often happens in Christians' unorganized connections as they carry out their God-given responsibilities. But the church as organized can issue declarations and confessions when appropriate—about sexuality and marriage, racism, poverty, abortion, or other public matters. Intentionally consulting other parts of the worldwide body of Christ concerning where they stand on matters of war and peace, for example, can shed light on our particular viewpoints and the unseen assumptions underlying them.[17] Local congregations can work within particular situations for justice on behalf of those who are disadvantaged or oppressed—for example, through empowering recent arrivals to the United States with English-language help. Cities provide particularly ripe opportunities for service, since different sorts of people are increasingly migrating to cities all around the world, including in the United States. Moreover, cities have a unique place in manifesting corporate human structures, art, and creativity, as well as sin and oppression—on the way toward the New Jerusalem of God's final re-creation of his world.

How my church and I will serve in our particular local situation is hard to predict. Situations are unique and ever-changing, as are local congregations. In all cases, each congregation is a local outpost of the worldwide body of Christ. We are to be "at home" and

16. The proliferation in recent years of U.S.-American pastors' and teachers' going elsewhere in the world to teach on short-term (one- to two-week) trips has a twin effect. On the one hand, students receiving the teaching benefit from both the material they are given and the contextualization process through which they must go in appropriating that unavoidably, at least to a certain degree, foreign material. On the other hand, those pastors and teachers who go—if they have the eyes and ears to see and hear—learn more of the universal God who brings them to those international settings.

17. One example of how U.S.-American Christians can do this very thing is to consult the Presbyterian Church in Japan's "Official Statement Concerning War," available online at http://www.covenantseminary.edu/pdf/Jennings_WarStmt.pdf.

involved with our local setting, but at the same time we are always to be a pilgrim, international group that keeps a certain prophetic, critical distance in order to live out and speak the gospel effectively. Too much "at home" comfort leads to syncretism; too much foreignness means quarantined irrelevance. Both local and global traits—being "glocal"—are key to maintaining a constructive position of prophetic reform.[18]

As Jesus instructed us in Matthew 28:18–20, as local congregations we are to be missionary communities by following "the missionary practice of Jesus and the disciples. . . . A missionary community is one that understands itself as being both different from and committed to its environment; it exists within its context in a way which is both winsome and challenging."[19] That is who we are as God's people, sent into his world. He has all authority in heaven and on earth, and he is most eager to share his might and grace with us.

Furthermore, Jesus told his disciples in John 20:21, "As the Father has sent me, even so I am sending you." By his Father's commission, Jesus was fully engaged in his Palestinian first-century world. He suffered greatly because of that engagement, being misunderstood and unjustly executed. As part of his worldwide following who have been sent into the world's various contexts, we in twenty-first-century America can expect Jesus' presence and power, even as we suffer internally and externally, after his example.

Jesus' promised presence and power should encourage us greatly as we move next to consider specific examples of the crisscrossing, multidirectional character of Christians' and churches' missions activities.

## Reflection Questions

- How might racism and nationalism be intertwined with my church's and my understandings (both theoretical and operative) of the Great Commission?

18. Lamin Sanneh, *Translating the Message: The Missionary Impact on Culture*, American Society of Missiology Series, no. 13 (Maryknoll, NY: Orbis Books, 1989), 28–48.

19. Bosch, *Transforming Mission*, 83.

- What helpful perspectives come from viewing the Christian life as a continuous missions trip?

- What are some unorganized ways in which you and your church participate glocally with Jesus in mission? Organized ways?

# THEME 4

## "Serve One Another"
### (1 Peter 4:10)

# 7

# Organizing Missions in Today's Multidirectional Mission Flow

Countless local churches in the United States have discovered in recent years the excitement of sending out their own members as short-term missions teams. In fact, there has been a virtual explosion of one- to two-week trips that groups take all over the world. These groups consist not of "professional missionaries" but of regular, lay church members who feel called to become directly involved in fulfilling the Great Commission to take the gospel to the end of the earth. The possibility is now there, so the trip announcements broadcast, for anyone to go and serve on the front lines of missions, not just pray and send others. (I hope, based on our discussion to this point, you question the *missions* framework of these last two sentences.)

As far as I can tell, increasing numbers of evangelical American churches are becoming involved in such short-term[1] missions projects, to one degree or another. (It is also interesting to note that many Korean churches are similarly involved. A few years ago I participated in a Wednesday night service in Seoul in which all the more than seventy people were leaving the next morning for a two-week medical missions

---

1. *Short-term* has come to mean "a week or so." A few decades ago "one to two years" was the normal meaning, in distinction from "career" or "long-term" missionaries.

trip to the Philippines. Also, the worldwide influence of both American and Korean Christianity is spawning similar short-term efforts from many other sectors of the worldwide church.) The vast majority of these churches seem to be continuing their traditional missions programs of supporting full-time U.S. missionaries. (As briefly discussed earlier, some churches have added the strategy of supporting non-U.S. "nationals," so much so that some churches have made the strategic decision to move toward supporting only national missionaries.) Whatever the particular combination of more traditional missionary support and short-term missions teams might be, short-term trips and projects have accelerated in ways unimaginable only a decade or two ago.

Short-term teams meet a wide range of needs. Many teams come alongside missionaries whom their churches support in evangelistic efforts. Medical and dental teams go and set up temporary clinics in remote areas. Opportunities for service range from ministries to street children, orphans, and prisoners, to school and church construction, theological education, and numerous other possibilities.

The rush toward short-term missions has not been without its critics. Some decry the amount of money involved in sending groups of five to fifty people on such trips. Whether real ministry can actually take place has also been questioned: after all, people going for such brief periods cannot know the local cultures, and if English is not the spoken language, that obviously presents a major barrier as well. Are not these trips just expensive, spiritualized vacations that can do more harm than good, given the lack of cross-cultural awareness that short-termers inevitably have?

Advocates have their answers. Sure, short-term trips cost money, but there are plenty of resources to go around if people will only give them. Training and preparation for trips can help deal with the built-in lack of cultural awareness. Post-trip evaluations by both the sending and receiving groups can facilitate learning and growth for all concerned. But the strongest argument given for short-term missions points to the payoff: significant ministries are taking place, career missionaries are being helped and encouraged (despite the obvious extra work they put in to accommodate teams that come), and—perhaps best of all, the defense goes—short-term missionaries themselves (and their local churches that send them out) are being transformed, even to the point that some of them become career missionaries.

The bottom line is that short-term missions are here, they are growing, and they show no signs of going away in the foreseeable future.[2] Some may continue to argue against short-term missions, but no amount of objecting will forestall this major development within contemporary Christian missions.

For our purposes, the central question I want to consider in this chapter is this: How can short-term missions, along with other organized missions efforts that we as American evangelicals carry out, take place within two-way, or even multidirectional, interdependent relationships with others? This question is crucial in light of the fact that we as Christians are an international, worldwide church. It is also crucial in light of what we were just discussing in the immediately preceding chapters, namely, that we as the worldwide church have been sent—to use a strange-sounding phrase—as glocal "nodes" into our particular settings. Since here we are wanting to break through an out-of-date, unreflective, yet often-assumed notion of "West-to-the-rest missions," how can we intentionally cultivate reciprocal, cooperative relationships within the worldwide church?[3]

*Partnership* has been the much-discussed buzzword in recent years used in approaching this important matter. In effect, such partnerships involve American Christians'[4] working together with Christians in another part of the world in a particular ministry project. Usually U.S.-based financial support is involved. Because money flow often

2. The seemingly limitless future of short-term missions going out from U.S. evangelical churches is due to more than such religious factors as Spirit-produced zeal and increased conviction that missions is the responsibility of local churches, not just missions agencies. (For a stimulating, if somewhat polemical, discussion of the latter of these two factors [as well as of many other issues], see James F. Engel and William A. Dyrness, *Changing the Mind of Missions: Where Have We Gone Wrong?* [Downers Grove, IL: InterVarsity Press, 2000].) As noted earlier, I would argue that at least as important in projecting the future of U.S.-based short-term missions, and indeed of U.S.-based missions in general, is the United States' economic and military superpower status.

3. One of the best new books seeking to cultivate a healthy learning posture among short-term missions teams is David A. Livermore, *Serving with Eyes Wide Open: Doing Short-Term Missions with Cultural Intelligence* (Grand Rapids: Baker, 2006).

4. Insofar as we are talking about U.S.-based partnership efforts. The same could be said about Korean missions, for instance.

carries with it authority flow as well, some have criticized using the term *partnership* to describe relationships that have such built-in imbalanced positions of power between the "haves" and the "have-nots." Nevertheless, countless U.S. churches and Christian organizations are involved in partnership relationships with corresponding groups elsewhere in the world.

Not long ago I asked a U.S. short-term missions team about their partnership with a group of ministries in a developing country. I specifically asked how their partnership could be a two-way relationship. At first the team members thought I was asking how the indigenous Christians were carrying out the ministries along with the expatriate short-termers, so they described for me how all that they as short-term missionaries were doing was "coming alongside the nationals" and encouraging them. But the team then realized that I was asking how the relationship between their home church in the United States and the churches and organizations in the developing country could be reciprocal and interdependent. Specifically, how did their U.S. church need their fellow Christians?

I expected the answer to focus on how the short-term missionaries were changed by their trip experiences, and then how the short-termers in turn affected their home congregation by sharing about those experiences. My own ideal answer would have focused on creative expressions of give-and-take between Americans and others, perhaps including two-way travel to each other's locations. Instead of either of those replies, however, the explanation was framed entirely within a we-are-Jerusalem understanding of Acts 1:8. Specifically, the people "on the mission field" to whom the U.S. church sent teams provided the Americans an opportunity to fulfill the Great Commission to take the gospel to the end of the earth.

Clearly, our conversation was misfiring at the levels of assumption and attitude concerning the Scriptures' message about how Christ exercises his unique Superpower status within his world mission. Who was in control of sharing the gospel, who had the right to go to whom, and who was in a privileged position in the international relationship were difficult questions that needed reflection and discussion.

## Historical Transition

Crucial to addressing these subconscious levels is developing a sense of the widespread *transition* that we as a worldwide Christian movement are undergoing. We have already considered the massive demographic shift that has taken place over the past few centuries: while once primarily located in Europe and North America, the Christian church is now dispersed throughout the world.

Such a major shift is nothing new in Christian history. Jesus' immediate followers were primarily Jewish. With Paul and others, coupled with the A.D. 70 destruction of Jerusalem, Christianity moved out of its Jewish heartland into various Gentile locations. Later shifts took place when Islam spread throughout the Middle East and north Africa, with Christianity experiencing focused growth northward and westward (and soon eastward among Slavic peoples) in Europe.[5]

The unthinkable transpired with these macro shifts in Christian presence. Peter could not conceive of Cornelius and other Gentiles' having equal legitimacy with Jews as God's people, but part of the gospel message was that Gentiles did have full legitimacy as God's people by faith alone. Later, Syrian Christian missionaries could have hardly anticipated Chinese embodying the Christian message—but they did after Alopen and other Christians arrived in China in the early 600s. What third-century Roman Christian would have really expected barbarian savages north and west of the empire to be fellow heirs with Christ? Little did they know that some of the greatest Christian emissaries would one day emerge out of northwestern Europe.

In our day, what was unthinkable only a century ago is now reality: those whom Westerners perceived as savage, subhuman, and uncivilized pagans of Africa and elsewhere in what is often called the "Global South" now constitute the majority of Christians worldwide. Jesus is followed and worshiped by peoples in countless locales and languages throughout the

---

5. Andrew Walls has been the seminal scholar in explaining these macro shifts as part of Christianity's "serial" growth, whereby the Christian faith thrives and then, in many cases, declines among cultures and civilizations. Cf., e.g., Andrew F. Walls, *The Missionary Movement in Christian History: Studies in the Transmission of Faith* (Maryknoll, NY: Orbis Books, 1996), 16–25, plus his *The Cross-Cultural Process in Christian History* (Maryknoll, NY: Orbis Books, 2002), 27–48.

earth. Many readers will be startled by the statement, "There are probably more Christians in China than in any [other] country on the planet"[6]—but it is true. Jesus is working among all sorts of his people to enable them to live out and spread his good news in all kinds of situations. He is also using different nationalities of Christians in cross-cultural missions activities, be they Brazilians, Nigerians, Indians, Koreans, Chinese, or many others.[7]

What the Christian faith looks like in these different situations, what issues are taken up, what styles of worship are employed, and any number of other matters will vary. On the one hand, there will be universal commonality: Jesus is supreme, the Bible is central, love of God and others are basic values, and so on. But while ongoing overt spiritual warfare, for example, is both appropriate and necessary for Christians who live in settings where the awareness of spiritual beings is part of life, for others battling the numbing effects of materialistic affluence must take center stage. Evangelicals in Japan have a bent toward peace that contrasts with American evangelicals' general willingness to support war.[8] Countless other examples could be cited of different emphases and concerns between Christians of different settings.

6. Paul McKaughan, "Framing the Future," *InVision* (December 2005), available online at http://www.mtw.org/home/site/templates/mtw_invision.asp?_resolutionfile=templatespath| mtw_invision.asp&area_2=public/Resources/Invision/2005/12/FramingFuture. McKaughan addresses several other themes with which we are dealing in this book, in the main how to structure missions efforts in light of the vast worldwide changes that have occurred over recent generations.

7. Examples are, of course, too numerous to even attempt to list. One noteworthy cross-cultural Christian enterprise (like many others, describable as charismatic) is "The Embassy of the Blessed Kingdom of God for All Nations" church, pastored by Nigerian-born Sunday Adelaja. Information available online at http://www.godembassy.org/en/index.php.

8. Why this is the case is an important consideration in its own right. The Japanese citizenry's abhorrence of militarist leaders' actions in the 1930s and 1940s is part of the explanation. Also, Japan's Pacific War experience of suffering carpet bombing and particularly the atomic bombs dropped on Hiroshima and Nagasaki is stressed to children in schools. Americans have the historical background of both world wars, into which the United States was reluctantly drawn in order to defeat German imperialism and Nazism.

The difference in attitudes between Japanese and American evangelicals regarding war and peace has several manifestations. For example, Christians in Japan uniformly dismiss the possibility that the decision to drop the atomic bombs could in any sense be justified; many American Christians, on the other hand, believe that decision to have been the best available for ending the war. Contrasting understandings of "just war" as well become evident through considering the aforementioned Presbyterian Church in Japan's "Official Statement Concerning War," an English translation of which is available online at http://www.covenantseminary.edu/pdf/ Jennings_WarStmt.pdf.

## Contextualization

To continue this line of discussion by borrowing an oft-used but confusing term, how the Christian faith is *contextualized* in different cultures and settings takes on different and often unpredictable forms.[9] Christianity is always concrete and particular. At the same time, it is always an expression of the transcendent and universal God working in specific contexts. The One God speaks his one Word in all languages—since the infinitely translatable Bible is articulated within the vast array of human communities, all of which have their own unique thought forms and traditions. God's people in turn respond to God as people who belong to their own particular and diverse communities.

Perhaps the clearest example of Christianity's diversity within its wider unity is how Christians worship. I am always struck by this when I travel back and forth between Africa and the United States. While there are plenty of exceptions to the rule, generally speaking churches in Africa are more lively and expressive. Dancing, congregational feedback during the sermon, and an overall heightened exuberance outstrip what happens in a typical American worship service (certainly one involving Caucasians). Most everyone would agree that such differences are appropriate and well suited to their respective contexts.

The plot thickens a bit when we consider how the Supreme Being that we English speakers term *God* is designated by about as many different labels as there are languages used in worship. These terms come right out of the Bible—as translated into various mother tongues. Arabic speakers use *Allah* in reference to the God of the Bible, Yoruba Christians pray to *Olodumare*, Christians in Korea worship *Hananim*, and on and on the list goes. All these terms (including *God*) were used before the Bible and Christianity entered their respective languages; yet the One living Creator and Ruler of the universe has been pleased to be designated by this multitude of labels, as evidenced by the Bible's own multilingual testimony. One divine Creator—*God*—is thus known through a host of

---

9. The subject of contextualization is crucial and massive. One entry-level, brief discussion is my "The Tapestry of Contextualization," in *Looking Forward: Voices from Church Leaders on Our Global Mission*, comp. and ed. Mission to the World (Enumclaw, WA: Winepress Publishing, 2003), 24–30.

terms. He truly is the universal Covenant-Creator who comes close to all of us, no matter where we live in this great big world.

This variety of God's communication with people throughout the earth points to the real players in the contextualization process. The central figure is God himself. He comes to people, addresses them in their language, and deals with them as his beloved creatures. Those people being addressed are next in importance. What it means to respond to God faithfully is something that indigenous, mother-tongue speakers must determine under God's direct leadership and guidance. Finally, the expatriate outsider (e.g., an American missionary) plays his or her important part as well. That role is not primary—so it does not help to say that missionaries must "contextualize the Christian gospel for others" so that they can understand it. God and the recipients do the primary contextualizing: the missionary outsider is a catalyst to help spur along that primary process.

## Implications

You may be asking yourself at this point, "How did we get off onto a discussion about contextualization—whatever that is? Weren't we talking about short-term missions?" We were indeed. What we did, however, was to take a detour into considering the historical transition that we are undergoing today within God's world mission. We did that, as well as discussed the primary agents in contextualization, so as to address the necessary matters of assumption and attitude about the Scriptures' message concerning Christ's world mission. If we fail to keep paying attention to these basic aspects of involvement in Christian missions, we will inevitably go awry in our attempts to organize activities in today's multidirectional mission flow.

As central as any message in this book is the bedrock conviction that *God alone is the Superpower* in carrying out his world mission. That conviction should temper and shape our instincts about our missions efforts—especially including *our* instincts as *American* evangelicals. As we have already discussed in various ways, we who are American Christians serve Christ in his mission *as Americans*. That is a good thing and part of God's plan. But as we have also already discussed, our evangelical perception of the United States' Christian heritage, coupled with the United States' current political-economic-military superpower status, reinforces the deep instinct that *missions* equals both "God's most meaningful work in the world" and "Westerners' (in particular, white Americans') going elsewhere to proclaim the gospel." Such an instinct is skewed and off base, and it gives rise to similarly warped assumptions, attitudes, and scriptural understandings. Attempts at organizing missions efforts will then reflect and indeed reinforce those misshapen and skewed instincts about God's mission and our place within it.

The point is this: God is the center and initiator of his mission, so my church and I must not unwittingly act as though we were the originating Jerusalem of Christian missions. Organized missions efforts that my church and I undertake are in fact joining in with all else that God is doing to remake his world.

Part of what that means is that my church and I will respect and learn through people of other cultural settings. My church and I may decide to go somewhere else and serve the cause of the gospel, whether short-term or more permanently. The ministry could be construction, medical, evangelism, economic development, or anything else. In all cases, God is the primary player in what is happening: he has already been dealing with the people who live where we have decided to go, and our decision to go there was part of God's initiative to take us there—in large part to shape and deal with us. While he wants to use my church and me to serve others, God is also particularly interested in working in *our* lives through placing us in a different cultural context. He will use the people there to teach us a great deal about himself, about his world (including the ongoing context into which he has sent our local church), and about ourselves.

A special word is needed about cross-cultural theological education. Especially with the phenomenal rise in one- to two-week short-term missions, legions of seminary professors and pastors go from the United States to offer short courses of all types. Sometimes these courses are taken for credit toward some type of degree (of varying accreditation standards), and sometimes they are just offered in stand-alone fashion. In all cases, those who go must not presume that they are offering instruction in some type of one-way transmission to blank-slate recipients. God has long been at work in the people taking in the instruction; moreover, those students have been wrestling with God throughout their lives. The teaching being offered is simply one more bit of stimulus that God is bringing to them for their good and equipping. The students will process that information through their own grids, in their own languages, and for their own purposes. The instructor is little more than a catalyst—who himself should be intent on learning through those to whom he has gone to pay such a brief visit.

The assumptions and attitudes just outlined will affect missions activities that we Americans plan and execute. With respect to all ministries, but with special regard to theological education, one question-set that must be asked with all seriousness is, "What can *we* teach *them*, and how should we do it?" The mirror question-set must also be asked: "What can *they* teach *us*, and how should we learn from them?" We need new and creative structures and processes, some examples of which will come up below, to help us embody Peter's admonition to "serve one another."[10]

The current period of historical transition, from a "West-to-the-rest" modus operandi to a multidirectional, cooperating worldwide Christian movement, demands nothing less.

## Unorganized Mission and Missionaries

God's overarching mission initiative has been driving and shaping the demographic shift in worldwide Christianity. As we create and execute missions activities that are appropriate to the ongoing transition, we must pay careful attention to how God is working in his "unorganized" mission, as we have called it earlier. God's mission is comprehensive; organized *missions* are only a part of his mission. Part of cooperating with God in his mission is to try to keep what we do in *missions* in step with the rest of what God is doing in his extensive unorganized mission initiatives.

10. A helpful article that draws on the contrasting experiences of American short-term lecturers and national recipients is Dave Livermore's "American or American't? A Critical Analysis of Western Training to the World," available online at http://www.intersectcommunity.com/pdf/AmericanorAmericant.pdf (and first appeared in the October 2004 issue of *Evangelical Missions Quarterly*).

Let's remind ourselves of what we do *not* mean by God's unorganized mission. We are not referring to the dichotomy that some Christian leaders were making in the 1950s and 1960s between God's work in the church and in the world, the latter meaning certain economic and political movements. Many were advocating abandoning organized Christianity altogether and finding God anew, as well as cooperating with his mission, by joining in various economic and political liberation campaigns. That is not what we are recommending here.

Instead, God's unorganized mission refers to his providential orchestration of world trends beyond and outside of Christians' intentional, organized activities. Our intentional, organized Christian missions efforts operate within and alongside structures (political, economic, tribal, etc.) and conditions (epidemics, violence, poverty and wealth, etc.) that surpass even our understanding, analysis, and awareness, much less our control. God the Sovereign Ruler, however, is at work behind, in, and through such structures and conditions, always with his ultimate redemptive purposes in view. God's providence that moves toward the new heaven and new earth is his mission that Christians don't and can't organize, but with which we should cooperate.

Here I want to focus briefly on just four aspects of how God is providentially working in the world—in what to us are "unorganized" ways—for his own redemptive purposes: immigration patterns, business flow, education, and urbanization.[11] Each constitutes a huge area of discussion, so we will only skim across the tips of these four icebergs.

## Immigration Patterns

People, whether individually or in groups, have been migrating to different places since the earliest times. In the Bible we read of the moving of the patriarchs, the Israelites, individual prophets, the baby Jesus' family, first-century Jews, and others—often out of necessity, always within God's providence—to new lands. Sometimes it was God's direct

11. The items on this list are similar to those that Roger Greenway terms "Population Movements": urbanization, international migration, refugees, and international students. Roger S. Greenway, *Go and Make Disciples! An Introduction to Christian Missions* (Phillipsburg, NJ: P&R Publishing, 1999), 4–5.

call, and many times economic hardship or political persecution pushed them elsewhere. Whatever the case, throughout the Bible and indeed all of human history, people have not simply stayed put in their separate locales.

Recent decades have seen an ever-greater acceleration in immigration movements. Wars have displaced millions of refugees (e.g., Afghanis, Sudanese, Liberians, Iraqis). The pull of economic possibilities has taken millions to more affluent regions (e.g., to Europe, the United States, Japan), whether near or far. The world has been increasingly shrinking in terms of peoples' interactions, again either by force or by choice.

Since the United States is a leading receiving country of immigrants and refugees, many American Christians have awakened to new possibilities close to home for cross-cultural ministry to internationals. The opportunities are practically unlimited for service to so many who arrive in America with little or no belongings, limited English-language ability, trauma from atrocities experienced, and other needs.

Alongside these ministry opportunities (and what I wish to stress here) is the posture that American Christians can take of receiving from God what he desires to teach us through those whom he has providentially brought to the United States. Much is to be gained, even if the lessons are painful, from listening to any number of perspectives that non-Americans have to offer. Lifestyle issues can be constructively challenged by learning from those newcomers who are much less affluent. Joy deepened through suffering can be shared from war refugees. Political views can be sharpened and refined as we learn of how non-Americans view U.S. foreign policy (and as we wrestle with political issues surrounding illegal immigrants in the United States). Encountering new languages can stretch the confines of typical linguistically limited Americans.

Especially since many new immigrants and refugees are Christian believers, but even including those whose religious faith is different, God has brought others to our doorsteps for mutual challenge, stimulation, benefit, and service. God's unorganized missionaries break the mold of our intentional structures and plans.

## Business Flow

God's unorganized missionaries also include the many Christians involved in today's global business and other corporate networks. Such globe-trotters represent many different nationalities and occupations. Ugandans—many of them Christians—scour Japan in search of used auto parts needed back home. Filipino nurses—again, many of them Christians—are working in health care centers throughout Asia, the Middle East, and the West. Korean Christian company men have been traveling into China and the former Soviet Union for decades. American Christians also dot the worldwide business landscape as executives, software designers, and countless other examples.

These Christians have not especially selected their jobs in order to travel as cross-cultural gospel emissaries. Nor are all of them even aware of their capacity as missionary representatives of Christ. Even so, God is moving his people around as his servants. As the Superpower Missionary intent on using his followers as salt, light, and proclaimers of his kingdom, God is sending and bringing his people into all kinds of situations through the complex exchange of goods, services, and money throughout the world.

## Education

Christians are also on the move within the world of education. Now even at pre-university levels, international exchange programs take and bring Christian students into contact with all sorts of distant peoples and situations. Often living with homestay families, Christians are witnesses for Christ, and are themselves shaped by Christ, as he puts them into high schools for a school term or an entire year. Christian teachers and exchange-trip chaperones can similarly serve as Christ's cross-cultural ambassadors.

At the university level, the ways in which God sends and brings his people only increase exponentially. Christian exchange students from many different countries (including America) come and go into all sorts of countries (including America). Postgraduate researchers and faculty members in various fields similarly take up residence for an academic term or even several years. Such individuals serve their heavenly King as they go, and churches all over the world (including in America) can receive and learn from them.

## Urbanization

As Christians, we are eagerly anticipating "the holy city, new Jerusalem, coming down out of heaven from God, prepared as a bride adorned for her husband" (Rev. 21:2). This central, urban feature of the new heaven and new earth shines its light into the present to help us to see how God's providential hand is behind the massive urbanizing trend in our world today. This is not to say that residing in cities and towns is more holy than tending a farm in Kansas or living in East Africa as nomadic hunters. It's just that within the biblical sweep from a garden to a city, God is bringing all sorts of people together for commerce and creative artistic development.

As you may have traveled (including through international airports), no doubt you will have noticed the many different language groups that have come together in cities in the United States, Latin America, Asia, Europe, or Africa. I have been struck by the different sorts of people even in smaller U.S. towns, regardless of the section of the country. Resident U.S. Christians can recognize and tap in to how God has brought Christians[12] from other parts of the world as part of his missionary force to stretch us, challenge us, and help us follow our Leader Jesus more appropriately and effectively.

## Missions-Sending and Missions-Receiving Churches

Perhaps your own local congregation has responded to God's bringing into your circles Christians from elsewhere as have some churches in St. Louis, where my family and I now live. One suburban congregation welcomed a Ph.D. biochemist from the University of Ghana in West Africa; he was conducting sabbatical research with Monsanto. This

12. Non-Christians come from elsewhere as well, but here we are focusing on the international movement of believers.

Ghanaian had been a Christian for decades, and he was on the lookout in St. Louis both for fellowship and for groups with whom his church in Ghana could cooperate in various ways. Through close, trusting relationships that developed between this biochemist missionary and a small fellowship group in the church (along with the church leadership), this congregation has spearheaded various efforts in St. Louis to travel to Ghana, help fund ministry projects there, as well as continue to receive subsequent church leaders who have been coming for mutual instruction and encouragement.

Another church, situated in an older, midtown part of the city, discovered a Brazilian pastor in St. Louis doing seminary studies (in a school that was nearby but with a different denominational heritage). This pastor and his family became involved in the life of this approximately 150-member congregation, occasionally leading in worship and even preaching. Since the pastor's return to Brazil, the congregation has taken multiple organized trips to his church, and individual church members have also gone in various capacities. Other seminary students from the same church in Brazil have come, the St. Louis church hosts a local Brazilian worship service, and several ministry networks go back and forth between here and several congregations in Brazil.

Another church in St. Louis was established about fifteen years ago with the expressed purpose of racial reconciliation (between blacks and whites). Totally unforeseen by the church leadership was the influx into the church's relational orbits of Latinos, Liberians, French-speaking Congolese, and various other Christian immigrants (as well as non-Christians). The church has been transformed into a representative example of the international people of God for whom Christ gave his life. The church leadership's openness to how God was at work—again through his unorganized missionary force—was key to their church's ongoing transformation. Part of that transformation has been how Paul's teaching in 2 Corinthians 8 and 9, about the need of the Christians in Achaia and Macedonia to share financially with the famine-stricken Christians in Judea, has compelled the church to become deeply involved with less affluent Christians elsewhere in the world.

None of these examples has been perfect or problem-free. There have been cross-cultural misunderstandings and uncertainties about how to proceed. But the point I want to stress is that there has been give-and-take in all the relationships that have developed. God brought to St. Louis a biochemist, a seminary student, and immigrants from various places around the world. At least part of what God intended was to use these servants to minister to people in St. Louis. The Christians and churches in that city were led by God's Spirit into the suffering process of relinquishing certain assumptions and attitudes about their rights and privileges. They have creatively come up with new applications and actions in starting down the road of becoming missions-*receiving* churches, in addition to the more familiar pattern of being missions-sending churches. Later we will look further at similar examples.

God alone is the Superpower in carrying out his mission. We who are citizens of the economic and political superpower United States of America—and thus tend to lean exclusively on our own resources—must recognize that part of what God is intent on carrying out is the sending of his cross-cultural, international emissaries into the American part of his worldwide mission field. Our nation (speaking both politically and ethnically), from which we who are Americans have been called to be his followers, is in need of further discipling. God has sent you and me as his indigenous missionaries into our particular U.S. settings, and he has been sending others from the outside into our situations to help. We can thus gladly receive these international missionaries, as well as cooperate with Jesus in his mission in other parts of his still-unredeemed world.

The picture of what a missions-receiving American church looks like is fuzzy—of course. To switch metaphors, any less-traveled path will be difficult to see and follow. Those in leadership positions—such as pastors, heads of missions committees, and missions executives—are usually just as inexperienced in this area (and sometimes more hamstrung as a result of unhelpful habits) as the next person. Even so, Jesus the great *Kurios* and Suffering Servant has proved himself to be able and willing to go where others have not been before. By his ever-living Scriptures and Spirit he will guide us, his suffering and pilgrim people, through the wilderness of the world that he aims to make right again in his mission.

144

## Reflection Questions

- What are some pros and cons of short-term missions?

- What signs of the historical transition within God's worldwide mission can you see in your local context?

- What unorganized missionaries has God sent into your local context?

# 8

# Organizing Missions Today
## as American Churches

The missionary movement from the West is only an episode in African, Asian, and Pacific Christian history—a vital episode, but for many churches an episode long closed. Missionary enterprise continues, but its Western, and especially its original European, component is crumbling. The great missionary nation is now Korea; in every continent there are Korean missionaries by the hundreds, and in coming years we can expect hundreds more, preaching from Tashkent to Timbuktu, and reaching where Westerners have long been unable to tread. In a more modest way, Brazil is now a major sending country. The eventual effect of such transformation in the sending structures can hardly be calculated.[1]

Today is an exhilarating time in which to live as a Christian. Struggles will remain, of course, until Jesus returns. Such difficulties notwithstanding, the worldwide character of the Christian church makes for an almost exotic situation full of new possibilities for a stimulating array of missions initiatives. Koreans, Brazilians, Indians, Nigerians,

1. Andrew F. Walls, *The Cross-Cultural Process in Christian History* (Maryknoll, NY: Orbis Books, 2002), 45.

Americans, and others are crisscrossing the globe as Jesus' international emissaries.

At the same time, as Andrew Walls (perhaps our day's most insightful missions analyst) has noted above, the modern Western contribution to Christian missions is "crumbling" and, for some at least, is an already completed "episode." To be sure, it is the European portion of Western Christianity that has dramatically dwindled over the past few generations. By contrast, American Christianity arguably has even rejuvenated in recent decades, and its sociopolitical influence is as potent as ever. Nevertheless, as I have already discussed, much of American evangelicalism is uncritically intertwined with U.S. patriotism-nationalism, a reality quite evident to others throughout the rest of the world. Many non-Americans would be hard-pressed to distinguish between Charles Briggs's yoking together of U.S. colonial and Christian missionary activities in the Philippines a century ago and today's widespread U.S.-evangelical support for America's military ventures.

Yet there have been welcome exceptions to the prevailing uncritical American evangelical-patriotic mind-set. Such a devoted North American as Herbert Kane, no doubt because of his extensive international missionary experience and intervening years of hindsight, had the eyes to see the damage done to gospel progress in China by nineteenth-century American and British extraterritorial laws that were finally abolished in 1943: "For exactly one hundred years these unequal treaties were a millstone around the necks of the missionaries," whereby all expatriates were judged by their own countries' laws instead of by those of China, their country of residence.[2] Furthermore, a conservative political commitment, often associated with U.S. evangelicals, does not necessarily mean unquestioning agreement with conservative political leaders: witness, for example, the conservative commentator George Will's capacity to speak critically regarding immigration issues and results of U.S. actions in Iraq.[3] Even so, Kane's Canadian heritage and

2. J. Herbert Kane, *Understanding Christian Missions* (Grand Rapids: Baker, 1978), 250.
3. George F. Will, "A Vote for English," *Washington Post*, May 25, 2006, available online at http://www.washingtonpost.com/wp-dyn/content/article/2006/05/24/AR2006052402433.html; "Bleakness in Baghdad," *Washington Post*, March 19, 2006, available online at http://www.washingtonpost.com/wp-dyn/content/article/2006/03/17/AR2006031701795.html.

Will's lack of evangelical identity shoot holes even in these supposed exceptions to the rule.

In short, American missionaries and Christians have often been unable to discern our alignment with America's international interests. Moreover, we are largely unaware of the degree to which the super-powerful U.S. economy and military support our still-vast missions presence and influence. Even if we do become aware of these realities, they are still there, including in the perceptions of everyone who sees us tightly clutching our U.S. passports.

The poignant question that many American evangelicals ask at this point is, "Well, what then can—or should—Americans do in missions? Should we back off, keep on with business as usual, or what? I feel frustrated!"

## Walking by Faith

This is another one of those wonderful crossroads where we so clearly need to look to Jesus our heavenly Commander in Chief to lead us forward. Some new structures and trends are indeed already emerging, as we will further introduce below. Even so, we American Christians are entering a new day in international missions, in which we do not have all the answers about what to do, or even how to frame our questions. "Should we support American missionaries or nationals?" is a hot-button issue, for example. As we noted earlier, however, the answer does not have to be exclusively either/or; there are problems with the category "nationals"; the nature of "support" must be examined; and a host of other questions must be asked.

Do we then fall into some sort of paralysis of analysis? No, we can ever look to Jesus to lead us forward. "Take my yoke upon you, and learn from me" (Matt. 11:29) is an appropriate invitation from Jesus to us who are eager to serve one another as the international church, but don't know exactly how.

### Uniquely American Contributions

God's good providence extends throughout the earth, including to Americans' cultural traits and to America's place in the world today. If you travel or follow the news, you'll know that much of the world has a love-hate posture toward Americans. Most everybody is happy to have us come to their country and spend our money, and many on a personal level like Americans' generally outgoing and friendly nature. On the other hand, many do not like what they perceive to be unilateral U.S. military ventures (some vehemently oppose all U.S. military actions; others, however, welcome them), and we Americans are often perceived to be shallow, shortsighted, and rather obnoxious. Many (but by no means all) aspire to come to America in pursuit of a better life, and much of U.S. pop culture is eagerly taken in. Many resent America's superpower status and influence, but most understand and accept America's importance in world affairs. Some Christians in other parts of the world have seen Americans as unfit to teach others about religious matters, reckoning us to be "this-worldly" and propagating "a religion of numbers and money and strategies."[4]

This entire complex situation is within God's sovereign rule over his world. It is also clear that God wants all his worldwide people—including those of us who are Americans—to participate with him in his mission. Much of how we participate with him is in unorganized ways, as we live "normally" by his gracious enablement while going into the world where he has sent us. Our present challenge—at this point in the book and at this point in history—is to discern how best to participate with God's mission in our intentional, organized missions efforts.

A very important point is to recognize some of the particular *American* contributions, within God's providence, that we can make within the worldwide Christian missions enterprise. One is the *experience* gained over several generations of organized missions experience. American churches and missions groups have much know-how to offer regarding organizational structures, financial oversight, personnel training, and many other areas. Another contribution is in the area of *financial resources*—although one must not presume that only Americans have money to share with others. American *academic institutions* can offer meaningful accreditation and valuable leadership training. One useful

---

4. Uchimura Kanzo (1861–1930), a prominent early Christian leader in Japan, was one such outspoken critic of American Christianity and missionaries. Ruth A. Tucker, *From Jerusalem to Irian Jaya: A Biographical History of Christian Missions*, 2nd ed. (Grand Rapids: Zondervan, 2004), 271–73.

trait that many Americans have to offer is an *entrepreneurial willingness* to try new ventures instead of simply sticking with tradition.

Some of these contributions are more uniquely American than others. All of them need to be tempered by others' input about how they can best be put to use. Americans lack much that others can contribute. But Americans do have ongoing gifts, qualities, and resources that will surely continue to be a part of the worldwide missions enterprise, as all of God's people trust Christ to empower and guide us in his mission.

## Missionary "Calling"

What about discerning whether or not I am "called" into missions? Particularly in today's changing worldwide Christian scenario, how are we to determine the roles that God wants my church and me to play, as Americans, in world missions?

These are vital questions, and we must be careful in how we think through their answers. I remember participating years ago in a meeting of missionaries and administrators. At one point we were asked to give our testimonies of how God had called us to Christ and of how he had called us into missions. I knew what the directions meant, but I recall the stark ambiguity I felt because of the conviction that all Christians, regardless of their occupations in life, had been called to participate in God's mission as part and parcel of being called to follow Christ. What was confusing me was the lack of distinction—both within myself and within the group—between what I've termed "unorganized" and "organized" missions.

That very distinction is of primary importance in wrestling with God's "calling" regarding missions. All Christians, including all American Christians, are called to cooperate with Jesus in his mission to make the world right again. In that sense we are all missionaries. Let's not forget that basic point when working through this important matter of God's calling and missions.

With respect to organized missions, many speak of God's special "calling" to become a missionary.[5] Some say that they are called to go to

---

5. Written materials on this subject are immense, as any Internet search or visit to a Christian bookstore or library will attest.

a particular country or people, while some say that they are called to be a missionary but that the location is not too important. Furthermore, some assert that a missionary calling is irrevocable, in that God calls a missionary to go to a "foreign field" for life, unless unexpected, undeniable, and unavoidable providential circumstances dictate a change.

I respectfully challenge this framework—emboldened by Herbert Kane's pointed remark, "The term *missionary call* should never have been coined. It is not Scriptural and therefore can be harmful"[6]—but I do so with an understanding of its importance for many godly people. For example, I have heard it stated publicly and privately that a strong sense of calling is necessary to carry a missionary through the inevitable tough times that one will face. Without a deep sense of God's calling, how else could William Carey have withstood the initial opposition to missions by church leaders in England, or the ongoing reluctance and poor health of his wife? How else could Hudson Taylor have pressed ahead with adopting a Chinese lifestyle, despite the ridicule of fellow missionaries?[7] "Just as God called Paul and his companions to go to Macedonia in Acts 16:6–10, you absolutely must have a strong sense that God has called you to those people, in order to persevere in preaching the gospel to them through much opposition and hardship," the charge rings out.

Here, briefly, is my respectful three-pronged challenge. First, in terms of biblical exegesis, Paul's Macedonian call was a night vision. Not all cross-cultural missionaries receive those, and not all such visions in the Bible are specifically for cross-cultural missionary service (think of King Solomon in 2 Chronicles 7:12ff., for example). Hence, to use that well-known incident as a normative model for a missionary calling is questionable at best.

Second, among Christians the notion of a special missionary calling strengthens the dubious assumption that organized missionaries are the pinnacle of spirituality—which missionaries themselves assert is not the case. On the one hand, setting organized missionaries apart in a special way is a helpful reminder of the intentional missions task that we as

6. Kane, *Understanding Christian Missions*, 41.
7. Tucker, *From Jerusalem to Irian Jaya*, 122–28, 188–89.

God's people are to be about under God's leading, in the manner of how Paul and Barnabas were set apart in Acts 13:1–3. Furthermore, the Bible, while affirming the goodness of all creation and the godliness of various vocations, does exhibit a preference for explicitly spiritual concerns and callings. Why else, for example, would Jesus have called a "fool" anyone "who lays up treasure for himself and is not rich toward God" (Luke 12:20–21)? Even so, Paul and Barnabas (and the countless missionaries ever since) had not, by virtue of being commissioned as missionaries, attained some superior level of holiness. Throughout his life and ministry Paul the missionary continually affirmed his own weakness and pride, so that God's power and grace could be on public display all the more: "For when I am weak, then I am strong" (2 Corinthians 12:10b).

Third and perhaps most seriously of all, claiming the necessity of a special missionary "calling," in order to press ahead while serving within the darkness of heathen lands, helps to perpetuate the out-of-date and unhelpful division of the earth into Christian countries and non-Christian ones. The assumed bottom-line reason that you need a special calling to help you persevere through mission-field struggles is the satanic opposition you meet while invading, as a missionary, his dark turf. Missions within such an alleged world remain a one-way move-ment "from the West to the rest." Later we will touch on the underlying and touchy issue of so-called territorial spirits, whereby it is believed that demonic powers have particular strongholds in certain areas of the world. Whatever one ends up thinking about all of that, for now I will reassert that the whole world is the mission field, no matter where one lives and works in this life. We draw strength from Jesus' abiding pres-ence with us wherever he has us, for "we know that we are from God, and the *whole world* lies in the power of the evil one" (1 John 5:19). All Christians are called to live in and serve on the mission field—in other words, in this world.

My suggestion is that we demystify the missions enterprise by think-ing not so much in terms of missionary "calling," but of a collective discussion as we decide how to follow God's guidance in our missions efforts. Jesus leads us by his Word and Spirit as we seek him and his will. Under his guidance we make the best decisions we can, we bear the consequences of making those decisions, and we trust him as our gracious Redeemer to shape and use us for his glory, our good, and the advancement of his gospel.

## Contemporary Trends and Examples

Given these preliminary considerations of how God leads or "calls" American Christians to make our particular contributions to the world missions enterprise, what are some current ways that American Christians are involved in missions activities in today's international, glocal ministry situation? Along with some of the examples we began to sketch in the previous chapter, no doubt you can list some right now (which I encourage you to stop and take a few minutes to do).

### Trends

Three elements can be identified in many contemporary missions initiatives: networks, team efforts, and collaboration.[8] With increased urbanization and globalization comes increased interconnectedness between people, or *networks*. Intentional missions efforts can tap in to these networks through *local* initiatives—for example, the linking of churches with ministry organizations and social-service agencies to help the poor and homeless. Such coordinated efforts can take place in a small town or section of a larger city, whether in the United States or elsewhere. There are also *specialized* network initiatives—for example, the Sonship material that emerged out of World Harvest Mission and has encouraged countless Christians, congregations, and ministries all around the world.[9] Examples of *global* network initiatives are two described elsewhere in this book: DAWN Ministries with its goal of

8. Cf. Michael Pocock, Gailyn Van Rheenen, and Douglas McConnell, "Working Together: Beyond Individual Efforts to Networks of Collaboration," in *The Changing Face of World Missions: Engaging Contemporary Issues and Trends*, Encountering Mission Series (Grand Rapids: Baker Academic, 2005), 247–78.

9. Cf. the World Harvest Mission Web page at http://www.whm.org/grow/sonship. I believe it is also accurate to note—as another example of the international interconnectedness of the Christian church—that much of the impetus for Jack Miller (and others who developed the Sonship emphases) experiencing and then stressing the joyful walk of repentance came from their contact with Ugandan Christians during the difficult 1970s under Idi Amin.

stimulating church-planting movements among every people group among whole nations, and the worldwide movement of evangelicals (Lausanne—see Appendix A). This last form of networks is by nature worldwide in focus and purpose.

Mission *teams* have been rediscovered during the last few decades, moving American missionaries away from individual, institutional responsibilities (in churches, hospitals, Bible colleges, and seminaries, for example) toward more mobile, catalytic, and equipping roles. Some missions agencies[10] stress the importance of teams' being international, to reflect the unity in diversity inherent to Christian fellowship. As we have already mentioned, short-term teams have skyrocketed in their volume and scope of ministry involvements.

Strategic *collaboration* has been aimed at facilitating churches and missions organizations to carry out their ministries more effectively. Relief and development assistance have been supplied to various efforts through World Vision and World Relief, for example. Demographics and other types of information are shared through such groups as Global Mapping International, the U.S. Center for World Mission, and journals such as the *Evangelical Missions Quarterly*. Initiative 360 (formerly Advancing Churches in Missions Commitment) seeks to "challenge and equip the Church to take its rightful place in missions" through speakers, materials, and seminars.[11]

These elements of utilizing networks, teams, and collaboration all reflect the trend from individual missionary activities to shared, collective missions efforts. Another similar trend, as noted in the previous chapter, is that of *partnerships*.[12] Many local churches have moved from simply extending their own ministries outward through missionaries (an approach reflected, perhaps, in the holding of "missionary conferences")

10. E.g., Send International (http://www.send.org/about/index.htm). Many agencies have become international in their makeup, even if they are not as explicit about having international teams per se. Cf. Wycliffe International (http://www.wycliffe.net/about/tabid/449/Default.aspx), YWAM (http://www.ywam.org/contents/abo_wha_ywamexplained.htm), OC International (http://www.onechallenge.org/index.php?option=com_content&task=view&id=15&Itemid=30), OM International (http://www.om.org/).

11. See http://www.acmcnetwork.com/.

12. The final chapter of Art Beals's *When the Saints Go Marching Out: Mobilizing the Church for Mission* (Louisville: Geneva Press, 2001) gives some helpful suggestions for local churches regarding "Partnership in Mission." This manageable book is a helpful, enthusiastic, and experience-based practical read for local churches, especially including missions committees.

to linking up with Christians and churches in other parts of the world. Sometimes the linkage is indirect through missionaries or missions agencies, and sometimes it is direct. In any case, money is usually central to partnerships in which U.S. churches are involved, and as we have already noted, there are spirited discussions about how money transfers should or should not take place. Also as previously noted, sharing finances is one particular contribution that U.S. Christians can make to the worldwide missions enterprise, so how to proceed is an important yet often confusing matter to consider.

Financial partnerships take place under different models.[13] Probably the easiest, yet most problematic, is the *personal support* model. In this method, U.S. churches or Christians give money to an individual indigenous ministry leader. If there is not much relational oversight and accountability, or if donors do not know the local situation toward which they are contributing, or if the recipient becomes dependent on outside funds for launching out in ministry, problems arise. An *indigenous* partnership seeks to make a new church or ministry self-supporting from the beginning. This could take place, for example, through a declining support schedule, perhaps creatively combined with some sort of matching support program. A formally established *structural* partnership model utilizes, instead of a direct recipient, a local, indigenous organization—church, independent board, school, or what have you—that administers funds sent from the United States.

Keys to whatever models are employed are trusting personal relationships and clear financial accountability. Cultivating a genuine interdependency (whatever that looks like) is a crucial challenge as well.

Partnerships consist of more than just money transfer, of course. Short-term trips by U.S. church members to the ministry situation are often part of what happens. Multiple U.S. congregations' coordinating their efforts with a missions agency, missionaries, and indigenous Christians can be a dynamic and central feature of partnerships.[14] How an

13. See Pocock, Van Rheenen, and McConnell, "The Changing Uses of Money," in *The Changing Face of World Missions*, 279–97.

14. Mission to the World is one agency that strongly encourages local U.S. churches to become involved in this type of international partnership ministry: http://www.mtw.org/home/site/templates/default.asp?ml_index=8&area_2=public%2FPartners%2Fpartners%2Dmain&objectid=BBF8D1F0%2D0&NC=5232X.

interdependent, give-and-take partnership can develop within a one-way money-flow situation, which is also heavily weighted toward the U.S. side in terms of numbers of people involved in decision-making, is a constant challenge that must be addressed.

## Examples

Even given just these few identifiable trends, the possibilities are endless for creative new expressions of interdependent, glocal missions initiatives by U.S. churches. What is often missing in the types of collaborative networking and partnering just described is a genuine sense among U.S. Christians that we are also on the mission field where we live now, and that our relationship with Christians elsewhere should facilitate our life and service here. Jesus has sent his international church into our settings around the world (all of which is still the mission field, including that part of the world known as the United States of America) as interconnected, interdependent nodes. How my church's and my needs are genuinely addressed by God through non-American Christians, or how we all can truly "serve one another" within the international body of Christ, is a crucial feature of the type of missions initiatives needed.

Thankfully, examples of such initiatives have been springing up.

One is the practice of an international pastoral-pulpit exchange. Such exchanges can emerge out of existing personal relationships, or perhaps a denominational liaison can develop and administer such a program. Language is an important factor, of course, so interpreters need to be available if the pastors cannot function linguistically in their respective foreign settings. Exchanges can be for a month, six weeks, or even longer. The congregations involved receive the benefit of God's ministering to them through a different national-ethnic channel. Various logistics must be worked out, of course, but such arrangements as finances, accommodations, and travel are by no means insurmountable.

Another fascinating new initiative is a partnership between Mennonite churches in Argentina and in Illinois. One of the two main ingredients in this two-way relationship is an Argentine church-planter's coming to Illinois to sponsor a new church-planting thrust that utilizes Argentine-style house churches. The other crucial component is an annual, alternating exchange of church members between Argentina and Illinois, all of which will involve missions projects. The mutuality embodied in this arrangement is exemplary for the type of interdependency that we as American Christians need to develop with others.[15]

This Mennonite partnership exemplifies the built-in global structures that many Christian denominations already have in place for networking and partnering. The Worldwide Anglican Communion is particularly noteworthy for its multidirectional flow of influences, including conservative Global South leaders' calls for U.S. Episcopalians to turn back from liberal positions on sexuality. Recently the archbishops of Singapore and Rwanda established the Anglican Mission in America, in many cases incorporating conservative U.S. Episcopalians (to use missiological terminology, native indigenous Christians) who have left the Episcopal Church.[16]

One nondenominational arrangement of mutuality is a Brazilian-U.K. network of churches and ministry organizations, called "Go to the Nations." Based on Brazil-U.K. relationships, mission partnerships develop as God leads. Another part of the thinking is that churches in Brazil are indebted to churches in the United Kingdom and Europe for having brought the Christian gospel to them generations earlier; now Brazilian Christians can return the favor in a time of Europe's spiritual need. The reality of being one worldwide church is also fundamental to this new and creative network.[17] While this particular network is not directly associated with a U.S. base, the example itself is appropriate for emulation.

The final example that we will consider involves U.S. churches that are in partnership with churches in Uganda. The TentMaker Project emerged out of a short-term missions trip that a Presbyterian pastor from southern Illinois took to Kampala in the late 1990s. After a similar trip by a Presbyterian pastor from Kampala to Illinois, key relationships that were developing led to discussions on how

15. Ryan Miller, "Mission Lessons for Illinois Come from Argentina," *Beyond Ourselves* 4, no. 1, available online at http://www.mennonitemission.net/Resources/Publications/BeyondOurselves/V4N1/article4.asp. Thanks to Dana Ergenbright for referring me to this ministry.

16. See the Anglican Mission in America Web site at http://www.theamia.org/.

17. Thanks to Gustavo Formenti for referring me to this ministry.

American Christians could share finances with Ugandans in a way that would not create dependency. Eventually what emerged was a church-administered micro-enterprise development program using revolving loans. Other similar ministries have begun as well, all in a way that is empowering to the Ugandans, shared out of a posture of mutual Christian care, and still small enough to be personal and manageable.[18]

All these examples emerged unpredictably and creatively. All embody (albeit imperfectly) important traits of trusting personal relationships, clear financial accountability (when applicable), bi- or multidirectional initiatives, and genuine interdependency. Jesus our Commander in Chief is creatively leading his people forward.

## Resources

In this whole matter of organized, intentional missions efforts in today's worldwide, interdependent Christian situation, one more fundamental underlying issue that we need to consider is that of resources. Assumptions about control, rights, and privileges necessarily arise. Let's approach the matter through three questions: What kinds of resources has God given his people, who has them, and how can they best be shared and be put to use?

### Types of Resources

When it comes to talk about "resources," the first thing that pops into many people's minds is *money*. After all, money is almost always part of ministry projects, and when you get right down to it, the assistance that ministry initiators usually are seeking from other Christians—particularly from American Christians—is financial support. While by itself "just writing a check" is rightly criticized as being an inadequate form of partnership, ministries often won't succeed if churches and individuals don't write those checks. Furthermore, those checks represent money consecrated to the Lord's work through the offerings made by

18. See the TentMaker Project Web site at www.tentmakerproject.org.

sincere, hardworking Christian people. Writing and sending checks is thus no mean thing to be disparaged in any way as insignificant.

Money, then, is a legitimate, necessary, and appropriate resource for Christian missions. So are what we might call "things," such as books, computers, projectors (whether old reel-to-reel types or newer ones for laptops), building materials, and 4x4s. These and many other items are needed and desired throughout the world in order to carry out strategic ministry programs.

Institutions are necessary resources as well. Academic institutions, including degree-granting universities, colleges, and seminaries, obviously provide educations for people. Degrees can provide the necessary qualifications for Christian leaders to serve in strategic and influential positions all around the world, as well as in many cases enable their newer institutions to move toward government recognition and accreditation. Hospitals and clinics serve thousands, even millions, across the globe in Christ's name. Orphanages, youth ministries (e.g., the YMCA and YWCA, at least in their founding purposes), and street-children houses are just a few of the many institutions, wide-ranging in age, size, and focus, that are a part of Christian missions.

Of course, people themselves—including their experiences, gifts, and myriad capacities—are this world's single greatest resource for Christian missions. God uses money, things, and institutions, but people are at the heart of how he works. We speak good news, serve others, and sacrifice our own desires for the sake of Christ and his gospel. We give the money, we make and use things, and we build and run the institutions. People are the top of the Christian missions resource list.

If we're not careful, we might restrict the range of people's experience, gifts, and capacities that are useful for missions. Such experiences as cross-cultural ministry, such gifts as preaching, evangelism, and counseling, and such capacities as medical and construction training might come to mind first. Also crucial, however, are such experiences as suffering and poverty, such gifts as dealing aggressively and overtly with the spirit world, and such capacities as speaking certain languages and being comfortable within certain cultural traditions. The range of people and how they can contribute in missions is vast within God's scheme of things.

Yet the greatest resource of all in missions is God himself. He alone is the Superpower. It is his mission to make the world right again, and he mercifully and graciously uses people and other resources that he himself gives for the whole task. We all know that, but we can too easily act as if it were not true. God is the beginning, middle, and end of his mission and of Christians' organized missions efforts.

## To Whom Has God Distributed These Resources?

The triune God is the owner of the cattle on a thousand hills and the King of his people, the church. He has richly given resources to his people scattered throughout the earth. Peter has thus written, "As each has *received* a gift, use it to serve one another, as good *stewards of God's varied grace*" (1 Peter 4:10).

As we survey the brief list of resources just reviewed, clearly on a worldwide scale the resources are not evenly distributed—which creates a wonderful opportunity for cooperation and sharing. It is immediately obvious (and regularly announced) that, generally speaking, those of us in the Northern Hemisphere have the lion's share of the financial resources. We thus have more ready access to "things" and have greater breadth and depth of technical training. American Christians spearhead the contribution of these sets of resources to the Christian missions enterprise. That's not to say that other parts of the global church do not have money, things, or technical expertise. Certainly, when you talk about institutions and business experience, the resources' location is not as clear (especially given the wide range of what can be termed "institutions" and "business"). Nevertheless, in large part because of the industrial and electronic revolutions, those of us in the Global North have the most money, things, and technology.

But what about experiences of poverty, suffering, and wrestling with spiritual forces? Here the tables are turned. Earlier we noted uniquely American contributions toward the worldwide Christian missions enterprise. The flip side is the range of uniquely American needs or lacks that others can help to meet and supply. Those of us who have grown up in relative comfort—and most Americans have grown up in relative comfort compared to much of the rest of the world—are generally poor in the kind of vital spirituality that only desperate struggle can produce. I, for example, have never known a day when I was not assured that I would have food (although as a student, some days I cut it close). I, for example, have little or no experience in overtly dealing with real, powerful spiritual forces, such as casting out demons. Other Christians I know, particularly those who live in less affluent parts of the Global South, do have those undeniably real experiences. They also readily speak several different languages, as do most other people outside the United States. Besides thus giving them access to a greater array of people, such multilingual people have a richness of experience that monolingual (or even bilingual) people cannot have.

I'd like to offer another special word about theology. Our actions—for example, who seeks to teach whom and whose theologies get translated into whose languages—would indicate that American Christians assume that we have an overwhelming advantage in theological resources that need to be shared with others around the world. Certainly, if one talks about libraries, books, and publishing houses, that advantage is clear (although the relative lack of advertising and distribution range of Global South publishers, not to mention the fact that many function in non-English languages, should not fool those of us who are unfamiliar with them into assuming their nonexistence). In reality, however, Christians all around the world, including the illiterate poorest of the poor, are bursting forth with theological formulations about God and his dealings in Christ with his world.[19] Jesus' followers who are in anywhere from first-generation to fifth- or sixth-generation Christian settings have more of an advantage of sensing the dynamics of gospel-culture interaction than those of us into whose language (in most Americans' case English, of course) the Bible was translated many more generations ago. How God is instructing his people in those newer Christian contexts holds much theological instruction for the rest of us. Hence, those of us who have the financial resources to possess broadband connections, CD-ROMs,

---

19. Kwame Bediako highlights this kind of grassroots theological dynamism in his analysis of an illiterate African midwife, "Cry Jesus! Christian Theology and Presence in Modern Africa," in *Jesus in Africa: The Christian Gospel in African History and Experience*, Theological Reflections from the South Series (Waynesboro, GA: Regnum Africa, 2000), 3–19.

and shelves of books should be careful about assuming that we have all or even most of the theological goods to deliver to others.

God has thus liberally distributed numerous resources into different sectors of the worldwide church in such a way as to set before us a wide-open situation for working together. How to do that is a major challenge we face at this stage of historical transition in the worldwide missions enterprise. Within the international church, who has the control, rights, and privileges is a set of questions that is especially incumbent on American Christians continually to ask.

## Utilizing Our Collective Resources

As we have already noted, it will take new, creative patterns and structures in missions to enable effective worldwide Christian cooperation. Our instincts—*our* referring to most Christians around the world—take us first to money and technical expertise when we think of sharing resources. Understandably so, many of our missions discussions focus on the best ways to share money. Yet how can we share and utilize those resources born out of situations of poverty, suffering, war, and overt spiritual activity? In a related way, how can we avoid thinking that sharing gifts is simply a redistribution of a finite set of items unevenly possessed, and instead realize that the Holy Spirit is freshly granting gifts and resources to his worldwide people?

One initial step is for an American congregation to recognize how God has sent such resources to its own doorstep. Maybe some international students or immigrants live in your neighborhood. How will you interface with these gifts from God so as to *share* life together, in a mutually enriching and interdependent way? How will you tap in to their linguistic heritages and frameworks? More than a fixed program, American Christians' postures and attitudes of compassion or "co-suffering," after the example of Christ who also suffered, will be key to how such relationships, structures, and ministries will develop.

Multidirectional theological instruction and exchange is an area in desperate need of development, especially among evangelicals. Written materials need to be translated not just from English to other languages, but in reverse direction as well. How publishers and distributors can make these translated materials available (and attractive) to American Christians is a vexing problem to overcome. How Global South theology students can have access to materials other than Western ones is another difficult challenge. How Global South Christian educators can instruct American theology students without contributing to a harmful "brain drain" is also an important consideration.

How international relationships can be furthered by multidirectional telecommunications and travel is another fresh opportunity. Short-term missions trips are largely "West to the rest." Is it viable to arrange short-term trips by others to our American locales? If so, what ministries would they conduct, or what activities would we do together? The Mennonite bidirectional missions program between Illinois and Argentina is one program to monitor for lessons that we all can learn.

Key to everything is the sense of our being sent into our respective contexts as a worldwide, interdependent church. As Jesus predicted in Acts 1:8, across the generations he has sent us, his people, throughout the world as his witnesses. It's not as though each of us were Jerusalem, radiating outward in missions; having radiated the faith out from Palestine during the earliest generations of Christian history, God the Holy Spirit is continually bringing Jesus' redemptive work into our various life situations. That mission continues in both organized and unorganized fashion. Jesus is ever leading us in ways that we could not have imagined or created even a single generation ago. More than ever before, we the worldwide body of Christ are positioned to "serve one another" as we serve the world into which we have been sent.

## Reflection Questions

- What are some of your experiences of learning how non-Americans viewed you as an American?

- In what senses do you both agree and disagree with this chapter's discussion about "missionary calling"?

- What additional examples do you know of interdependent, glocal missions efforts?

- What resources can you and your church receive from non-American Christians? What resources can you and your church appropriately share with non-American Christians?

# THEME 5

## "Throughout the Time of Your Exile"
### (1 Peter 1:17)

# 9

# The Ongoing Nature of Missions

Life on the mission field: exhilarating, humiliating, fascinating, and—to employ an overused, undercharged, but appropriate term—challenging. Adjusting to ever-changing, beautiful yet sin-filled, and exotic situations takes creativity, perseverance, a good sense of humor, and spiritual insight.

We all should know—because each one of us lives on God's mission field every day.

Please forgive me for beating this same drum, but the perspective that the United States (suburbia included) is part of "the mission field" is both a matter of fundamental importance and an assumption that is contrary to our inherited American-Christian instincts.[1] It is important because it keeps Americans (and others whom God has sent to the United States) alert to our ongoing encounter with our

---

1. The prevalence of these inherited instincts that exempt North America from "the mission field" is exemplified in J. Herbert Kane, *A Global View of Christian Mission: From Pentecost to the Present* (Grand Rapids: Baker, 1971). In the book's discussion of missions as they have taken place during the last two centuries, every inhabited region of the world is considered—*except* North America. Kane's later, more concise historical volume entitled *A Concise History of the Christian World Mission: A Panoramic View of Missions from Pentecost to the Present* (Grand Rapids: Baker, 1982) follows the same outline. Even such a recent and helpful book as Bryant L. Myers's *Exploring World Mission: Context and Challenges* (Monrovia, CA: World Vision International, 2003) similarly omits North America in its regional depictions (on pages 58–61) of "The Church in the World."

own sin-racked settings; it also checks our tendency to export to other contexts, in unhealthy and uncritical ways, "our way of life" in the name of Christian testimony. The perspective is contrary to our unspoken, powerful, and instinctive modus operandi that *missions* = American Christians' going elsewhere (along with the massive infrastructure required for recruiting, training, praying for, financially supporting, envisioning, caring for, and otherwise enabling people to go).[2] That M.O. is intertwined with destructive racist and nationalist sentiments, and if left unexamined it can be out of touch with today's worldwide, multidirectional Christian ministry situation. Missions today involve the whole, global church's cooperatively following Jesus in his continuing mission to remake the world.

## Recap and Final Theme Introduction

This chapter and the next make up the fifth and final couplet of the book's ten chapters. We have come a long way together through some weighty material that has not always been easy to navigate. Here are summary statements of the four main themes we have discussed so far (together with the corresponding references in 1 Peter):

- God is the Superpower in Christian mission (1:21).
- The church is inherently (and today more than ever, in fact) international (5:9).
- God has sent all of us who make up the church into our respective life contexts (2:12).
- Christian missions efforts should be bi- if not multidirectional (4:10).

2. One critique of this infrastructure pejoratively calls it "Mission, Inc." While I agree that the vast extent of the resources put forth toward the organized, U.S.-based missions enterprise needs continual reevaluation, I regret the destructive polemics that have often characterized the critique aimed at "Mission, Inc." and its "managerial missiology." Cf. Samuel Escobar, "Evangelical Missiology: Peering into the Future at the Turn of the Century," in *Global Missiology for the 21st Century: The Iguassu Dialogue*, ed. William D. Taylor (Grand Rapids: Baker Academic, 2000), 109–12, and James F. Engel and William A. Dyrness, *Changing the Mind of Missions: Where Have We Gone Wrong?* (Downers Grove, IL: InterVarsity Press, 2000), 69, 87, 167.

Each of these themes, of course, has its own nuances and subthemes, and it might behoove you to flip back and remind yourself of some of those finer points. In any case, if we can "wrap our minds around" (to use an indigenous phrase that was new to me when we moved back to the United States a few years ago) these four summary themes, we should be set to tackle our fifth major topic.

Together these final two chapters will consider the claim that missions should be more than just a one-time occurrence in a certain area or among a certain people. An understanding of missions as one-time sees evangelization and church-planting (and perhaps even social ministries and transformation) as the essence of missions, and when a certain stage is reached, missions therefore ceases to be needed in that area or people and moves on elsewhere. Instead of that prevalent evangelical view, the understanding I am advocating is that missions involve an ongoing and ever-changing process. I believe it is helpful, for any number of reasons that have already arisen and that we will be examining further, to view and conduct missions in such a way that every place and situation is treated as a mission field—regardless of how long the Christian gospel has been present there or of the extent to which the gospel has had its impact.

One thus cannot "go to the mission field" as if one's place of origin isn't the mission field. Christians live on the mission field until they die or until Jesus returns. That's the way it was with the original readers of 1 Peter, who were instructed to "conduct yourselves with fear throughout the time of your exile" (1:17). We, too, as twenty-first-century Christians, are "sojourners and exiles" as we "go" about our lives in this world. Where God has already sent us, along with wherever else he might send us throughout our lives, is the/his mission field.

I don't think this claim is simply semantic hairsplitting. It is also more than just being careful about how to use the terms *missions* and *mission*, as important as that distinction is. Working through the counterintuitive reality that where my church and I live is part of the mission field involves the kind of issues we raised in chapter 2 about different facets of God's mission, all under the umbrella of God as the ultimate mission Superpower. It relates to God's dealing with my church and me as *objects* of his mission to remake the world: he uses us as instruments of his grace, yes, but he is always intent on shaping us as well, often through others who are quite different culturally and otherwise. Reminding ourselves as American Christians that our own settings are just as much a part of the mission field as are the settings of others with whom we partner in missions helps to enable us truly to be partners in need of each other. New, creative missions structures and patterns can thus develop that facilitate two-way (even multidirectional) traffic, as we all seek to serve our Commander in Chief in the ongoing battle for the gospel throughout this sin-racked world.

## Mission Fields and Mission Fields

"Fair enough," you might be thinking. "But aren't some areas of the world more 'the mission field' than others? After all, Christians are more numerous in certain places than in others, and some societies reflect gospel values more than those relatively unaffected by Christianity. And to be frank, even though values have deteriorated in America over the past few decades, 'No state in the world has been so strongly influenced by biblical Christianity,'[3] so we need to fight for the preservation and revitalization of that influence." Or as one descriptive layout of the world puts it:

The world's population can be divided into three [roughly equally populated] segments:

- Christian World—that part which has heard the gospel and been influenced greatly by it . . .
- Evangelized Non-Christian world—that part in which up to 50 percent of the people have been evangelized, but are still resistant . . .
- Unevangelized world—that part which has never heard the gospel and is often removed geographically, culturally, and linguistically from Christians . . .[4]

3. Patrick Johnstone, Jason Mandryk, and Robyn Johnstone, *Operation World*, 21st century ed. (Waynesboro, GA: Authentic Lifestyle; Gerrards Cross, Bulstrode, England: WEC International, 2005), 657. I question this kind of evaluation's being made about any country, and I question what underlies this particular evaluation of the United States.

4. Fred Markert, "The Challenge of the 10/40 Window," in *Praying through the 100 Gateway Cities of the 10/40 Window*, ed. C. Peter Wagner, Stephen Peters, and Mark Wilson (Seattle: YWAM Publishing, 1995), 17–18.

That is, "Isn't 'the mission field' most especially the 'unevangelized world,' along with the 'evangelized non-Christian world' (and not the 'Christian world,' preeminently the United States)?"[5]

Such honest wrestling merits honest discussion, and that's what this chapter is all about. Let's press ahead even as God, the global Superpower, presses in on your heart and mine, as well as on the hearts of your and my kind of people.

## 10/40 Window

In evangelical circles, the best-known wider "mission field" is the rectangular swath of the globe stretching across northern Africa, the Middle East, India, China, and adjoining areas, together known as the "10/40 Window." This vast region is so-called because of its location between parallel, latitudinal lines running 10 and 40 degrees north of the equator. The vast majority of least evangelized peoples—particularly Buddhists, Hindus, and Muslims—live in this part of the world. There is great poverty as well, along with burgeoning megacities.[6]

The 10/40 Window idea was formulated in the late 1980s, and it took shape together with the AD2000 Movement with its purpose of "A Church for Every People and the Gospel for Every Person by the Year 2000."[7] In terms of its usefulness for evangelicals, the 10/40 Window focus has been "brilliantly successful." In fact, "the concept became almost too successful—sometimes in being applied to invalidate any mission activity outside the Window!" In recent talk about missions, "The unusual phrase became a household phrase across the evangelical

---

5. Some thus distinguish between "Regular Mission" that takes place among reached peoples and "Frontier Mission" among the unreached. For a helpful, down-to-earth, and concise description of these and other such common evangelical missiological categories, see the "Missions Definitions" Web page of the New Song Christian Fellowship of Brentwood, Tennessee, at http://new-song.ccbchurch.com/app/w_page.php?id=32&type=section.

6. Information about the 10/40 Window can be found at the now-nonupdated AD2000 Web page, "AD2000 10/40 Window Overview—Getting to the Core of the Core," written by Luis Bush, International Director of the AD2000 & Beyond Movement, available online at http://www.ad2000.org/1040broc.htm. Other Web sites that are active and updated include "1040Window.org" (http://1040window.org/) and "Window International Network" (http://www.win1040.com/).

7. With the passing of the year 2000, the AD2000 Movement has been renamed the "AD2000 & Beyond Movement." Cf. its Web site at http://www.ad2000.org/.

world."[8] I want to add that the central motive behind the development of the 10/40 Window framework has been a zeal for the spread of Christ's gospel. That practically goes without saying, but the criticisms that have been leveled against the 10/40 Window require an affirmation of its overarching goal and purpose.

*Background threads.* As we seek to understand more deeply this immensely influential concept by unraveling its background, I believe we can find at least two major threads. One—and this point is particularly relevant to understanding how the concept has taken root so widely among U.S. evangelicals—is the outdated but still-influential medieval European Christendom framework that we considered earlier. Having come to the New World with European immigration, this subconscious territorial notion underlies the powerful U.S.-evangelical view of missions as going to the nations "out there," something that we have also previously discussed. One can note that the United States is obviously *not* one of the areas of the world contained within the 10/40 Window. There is also a remarkable coalescence with the non-Christian world as viewed by the early-twentieth-century international missions community (i.e., at the 1910 Edinburgh World Missionary Conference). The notion of a Christian Europe and North America, as compared with a non-Christian non-West, was self-evident to the Western world in its optimistic global outlook prior to its self-inflicted two world wars.

This thread of a territorial European Christendom by no means constitutes the entire backdrop of the generally happy story of the 10/40 Window. Nevertheless, it does help to explain how the 10/40 Window framework has resonated with so many U.S. evangelicals. On top of that, it bears repeating, in the strong language used earlier (speaking as an American to Americans), that God in his mission is interested in exposing and dealing with the intertwined monstrous racist and nationalistic assumptions that underlie such a territorial Christendom notion. Relinquishing such subconscious assumptions is central to the suffering process through which Christ would lead us.

8. Johnstone, Mandryk, and Johnstone, *Operation World*, 6.

A second thread is the teaching about "unreached people groups." Ralph Winter, founder of the Pasadena-based U.S. Center for World Mission, has spearheaded the development and use of this now-widespread and foundational concept for evangelical missions. Winter combined the linguistic-group focus of Cam Townsend (who helped to found Wycliffe Bible Translators) with the ethnic-group focus of Donald McGavran (founder of the so-called Church Growth school). Fueled by a Pauline "ambition to preach the gospel, not where Christ has already been named" (Rom. 15:20), the result was a nongeographic strategy to reach ethnolinguistic groups—peoples or biblical "nations"—with the gospel, with the goal of starting indigenous churches.

Further background of Winter's thinking is his scheme of analyzing the modern missions movement. Marking the beginning of modern missions at the time of William Carey in the 1790s, Winter divides the past two centuries into three eras. First, coastal regions were reached by Western missionaries. Hudson Taylor and others then penetrated various inland areas.[9] Now, with the focus on people groups, "I think we are living in the third and final era of mission history," Winter has written.[10] This eschatological expectation, associated with Jesus' declaration that "this gospel of the kingdom will be proclaimed throughout the whole world as a testimony to all nations, and then the end will come" (Matt. 24:14), is evident here and in much of the focus on reaching all peoples (for example, in the AD2000 Movement and its associated programs, e.g., the Joshua Project, devoted to gathering demographic information about the world's peoples). While the precise definition of *unreached* has undergone regular revision, the capacity of an indigenous Christian community to spread the gospel to its own people without outside assistance has been the central criterion for declaring a people group *reached*.[11]

9. An instructive graphic of Winter's scheme is "Three Eras of the Modern Mission Movement," in *Perspectives on the World Christian Movement: A Reader*, ed. Steven C. Hawthorne and Ralph D. Winter, 3rd ed. (Pasadena, CA: William Carey Library, 1999), 259.

10. Ralph D. Winter, "Unreached Peoples: What Are They and Where Are They?" in *Reaching The Unreached: The Old-New Challenge*, ed. Harvie M. Conn (Phillipsburg, NJ: Presbyterian and Reformed, 1984), 56.

11. The definition-pair of *unreached* and *reached* seems to have settled on a dividing line of approximately 2 percent of the general population. Cf. "Joshua Project," available online at http://www.joshuaproject.net/definitions.php#unreached.

The emphasis on unreached peoples has galvanized evangelical missions and our strategies. Local churches have adopted certain peoples for prayer, taken corresponding short-term trips, and implemented other targeted efforts. Increasing numbers of (organized) missionaries have entered "creative access" areas within the 10/40 Window, often in tent-making or even more clandestine ways. The focus on church-planting has evolved into igniting church-planting movements, in which the hope is for indigenous churches to spread spontaneously and rapidly throughout people groups.

Critics have voiced such objections as the interpretation that, biblically speaking, *nations* (*ethne*) collectively refers to nonbelieving peoples, not sociologically defined groups.[12] Certainly the dating of the second coming to coincide with 2000, which some evangelicals inevitably espoused in light of Matthew 24:14, was an unbiblical excess. I fear that subliminal racist and nationalistic notions can abuse the helpful categorization of people groups by unhelpfully objectifying them as "those people out there" and, correspondingly, by trying to keep God at arm's length in dealing with one's own kind of people. Whatever one makes of this last particular warning, the notion of *unreached* clearly needs at least some sort of clarification in light of God's ongoing, universal dealings with all peoples: no one has ever been out of God's reach, even those to whom he has not yet brought his specific gospel message.

The important ideas of the 10/40 Window and unreached people groups thus need some measure of qualification. Please recall as well that the point of this chapter and the next is that missions are to be ongoing in all settings, not just select portions of God's worldwide mission field. Even so, however one evaluates the overall 10/40 Window focus, its "almost too successful" character of channeling evangelical passion for the spread of the gospel is a most welcome development.[13]

---

12. Richard De Ridder, *Discipling the Nations* (Grand Rapids: Baker, 1971), 189. Cf. Pieter Tuit's further explanatory comments in his "The Relationship between Church and Kingdom Within the Missionary Theology of Johan H. Bavinck," *REC FOCUS* 1, no. 4 (December 2001): n15, available online at http://rec.gospelcom.net/index.php?section=126.

13. One well-researched, and critical, analysis of the 10/40 Window—that in the end suggests an overhaul of the concept and its foundations—is Michael A. Rynkiewich, "Corporate Metaphors and Strategic Thinking: 'The 10/40 Window' in the American Evangelical Worldview," *Missiology* 35 (2):217–41.

*Territorial spirits.* As we wind our way in this chapter toward making the claim that God's mission (and thus Christian missions) is ongoing in all parts of the world, we need to raise one more important point before leaving this brief discussion of the 10/40 Window. Intertwined with both of these just-considered fundamental threads—of a territorial, European (now U.S.) Christendom and of unreached people groups—that help to form the backdrop of the 10/40 Window concept is the belief in "territorial spirits." As Luis Bush, the central architect of the 10/40 Window framework, has written, "The 10/40 Window . . . is a stronghold of Satan. . . . It appears from a careful observation of the 10/40 Window that Satan has established a territorial stronghold with his forces to restrain the advance of the gospel in that territory."[14] The connection between the 10/40 Window and demonic forces is an easy one to make, and many have done just that.

A mild form of the belief in territorial spirits, but I suggest a pervasive one among U.S. evangelicals, was articulated by a missions conference speaker whom I heard years ago. He noted how demonic forces had been beaten back in the United States to the extent that they were no longer able to be as active here as they once were and still are elsewhere. Others express this belief when they comment on how they feel darkness and oppression in certain other parts of the world, unlike anything they have ever experienced at home. Some American missionaries claim that it is easier to live as Christians in the United States than "on the field." In other words, this mild form of belief in territorial spirits sees Satan and his forces as specially and overtly active in various contexts around the globe in ways in which they do not, or perhaps cannot, operate in Christianized areas such as the United States.

A more explicitly formulated view of territorial spirits cites scriptural precedent, as well as numerous contemporary anecdotes, in claiming that the key to advancing world evangelization lies in explicitly confronting demonic powers that have specific geographic strongholds. These forces of darkness are to be identified; people within their grip must repent of related corporate sins; then specially gifted, trained, and

14. Luis Bush, "What Is the 10/40 Window?" in *Praying through the 100 Gateway Cities of the 10/40 Window*, 15.

experienced prayer warriors must wage spiritual warfare to free an area for it to become receptive to the Christian gospel.[15] Peter Wagner has been one of the major proponents of this view and its associated practices of "Strategic-Level Spiritual Warfare." Many others[16] have significantly contributed to the wide and varied beliefs and practices associated with territorial spirits (e.g., identifying their hierarchical chains of command), although Wagner's peculiar influence as coordinator of the AD2000 United Prayer Track is worthy of special mention.[17]

As with those who formulated the 10/40 Window framework, the central motive of world evangelization is to be recognized and affirmed among the proponents of the reality of territorial spirits. Whatever one makes of the movement biblically, theologically, or methodologically, that crucial, common cause is to be kept at the forefront of any discussion. Furthermore, at a minimum, the emphasis on strategic spiritual warfare has helped many Western Christians recover a sense of the undeniable biblical reality of the unseen, spiritual world. We who live in the lingering wake of the Enlightenment and its scientific worldview must be reenlightened to the totality of forces at work in the universe.

At the same time, the difference of views among Bible-believing Christians concerning this topic is undeniable. There have been animated disagreements.[18] Many conferences, articles, books, and book reviews

15. Clinton E. Arnold, *3 Crucial Questions about Spiritual Warfare*, 3 Crucial Questions Series (Grand Rapids: Baker, 1997), 146–50.

16. Among the highly respected notable proponents are Charles Kraft and George Otis Jr.

17. This focus on territorial spirits is part of what Wagner himself termed the " 'third wave' of signs and wonders" of twentieth-century church history, following the first two waves of Pentecostalism and charismatic Christianity. Books dealing with territorial spirits that Wagner has written include *Warfare Prayer* (Ventura, CA: Regal, 1991) and *Confronting the Powers: How the New Testament Church Experienced the Power of Strategic-Level Spiritual Warfare* (Ventura, CA: Regal, 1996). It is also important to note Wagner's continued leadership in global prayer coordination through Global Harvest Ministries and its focus northward in the 40/70 Window (which we will touch on shortly). See in particular the "About Us" GHM Web page at http://www.globalharvest.org/index.asp?action=about.

18. One is the Evangelical Missiological Society's annual publication of 1995. The second of three total chapters, written by Charles Kraft, begins with the agonizing acknowledgment: "The [first] chapter . . . to which I am replying leaves me incredulous and makes this a very difficult chapter to write." Charles H. Kraft, " 'Christian Animism' or God-Given Authority?" in *Spiritual Power and Missions: Raising the Issues*, Evangelical Missiological Society Series, no. 3 (Pasadena, CA: William Carey Library, 1995), 88.

have been devoted to the matter.[19] Heightened appreciation and respect among those who differ concerning territorial spirits has resulted in some instances, but there are still many points of disagreement and tension.

I will not attempt to sort out the difficulties of interpreting Daniel 10 and the appearances there of Gabriel, Michael, and the princes of Persia and Greece. Nor do I want to debate the legitimacy or efficacy of claiming cities for Christ through prayer walks. I do, of course, reject an extreme blaming of demonic forces for all ills, whether personal or social, whether by "looking for a demon under every rock" or absolving people of their responsibility with a Flip Wilson–like "The devil made me do it" attitude. The best stopping-off point for our purposes is to note the comprehensive, careful, and constructive approach to this whole subject taken by the helpful "Deliver Us from Evil Consultation Statement." This substantial formulation was unanimously approved by a wide range of participants in an important consultation held in Nairobi in August 2000, and it is a helpful guide for evangelicals looking for some constructive guidelines.[20]

Hence, instead of further discussing the subject of territorial spirits per se, in keeping with this chapter's central claim of the ongoing nature of missions in all parts of the worldwide mission field, I would like to suggest another underlying component of such a major missions topic that psychologically contributes to exempting the United States, and specifically Anglo-Saxon Americans, from being part of "the mission field." I have already referred to the influential medieval, territorial European Christendom inheritance. I have suggested as well subtle ways that racism and nationalism can seep into and misuse missions frameworks. Here I will add a contributing *political* element.

19. One of the most widely read and reviewed critiques is the thoughtful biblical analysis by Chuck Lowe, *Territorial Spirits and World Evangelisation?* (Fearn: Mentor/OMF Publication, 1998). Reformed contributions have not been as numerous as one might hope, although one of the most comprehensive—varied as it is—is the December 1995 issue of the now-defunct Westminster Theological Seminary–based journal *Urban Mission*, edited by Harvie Conn.

20. A. Scott Moreau et al., eds., *Deliver Us from Evil: An Uneasy Frontier in Christian Mission* (Monrovia, CA: MARC, for the Lausanne Committee for World Evangelization and the Association of Evangelicals in Africa, 2002), xvii–xxviii. The statement is available online at http://www.lausanne.org/nairobi-2000/consultation-statement.html.

Specifically, the twin facts that the western half of the 10/40 Window almost totally comprises Islamic countries and a large portion of the eastern half is made up of communist China buttress an evangelical missions outlook (especially including an American evangelical outlook) on that section of the world as dark and held in demonic bondage. To overgeneralize but to get to the heart of the matter, the overlap between blocs of countries politically hostile to liberal democracies (preeminently, for Americans, the United States) and the non-Christian world as medieval Europe understood it is in effect the therefore easy-to-demonize 10/40 Window.[21]

Interesting in this regard is the shift in prayer focus that Peter Wagner urged, at the beginning of the new millennium, northward by 30 latitudinal degrees to the so-called 40/70 Window: "Our new assignment for the next five years is to launch a massive worldwide prayer and spiritual warfare thrust targeted on the 40/70 Window. We feel that the Lord has indicated that we have five years for Target 40/70 Window—2001 through 2005."[22] This new window stretches over all of Eurasia, from the United Kingdom across central Asia to the easternmost coast of Russia. While the westernmost portion of this more northern window consists of western Europe, the bulk of the new target—and what certainly catches an American evangelical's eye—is the former Soviet Union.[23] Just as was the case when U.S. evangelicals' missions efforts poured into the former "Evil Empire" (which all baby-boomer Americans had grown up fearing) following the fall of the Berlin Wall, such a new 40/70 Window fits into a mental political map that provides fertile spiritual-psychological ground in which it can readily take hold and flourish.

An inherited European Christendom framework, our racism and nationalism, and long-cultivated political instincts thus strengthen

21. I realize that the belief in territorial spirits does not restrict them to the 10/40 Window. Indeed, one of the most oft-used anecdotes cites a strong difference in gospel-receptivity right across the Uruguay-Brazil border, and many of the strongest advocates of dealing with territorial spirits are non-Westerners functioning in Africa and Latin America. Here, however, we are focusing on the belief in territorial spirits in specific relation to the 10/40 Window and on how such a belief relates to understanding where "the mission field" is—and where it is not.

22. "The 40/70 Window," available online at http://www.watchmannetwork.org/The_40_70_Window.htm.

23. Such a map can be viewed online at http://www.watchmannetwork.org/40_70_map.htm.

American evangelicals' understandings of where "the mission field" in general is, and where more specific "mission fields" are situated. The flip side of where targeted mission fields lie, and where Satan is understood to have his strongholds, is where it is allegedly different: Christianized lands that are relatively free of enveloping demonic power. For American evangelicals, even with its downward moral spiral of recent decades, the heartland of such territory is the United States of America.

## Has America Become a Mission Field?

The United States, for many American (and other) Christians, shines forth as the brightest beacon of what a Christian country should be. Over a century ago, the Dutch theologian and politician Abraham Kuyper "saw in America a liberty based on a commitment to divine sovereignty, a separation of powers, and a rich, pluralistic associational life, and he wanted to hold America up before his compatriots as a model for what a great Christian nation could and ought to be. . . . For Kuyper, America represented the future of liberty on our planet. America was providence's destiny."[24] Much has changed over the last century, and while there is, of course, a wide spectrum of American (and other) Christians' views of the United States, many still feel similarly to Kuyper in the unique place they give to America in God's dealings with the world.

Even so, many U.S. evangelicals regularly make the statement, "America has become a mission field." Sometimes preachers preach about it; sometimes individuals casually toss out such a remark. The statement can have an encouraging ring of opportunity, or it can carry a pessimistic tone of lament and even resignation. What do people mean when they offer such an analysis of the need for missions in America?

*Meanings.* One line of meaning highlights the accelerated stream of immigrants who have flowed into the United States since the 1960s.

---

24. John Bolt, "Abraham Kuyper and the Search for an Evangelical Public Theology," in J. Budziskewski, *Evangelicals in the Public Square: Four Formative Voices on Political Thought and Action* (Grand Rapids: Baker Academic, 2006), 146.

Lyndon Johnson signed the Immigration Bill of 1965, thus openly granting asylum to Cuban refugees. The Vietnam War brought thousands of refugees from southeast Asia. African immigrants have fled here from crises of war and famine, refugees from the Balkans have exponentially increased, and Latinos from farther south have begun to outpace African Americans as the largest minority group in the United States. Of course, no matter where Americans live, one also encounters other recent arrivals from south Asia, the Middle East, east Asia, and elsewhere.

In short, internationals of non–northwestern European stock are more prominent in America than ever. In that sense, "the mission field" (or "the nations") has come to America.

Another sense of the claim that America has become a mission field relates to the sweeping social and cultural changes that Christians have battled since the 1960s. The so-called sexual revolution headed a list of seismic shifts in values from an apparent Christian consensus to a pluralistic, and even what has seemed to many to be an anti-Christian, onslaught. Hence, proactively bringing biblical values to bear on a secularized and ungodly American society—what some evangelicals have termed "reclaiming" America for Christ—as well as the seemingly increased number of non-Christians has constituted a shift for some to viewing America as a mission field in desperate need of gospel ministry.

*Evaluation.* As far as the purpose of this chapter is concerned, there is an obvious upside to the analysis that America is now a mission field. *Nowhere*, I want double-negatively to claim, is *not* the mission field, and missions thus continues throughout the earth and its myriad contexts, including all of America.

Moreover, the needs of new immigrants and refugees in the United States, and the opportunities for American Christians to meet those needs, are clear. (So is the opportunity, as we noted earlier, for mutual enrichment for Americans and more recent arrivals when we interact constructively.) Similarly, U.S. evangelicals face tremendous challenges in meeting the societal and cultural challenges thrown up by early-twentieth-century American values and behaviors.

There are, however, downsides to claiming that America has *become* a mission field in either of the senses explained above. For one (again, please forgive the strong language), to assert that non–northwestern European peoples constitute "the mission field" is patently racist and nationalistic. The fact of the matter is that most Christians now are non-Caucasians and non-Westerners, and many, many immigrants to the United States are Christians. The corollary, subliminal assumption that Anglo-Saxon Americans (or "real" Americans present before waves of immigration during the last hundred years or so) are *not* part of the mission field is also racist and nationalistic. Besides the fact that many Americans of northwestern European lineage are not Christians (as has always been the case), we have traits, tendencies, histories, and other qualities (varied as they may be) that are imperfect and sinful. To claim that our kind of people are now "Christianized" is, I believe, a racially and nationalistically fueled delusion (even if more than 2 percent of the population—the current threshold differentiating "reached" and "unreached" peoples—are professing Christians).

In the language of "people group" analysis, to say that "mainstream Americans" are not part of "the nations" is both sociologically and theologically impossible. (Just stop and think about that for a minute.) Applying that meaning, "*The nations* have come to *us*" is a nonsensical statement.

A second downside is that claiming that America has socially and culturally *become* a mission field implies that it once (prior to the 1960s) was not. That is, allegedly from the time of the country's founding (or even earlier, say from the time of the Pilgrims in the early 1600s) up through World War II, colonial and then mainstream U.S. society was Christian.

My intent in fundamentally disagreeing with that analysis is not to launch into an American-bashing tirade. That is an all-too-convenient and destructive approach. Nor is it to ignore or deny the gospel's impact in American social and cultural life. Just as Jesus has brought his values to bear in all settings into which he has shouldered his way, so, too, has the gospel had its impact in various aspects of how the United States has developed. Nor do I disagree with the assertion that the 1960s had significant destructive impact in the United States (although I wish to point out as well some of the positive developments from the 1960s, not the least of which were many of those associated with the civil rights movement). Indeed, one can trace stages of the gradual disestablishment of Christianity from the mainstream of colonial and then national public life, starting generations prior to the 1960s.[25]

Rather, as a biblical principle I reject the possibility of any society or culture's becoming, before Jesus' return, "discipled" or "Christianized" to an extent that it ceases to be in need of growth and improvement—that is, that it ceases to be a "mission field." Furthermore, one does not need to stop at continuous ill-treatment of Native Americans, institutional slavery, the Civil War, the rise of imperialism in the late nineteenth century, the development of an unhealthy and extreme individualism, racism, nominal religiosity, materialistic greed, flippant pop-culture glorification of romantic "love," or other ills to describe the particular deep-seated shortcomings of pre-1960s America. While some may have perceived a Christian consensus that has been lost, I suggest that America—in principle and in fact—has always been a mission field.

Continuing in that same vein, how the Christian faith has fleshed itself out in American life is our next topic of discussion.

## Contextualization and Syncretism

We discussed earlier (in chapter 7) some of the important facets of understanding the process that we have come to call *contextualization*. There we noted how the universal Christian faith always takes on particular and ever-evolving shapes, depending on the ever-changing contexts involved (language, history, sociopolitical realities, etc.). We also noted that the primary agents in the process of contextualization are, rather than a missionary outsider charged with contextualizing the gospel for people to whom he has been sent, God himself and the people to whom he speaks in their particular heart language. In his ongoing dealings with people, God brings to them outsiders as catalysts

25. A succinct analysis of this process is in Darrell L. Guder, ed., *The Missional Church: A Vision for the Sending of the Church in North America*, The Gospel and Our Culture Series (Grand Rapids: Eerdmans, 1998), 48–55.

and facilitators (with whom he is also continuously dealing as objects of his mission).

## Christianity's Ebb and Flow

That dynamic understanding of the ongoing contextualization process is important for understanding how missions have been ongoing in all settings throughout the history of the world, including in America. To further see this ongoing character of missions in all settings, it helps to consider the earliest cross-cultural movements of the gospel. The New Testament focuses on what happened in Palestine during Jesus' lifetime, and then how the Christian faith spread into wider Greco-Roman circles, particularly through Paul but others as well. We also know that the gospel spread early on eastward as far as India, as well as into northeastern Africa. In subsequent generations this multidirectional, multilingual, and multicontextual spread and growth of Christianity continued.

*God's mission, and missions, continue.* Our purposes here involve two important points. First, God's dealings with people in Palestine—in terms of evangelism, church maturity, and bringing gospel values to bear on public society, all three of which together make up God's mission throughout the earth—were ongoing up until Jesus' time, throughout his life, as well as afterward, even through Jerusalem's destruction in A.D. 70. Similarly, God's *mission*—in the comprehensive, three-pronged sense in which we are using that term here—in Rome, Ephesus, Alexandria, Edessa, and elsewhere did not cease once a certain threshold of Christian believers was achieved. God's mission in those cities and among those peoples has continued up until this day. Correspondingly, Christians' organized efforts at cooperating with God's mission—*missions*—in those cities and among those peoples have continued up until this day.

To continue for a bit about this first important point, we must be careful to be both clear and nuanced. Please recall how, in the "Checkup" after chapter 4, we noted that "with respect to God's mission, missions are organized Christian activities, particularly cross-cultural activities. Conceptually, God's mission is all-comprehensive; Christian missions are part of that greater whole." That point was made in the discussion about checking the default U.S.-evangelical notion of *missions* as "Americans' going elsewhere." An opposite extreme—to which some have gone in connection with the idea of "God's mission" or *missio Dei* (see Appendix A)—is to call everything *missions*. Hence, Christian education, counseling, or all other forms of Christian ministry become *missions*, or perhaps *mission*.

I am not advocating that extreme. Preventing us from going that far is noting the *cross-cultural* distinctive in missions. Part and parcel of God's mission in the world is to send and bring people into different cultural settings for the mutual benefit of all who thus interact cross-culturally, whether as goers or receivers. I do want to claim this: wherever we are, and irrespective of the specific ministry in which we are involved, insofar as we are operating with multiple cultural contexts in view, we are involved with *missions*. Intercultural education, counseling, evangelism, preaching, administration, and so on are *missions*. Insofar as God is intensely interested in having us operate cross- and interculturally, our missions activities are thus ongoing and quite varied.

Yes, this is a revised and expanded understanding of *missions* as commonly tossed about. Yes, the lines of distinction between *missions* and other Christian activities become fuzzy. But since the lines of distinction between God's *mission* and *redemption* are similarly fuzzy, and because of the valuable benefits and checks that come from blurring the compartmentalized distinctions between *missions* and other activities, we need to see the ongoing nature of missions in connection with God's intercultural mission in our various settings.

*Christianity's contextual development.* The second important point (about Christianity's growth pattern in an area, and how that relates to the ongoing nature of missions) concerns how Christianity develops or takes shape in particular linguistic and cultural contexts. Take, for example, the growth of Christianity in the Roman Empire. An easy way to understand that process is to view a gradual numerical growth of Christian believers, despite periods of intense persecution. The Christian population finally reached a point at which the Emperor Constantine himself led the whole empire in officially adopting Christianity.

Christian theologians and churchmen were then able to construct the edifice of official church doctrine, starting with the Trinity and then Christological formulations. Orthodox Christianity hence took shape, and subsequent expressions of Christianity must therefore conform to that standard of doctrine and basic practices.

Accordingly, per this face-value understanding, missions in the Roman Empire ceased with the church-planting and early evangelistic efforts of Paul and others of his generation (plus a few closely following generations, perhaps).

On the one hand, such a commonsense view may resonate with a popular understanding of early church history. Its main flaw, however, lies in not accounting for how the gospel continues to work in a particular and ever-changing culture. To use language employed already, Jesus shoulders his way into a setting to disciple it as its Redeemer-King-Boss. People in that ever-changing setting must wrestle with his claims, demands, and re-creating initiatives. He deals with particular, whole people—not just acultural souls. He takes our particular issues, questions, faults, and quirks and he works with us as concrete people.

In the Greco-Roman philosophical world, this meant that questions about who Jesus was in relation to God, as well as who the Holy Spirit was, demanded answers. Hence, church leaders had to wrestle with how to testify to their particular setting—using indigenous terminology and categories—regarding who God is. Thus, the particular doctrines of the Trinity and the divine-human natures of Christ were articulated. More than a foundation of a doctrinal superstructure, those doctrines and others like them were confessions of faith in a fresh cultural missions setting that required explanations. In the words of 1 Peter, such confessions were "a defense to anyone who asks you for a reason for the hope that is in you" (3:15). They were precedent-setting, to be sure, not only in establishing categories requiring conformity but also in giving the rest of us instructive patterns of how to speak to our various indigenous settings.

Those confessions were achievements, but not laurels on which to rest. Issues of witness and reforming work remained on various fronts, not the least of which was how to handle newfound imperial approval. How to relate to other Christian communities who lived farther away arose when doctrinal controversies emerged. New generations of believers had to be instructed afresh, all the while adjusting to their ever-changing contexts (e.g., when the Roman Empire fell). Even with an increased number of believers, witness to surrounding unbelievers was an ongoing task.

In other words, missions continued.

As generations came and went, the tendency in Greek- and Latin-speaking settings was to freeze those expressions of Christianity as timeless and normative. Northwestern European peoples thus came into the faith and had to worship in Latin. Peoples in the eastern Mediterranean world had to worship in the Greek of their forefathers. Even after the revolutionary translation of the Scriptures and liturgies into Slavic by the ninth-century missionary brothers Cyril and Methodius, the trend was to preserve that form of Slavic worship over generations as the normative standard to which all subsequent Slavic speakers had to conform.

## Combating Syncretism

The rise of the northwestern European Reformation challenged the foreign imposition of a static Latinized Christianity. Translations of the Scriptures by John Wycliffe (1324–84) and others into contemporary English, as well as the translation of Martin Luther (1483–1546) into contemporary German, helped to spark a fresh gospel-culture interaction whereby Jesus dealt with people in their mother tongues. The syncretism of an encrusted affirmation of the status quo, in which power and oppression went unchallenged and abuses of religious realities stagnated spiritual vitality, had to be confronted.

*Syncretism* is a common term with a nuanced meaning. When we evangelicals use the term, we normally mean some sort of religious mixture that distorts the Christian gospel. That meaning flows out of the word itself: *syn* refers to combining, *cret* to creed or belief. But as I have discussed elsewhere, syncretism is best understood as a distortion of a healthy contextualization process:

> Syncretism then becomes the loss of universal, transcendent and normative traits of the Christian faith, due to a culture's "pull" towards au-

tonomy. Outside (etic) input becomes marginalized or even eliminated. Sins of omission, e.g., not loving one's enemies, result from this failure to pay attention to God's transcendent and normative commands; sins of commission, e.g., sexual perversions, flourish due to the lack of restraint that should be brought to bear on people's lives by God's transcendent and normative commands. There is a protection of the status quo against all critique, no matter what normative standards of justice and mercy might attempt to speak into the situation. Finally, what is genuinely local and flexible is reified into something allegedly universal and normative—which becomes problematic when other local situations are encountered.[26]

In this multifaceted and nuanced sense, syncretism is an ongoing threat against which Christians in all contexts must be on guard—in partnership with Christians from other contexts—with Spirit-led vigilance.

As exemplified in pre-Reformation Europe, syncretism that arises generations after Christianity has entered an area has been a continual problem throughout Christian history. That is because Christians, weak and sinful as we are, want to ease the discomfort and threat of Jesus' ongoing reforming mission in the midst of our ever-changing contexts. Freezing what has become settled is safe. Our subconscious assumptions can seek to preserve our own control, rights, and privileges. When that happens, abuse, comfort, and intergenerational conflicts will arise and squelch life and vitality. Our missions efforts are familiar with challenging the type of syncretism, or religion-mixing, that can occur at the front end of Christianity's development in contexts. Just as important for missions is the need to challenge, for the sake of ongoing gospel impact, the type of syncretistic fossilization that can arise among people who have a multigenerational familiarity with the Christian faith.

As we consider Christianity in the United States, we thus can see why missions—that is, cross- and intercultural stimulation of what the gospel is all about—have been needed. As is the case in all settings, there is the continual need to keep fresh the linguistic expressions (in our case in English, primarily) of who Jesus is and of the nature of the Christian

26. "Suburban Evangelical Individualism: Syncretism, (Harvie) Conn-textualization, or Something Else?" *Global Missiology* 2, no. 4 (July 2005), available online at http://www.global missiology.org/english/docs_html/featured/Suburban_Evangelical_Individualism.htm.

gospel. Historically speaking, Christians from Europe brought over their versions of Christianity to the New World. They settled and passed on the faith to their children, who did the same for their own children. One religion per territory (a transplant of European Christendom) was the order of the colonial day—until different peoples having to live together, a result of God's unorganized mission, forced a move toward religious tolerance. Racial abuses became codified in various ways: toward Native Americans during westward expansion, toward African Americans in slavery, toward East Asians and Jewish people in the 1924 Immigration Act.[27]

As post–World War II America developed, excessive materialism and individualism took more definite shape. One result was a syncretistic obsession with personal well-being that has preoccupied many a Christian ministry.[28] A myopic patriotism—again, arguably better termed *nationalism*—clouds much of U.S. evangelicalism's needed capacity at least to hear what the bulk of the worldwide church criticizes as America's inordinate military ventures and bullying foreign policy. (For example, can we as American Christians at least consider one international Christian's assertion of "the self-serving and often immoral nature of [America's] interaction with the rest of the world"[29]?) We are thus hamstrung in cultivating the capacity to respond domestically with a prophetic and constructive stance—as part of Jesus' global followers. The path of least resistance is simply to affirm what appears best for our own national interests.

"Christ also suffered" must be at the forefront of our interest as international Christian people, so that we as U.S. Christians can risk heeding 1 Peter's encouragement truly to "live as people who are free . . .

27. Kevin MacDonald argues for *ethnic self-interest* instead of *racism* for understanding the motivation behind the 1924 Immigration Act. See his "Was the 1924 Immigration Cut-off 'Racist'?" June 19, 2004, available online at http://www.vdare.com/macdonald/040619_1924_immigration.htm.

28. Harvie Conn used the term *syncretism* to describe American evangelicalism's enslavement to personal comfort, which has inhibited needed attention to wider issues of poverty and injustice. See his *The American City and the Evangelical Church: A Historical Overview* (Grand Rapids: Baker, 1994), 191–94. I address why Conn uses that label of *syncretism* in this instance, and the resulting importance for understanding *contextualization* and *syncretism*, in my article cited in note 25 above, "Suburban Evangelical Individualism."

29. Jonathan J. Bonk, *Missions and Money: Affluence as a Western Missionary Problem . . . Revisited*. Revised and expanded edition. American Society of Missiology Series, no. 15 (Maryknoll, NY: Orbis Books, 1991 and 2006), 33.

[to live] as servants of God" (2:16). We who are Christ's international followers are to be free from our surrounding, enveloping nationalistic pressures to serve the cause of Christ's gospel for all people and societies, including our own.

Missions efforts directed toward U.S. contexts help to point out syncretistic shortcomings and blind spots, and thus in turn pathways toward redemptive gospel progress. Accordingly, God in his mercy has brought all types of people together in America for cross-pollination and fresh familiarity with the breadth and depth of the gospel. All Christians, including U.S. evangelicals, must have ongoing reminders that our identity as Jesus' international body trumps and affects all other slices of our identity, including those of ethnicity and nationality. Now more than ever, missions are needed in the United States to deal with such urgent issues as poverty, imperialistic tendencies, unbelief, and skewed sexuality. May God in his mission use Christians' missions efforts all around the world, including in America.

## Reflection Questions

- What is your familiarity with the concepts of "10/40 Window," "unreached people groups," and "territorial spirits"?

- Has America become a mission field? Why or why not?

- In what ways do you see missions efforts taking place that target your church and community, as well as the United States as a nation-state?

- As you think about applying 1 Peter 2:13–17, how do you compare the political situation of the original first-century readers with that of contemporary American Christians?

# 10

# The Comprehensive Scope
# of Missions

Crucial to believing that missions are to be ongoing among any given society is a revised understanding of what *missions* is—or are. As we have already asserted, they are part of God's overarching mission. They are Christians' organized initiatives, efforts, and activities. They are *not* simply *going* somewhere, together with the supporting infrastructure (although missions include those efforts as well). As we have already suggested—and this bears repeating because it goes against a well-established grain in our assumed understanding of *missions*—what sets missions apart from other, overlapping types of Christian ministry is the intentionally cross- and intercultural aspect of missions activities.

On the one hand, I believe that it is *not* necessary or even helpful to make crystal-clear distinctions between *missions* and other Christian ministries, since there is indeed a great deal of overlap. Christian worship, for example, is worship, wherever and among whomever it takes place. So is education, counseling, mercy and justice work, evangelism, and other ministries. Thus, as a Christian pastor and leader, I view the nature of my Christian calling and ministry as essentially the same, regardless of the people or place I am serving.

At the same time, as we deal with multiple cultural dynamics—which are at the heartbeat of the universal, biblical God's redeeming an international people and entire creation—we are involved with *missions*. So, for example, a culturally different person shows up at your rather homogeneous church's Sunday worship service: I say that is missions in action. God has brought that culturally different person to your church to somehow teach and stretch you, and as your church serves that cross-cultural visitor, you are engaging in missions. Or take a completely different situation, say in Ghana's capital city of Accra, located in the south. A large slum area there is known as the Yam Market, where many northern Ghanaians have migrated. Southern Ghanaian Christians who minister there are involved in cross-cultural interaction, sometimes in evangelism, sometimes in joint worship services, sometimes in counseling or education, sometimes in justice and mercy advocacy. All those activities are missions—as are the efforts of the northern Ghanaians who have become Christians to serve and otherwise work with the southerners.

Any Christian ministry activity involving more than one cultural setting is therefore *missions*, I am suggesting. Such an understanding of *missions* is a shift from how the word is tossed around, but I believe it is a healthy one, especially for us American evangelicals. More than simply a semantic adjustment, what is really important here are the posture and assumptions that underlie what we *mean* when we talk about, and more importantly participate in, missions. In line with this book's plumb line of American Christians' suffering after Christ's example, I believe that *missions* primarily implies the recognition of God's ongoing control, right, and privilege to keep on conducting his mission—including how the various nationalities of his people share, in derived fashion, the control, rights, and privileges necessary for carrying out missions activities.

## Two Qualifications

Let me make my case again for why the default notion of *missions* needs some adjustment. Most fundamentally for Caucasian-American evangelicals, our latent racism and nationalism can run unchecked as we go "out" (allegedly from Christian territory) to serve

191

"others." Thankfully, by the grace of God, that does not always happen. Thankfully, missionaries normally go with humility and in the posture of learners as well as proclaimers. Nevertheless, subconsciously "the American way of life"—politically, economically, and otherwise—is considered the Christian standard, to which others are to be elevated. The deep fault lines that run through who we are can remain unexposed.

For example, it took years before my close friend in Japan mustered up the courage to ask me, "Why are all of you American missionaries white?" That sort of penetrating question was, of course, God's way of forcing me to reconsider myself and my group before him and the Bible. It is only one example of how Americans need the input of others—missions directed toward us—to see ourselves for who we are, in need of continual reform, repentance, and growth.

Adjusting the notion of missions from simply going out to the nations is necessary for non-American Christians as well, since all people can unwittingly carry their own superiority complexes to folks in need— for example, southern Ghanaians with respect to northern Ghanaians. Americans by no means have a monopoly on that practice: Koreans, Nigerians, Indians, and everyone else do the same thing. In this book, however, we are particularly dealing with American notions. Moreover, the United States' superpower status renders us especially vulnerable to thinking, even though we would deny as much, that we really don't need other kinds of people.

Two more points in reiterating my case. First, in assuming that *missions* = going out to "the nations," we Americans unwittingly overlook the sociological and theological (as well as geopolitical) reality that we, too, are part of "the nations." Second, the church is now in fact more worldwide than ever before. The inherent international character of Jesus' followers has become a truly global reality, so Christians everywhere are to cooperate with other Christians in serving Christ together in the settings into which God has sent us. Genuinely believing that my kind of people are just as much in need of missions efforts as others (even though the particular needs may very well be different) helps to cultivate a situation in which genuine, cross-cultural partnerships can develop.

*Missions*, then, are Christians' service efforts that involve multiple cultural realities. They can take place anywhere and among any type of people, including my own kind of folks. They will continue "throughout the time of [our] exile" (1 Peter 1:17), or until "after [we] have suffered a little while" (1 Peter 5:10)—that is, until Jesus returns. Getting used to the whole idea takes some time and effort, but the rewards are worth it, as I hope we will continue to see.

Having made that case again, let me add one more important qualification. Here I want to draw on the historical insights of the American evangelical missionary statesman Ralph Winter. He reminds us that if we are not careful, by asserting the comprehensive character of mission, then in the end missions may lose their edge and focus. That became apparent when the World Council of Churches absorbed the International Missionary Council in 1961 (see Appendix A), in the name of "the church" and its various churches carrying on in mission. The theory sounded good, but in fact specifically missions-oriented structures continue to be necessary.[1] Otherwise, *mission* can degenerate into simply serving where the church is already present, instead of pushing into societies where the church has yet to come into existence.[2]

These instructive words of caution are well taken. We need special structures and people to keep us focused on the unique character of missions. We also need the continual push to set our eyes on peoples among whom there is not yet a viable Christian presence and witness. We must share Paul's "ambition to preach the gospel, not where Christ has already been named" (Rom. 15:20). Left to our own settings, the black hole of our own immediate needs will inevitably draw our focus onto ourselves.

It is precisely here that the comprehensive character of Christian missions, as part of God's world mission, can serve us well. Thankfully, God has not left us, his people, to our own devices: he gives us his own presence, and he regularly demonstrates his commitment to bring

1. Ralph D. Winter, "Historical Precedents and Foundations for the GNMS," *Mission Frontiers* 27, no. 4 (July–August 2005): 11, available online at http://www.missionfrontiers.org/2005/04/pdftoc.htm.

2. Ralph D. Winter, "The Meaning of Mission," *Mission Frontiers* (July 1987), available online at http://www.missionfrontiers.org/1987/07/j872.htm.

missionaries to us and to all other kinds of people. His redemption of his world is inherently inter- and cross-cultural, so missions is at the heart of what his people are to be about. Much—or dare I say most—of how he works in his mission is via what we have called unorganized missions; we need God's continual help to see how he is at work in these often unrecognized, but crucial ways. Here we are considering our organized efforts at serving Jesus and people within the ever-present reality of multiple cultures' interacting.

For the rest of this chapter, then, I want to think together with you about three main areas of missions focus, as they relate to God's overarching mission to grant, among all the world's peoples, (1) faith in Jesus Christ, (2) maturing of the church, and (3) foretastes of the heavenly city.[3] Against the backdrop of the four themes we have covered so far—God's unique Superpower status in his mission, the international character of the church, our having been sent by Christ into our respective corners of the world, and the preferred bi-/multidirectional movement of missions—we will consider the ongoing nature, in all settings, of Christian missions.

## Evangelization

As we noted earlier, and as you will probably confirm from your and your church's own experiences, evangelicals have always majored in proclaiming the Christian gospel, through both word and deed (unequivocally the former), to unreached peoples. The last few decades have seen an evangelical focus on unreached people groups (UPGs). Now world evangelization = planting churches (and sparking church-planting movements) among UPGs = completing the task = fulfilling the Great Commission.

### Reaching UPGs

Because of the incredible focus on UPGs, an abundance of resources are available to U.S. congregations for becoming involved with helping to bring the gospel to people even halfway around the world. Perhaps

---

3. These same three areas have already appeared several times—for example, in chapter 1 (under "God's 'Mission' and Our 'Missions'") and under slightly different labels at the end of chapter 6 (under "Organized Efforts").

the most obvious first step is to consider adopting a UPG for prayer and other involvements. This campaign is out of the U.S. Center for World Mission in Pasadena, which provides a step-by-step explanation of how churches can participate.[4]

Evangelical denominational missions agencies give helps to congregations for various worldwide missions involvements, including those directly related to reaching UPGs.[5] ACMC—Advancing Churches in Missions Commitment (now called Initiative 360)—is a resource mentioned earlier that is specifically designed to help local U.S. congregations become more internationally active.[6] The U.S. Center for World Mission is a clearinghouse for any number of organizations and databases that churches can use as well.[7]

In short, if churches want to be internationally active in evangelical missions, particularly for helping to reach UPGs, there are plenty of resources to help.

### Ongoing Evangelization

While affirming this evangelical zeal to focus on UPGs so that they might hear about Jesus and become his followers, here I am advocating a broader—geographically and otherwise—understanding of world evangelization: "the task" and the Great Commission. I also wish to broaden the understanding of evangelization of a people group beyond just a one-time task that has certain threshold benchmarks for determining when a UPG becomes evangelized. I understand the eschatological, biblical, and strategic motivations for focusing missions-evangelization this way. Even so, I believe that narrow understanding is on the one hand reductionist of the ongoing character of evangelization. I believe it also neglects the ongoing need for cross-cultural input—missions—into all settings with respect to evangelization.

4. See the Adopt-A-People Campaign home page at http://www.adopt-a-people.org/.

5. See, for example, the PCA Mission to the World's Web site (http://www.mtw.org), the Southern Baptist International Mission Board Web site (http://www.imb.org), and the Evangelical Free Church of America's International Mission Web site (http://www.efca.org/international/).

6. Again, see the ACMC Web site at http://www.acmcnetwork.com/.

7. See the U.S. Center for World Mission Web site at http://www.uscwm.org/.

We all agree on the need for evangelistic outreach among people where the church does not yet exist, or still has only a negligible presence. While not at all wanting to diminish the need to focus in those areas, we all know as well that there are people living within earshot of Christian churches all over the world who do not yet believe in Jesus. God has sent his people into those settings to witness to those friends and acquaintances as well.

"But preaching the gospel to those folks is called evangelism, not missions," many explain. Or, to put it in a more precise evangelical-missiological way, "Evangelism means winning individuals to Christ—whoever they are. . . . Missions reaches into groups not yet having an adequate internal witness."[8] Yes, but why do we make that distinction?

One reason is strategic and takes into account cultural differences between the gospel proclaimer and the hearer(s). Missiologists have used the "E-scale" to describe these distinctions, whereby E-0 and E-1 represent situations of relative cultural similarity, while E-2 and E-3 are those of cultural difference. By this scheme, evangelism occurs in E-0 or E-1 relationships, and missions takes place when the communicator's and hearer's cultures are different.[9] In a related way, strategically distinguishing between evangelism and missions helps to preserve the unique place of UPGs in missions efforts.

On the downside, earlier (in chapter 4) I rather brazenly asserted that racial prejudices are at least part of the underlying reason for the evangelism-missions distinction, thereby keeping *missions* to my kind of people at arm's length. I am going to stick by my guns on that point. I also want to add into the mix the way in which God brings fresh outsiders into Christian contexts—unorganized missions, if you will—for the sake of biblically revitalizing evangelism.

Take two time periods of Caucasian American-Christian experience as examples. The first is that of institutional slavery. White slaveholding and slavery-supporting Christians preached the Christian message to the

8. Ralph D. Winter, "World Evangelization—AD 2000 and Beyond," *Mission Frontiers* (March 1989): 10, available online at http://www.adopt-a-people.org/articles/world_evangelism.pdf.

9. See again the New Song Christian Fellowship "Missions Definitions" Web page at http://new-song.ccbchurch.com/app/w_page.php?id=32&type=section.

very blacks they were oppressing. What an incongruent situation! God brought black slaves (many of them Christians) to those white Christians to revolutionize their domesticated, individual-spiritual understanding of the scope of the gospel message.

Next consider situations of contemporary American Christianity. One major segment comprises suburban churches—primarily white, but also black, Asian, and other monoethnic churches. By and large these suburban churches, many of which are quite active in evangelism and missions (to use the standard, bifurcated paradigm), have preached an individualistic, overspiritualized gospel message—which has needed reforming. God has therefore been bringing various others into suburban communities to challenge the safe, settled notions of the gospel that had developed.

What turns such dynamics into missions is when the reformed, internationalized Christian churches, as particular parts of the worldwide church sent into their settings, thereby take their freshly empowered gospel message into their communities. They have been given a certain critical distance from their context so as to preach about Jesus' kingdom with penetrating power.

Earlier (in chapter 7) we cited an example of a St. Louis congregation that began with a central focus on racial reconciliation between blacks and whites, and then unexpectedly expanded to encompass a wide array of immigrants, refugees, and internationals from all over the world. This church has thus been evangelistically able to proclaim and demonstrate to the surrounding communities the gospel's power to bring people together, despite vast differences. This missions-evangelism thrust has involved multiple cultural realities, flowing out of the church's internal makeup that has resulted in cross-cultural relationships between the church's resulting hybrid-eclectic cultural character and the surrounding communities (as well as other area churches).

We also cited earlier (in chapter 8) a creative attempt to employ Argentine house-church methodologies in Illinois. The purpose is for renewed evangelism and church-planting, or missions, given the cross-cultural dynamics involved.

I know of another St. Louis congregation, this one more typically suburban (and white), that actively employs Evangelism Explosion[10] in training its membership and others for personal evangelism. One interesting feature of their program is the number of non-Caucasians who have been involved as goers, for various reasons and through various connections. The resulting outreach has been a cross-cultural, international approach to many in the surrounding community—in other words, a missions outreach.

We could cite countless other examples of churches internationalized, to small or large degrees, in Caucasian-American situations, African-American contexts, Asian-American ones, or other situations all around the world. The point is that people, in America and elsewhere, need to see the gospel's transforming power put on display in the coming together of formerly distant people.[11] Jesus himself prayed for his followers' unity, "so that the world may believe that you have sent me" (John 17:21). That sort of gospel demonstration, no matter the setting, is a missions activity.

Furthermore, such missions activity should be ongoing in all settings into which God has sent his people. God will faithfully bring different folks into the picture. (I was always amazed, for example, to discover at least one or two Korean Christians in almost every Japanese congregation I knew. The history between Korea and Japan is riddled with sad, abusive encounters, and Koreans and Japanese coming together in Christ is a powerful testimony.) Each church's challenge is, by the Holy Spirit's enabling power, to rise above its squelching context and be a signpost of Jesus' international kingdom breaking in to a lost world that needs to learn of God's grace and mercy.

## Church Maturity

That ongoing challenge of manifesting God's international kingdom within stifling and ever-changing contexts matches Jesus' continuous

10. See the Evangelism Explosion International Web site at http://www.eeinternational.org/.

11. As one Sri Lankan evangelical theologian has put it, "The gospel creates new human community, and that new human community is itself part of the gospel to be proclaimed." Vinoth Ramachandra, *The Recovery of Mission: Beyond the Pluralist Paradigm* (Grand Rapids: Eerdmans, 1997), 266.

mission to refine, shape, and mature his people within the situations into which he has sent us. Jesus prayed for his disciples, "They are not of the world, just as I am not of the world. Sanctify them in the truth; your word is truth. As you sent me into the world, so I have sent them into the world" (John 17:16–18). Thankfully, Jesus continued by affirming, "And for their sake I consecrate myself, that they also may be sanctified in truth" (John 17:19). That reality of Jesus' resurrection, ascension, enthronement, intercession for us, and ongoing presence by his Spirit backs up his Great Commission promise to be "with you always, to the end of the age" (Matt. 28:20).

In a way already mentioned, 1 Peter couples churches' ongoing evangelistic missions responsibility toward surrounding communities with our continuous maturing process when he points to our foreign, international character: "Beloved, I urge you as sojourners and exiles to abstain from the passions of the flesh, which wage war against your soul. Keep your conduct among the Gentiles honorable, so that when they speak against you as evildoers, they may see your good deeds and glorify God on the day of visitation" (1 Peter 2:11–12). "Passions of the flesh" are not just outrageous, sexual cravings. They can also be subtle longings for comfort, security, and conformity—good things in and of themselves that can nevertheless wage war against our souls by dulling us to Jesus' standard of being sanctified, or set apart, for his service.

## Numerical Growth

One form of church maturity for which Jesus is working in his mission is numerical church growth. That is not to say that bigger numbers necessarily mean spiritual maturity. It simply is to affirm Jesus' expressed intent to gather his people from "every nation, from all tribes and peoples and languages" (Rev. 7:9). The book of Acts records numbers of people coming to faith, so while it is not to be of sole importance, observable church growth is part of what Jesus is after.

Wherever we are in the world, as Jesus' followers we are similarly to long and labor for new believers to join God's people. Insofar as all kinds of people are to be invited and welcomed, missions aiming toward numerical church growth will always continue.

## Growth through Venturing Out

Part of Christian missions activities involves daring to move toward people who are different culturally, linguistically, and otherwise. As we have argued, that is not all there is to missions. At the same time, following God's lead to move out somewhere new—whether "short-term" or more indefinitely—is surely an ongoing aspect of organized Christian missions. Paul's missionary journeys are perhaps the ultimate biblical example of this concept, and historical and contemporary examples of missionaries' going elsewhere to serve cross-culturally are, of course, countless.

What I wish to stress is something that every cross-cultural missionary worth his or her salt knows all too well, namely, the growth and maturing that occurs in the missionary. Even with extensive training prior to going, there is no way to predict or control all the ways in which God will shape you when you move into a new cultural setting. Particularly when learning a new language is involved (especially for many of us monolingual Americans), the personal upheaval through which God takes you can be quite profound. Latent expectations turn out to be different from reality. Subconscious sin patterns come out at the most unpredictable moments. At times you may feel quite at home, and at other times you feel as though you have arrived on another planet.

And then there is the so-called reverse cross-cultural experience, when a missionary reenters the context that used to be "home." That experience can be even more painful than the previous one, perhaps because we are not trained to be gracious, patient learners ("It's just different here; give it some time") as we were before going to a new setting.

In any case, part of God's ongoing mission concern, and part of ongoing missions, is the maturing process that organized missionaries, as well as everyday Christians living at home, experience by going out and encountering different people.

## Growth through Cultural Outsiders' Coming In

From an American missionary perspective, think of how people who meet you and get to know you are affected by your coming into their home setting. Typically, they will be hearing you stumbling over words and using a funny accent when you speak. You will not know the simplest of tasks, for example, how, where, and when to put out your trash. They will associate you with whatever facts they know about America—perhaps the president, famous athletes and entertainment celebrities, other Americans they might have met, and certain products and foods they know.

Sooner or later they will encounter your religious faith. Depending on their setting, they may be quite familiar with Christianity, or they may know basically nothing. In Japan, I often met people who were initially puzzled about why I was married, since their only acquaintance with Christian leaders had been with celibate Catholic priests. How, therefore, could I be a "priest" or "pastor" and also have a family?

I also sympathized with regular Japanese people who had such a difficult time sorting out all the different Christian churches and denominations, a reality that inevitably had to become a topic of conversation. They might have known of a church here and there, or perhaps a Christian kindergarten that either they or their child had attended. But to sort out the vast array of such strange-sounding groups was an incredibly daunting task for almost everyone. What helped me to sympathize was to turn the tables on myself and see how utterly bewildering it was, especially at first, to encounter the incredible number of Japanese Buddhist traditions that exist. Wasn't Buddhism just Buddhism? It was instructive to learn how those traditions have their own histories, splits, personalities, and distinctives, just as is the case with Christian traditions.

It helps to turn the tables on ourselves to see how missions *to us* can be part of how God in his mission remains interested in maturing us through those he brings into our settings. We have already spoken much about how this happens in various unorganized ways. Here I am speaking of those still largely unfamiliar cooperative activities that we might undertake to have missionaries from elsewhere come for missions work among us and our kind of people.

Many of us will have had the experience of hearing a guest preacher who has come from somewhere else in the world. Perhaps most memorable was the struggle to understand his English. Or maybe it was some other aspect of his personality—his exuberance, perhaps, or an incredibly global perspective that came through. Maybe he preached *way* too long, which was fine on the one hand, but which delayed other scheduled events (making our time-conscious stomachs turn somersaults).

I remember very distinctly the first few times that, as a theology student, I ever sat under black African instructors. I had been taught by English and Scottish lecturers, which was, of course, cool and stimulating, hearing them speak English in such sophisticated accents and vocabularies. What, though, could these African men—well pedigreed as they were—have to offer me?

It is in that kind of moment that God works to shape and mature us through different Christians he brings to us. Those African instructors indeed had much to offer me, especially including the content of their course material (e.g., about Christian theology and history). But for me as a person, actually encountering them and dealing with my racism and nationalism was a painful but necessary growth point to which God wanted to take me as I experienced those particular missions arrangements.[12]

How such cross-pollinating missions arrangements can take shape is still emerging for most of us. With respect to non-American partners traveling to churches in the United States, as Americans we must, of course, avoid parading converts before supporters, like trophies to be admired so as to raise more money. How to work together in mutuality and respect is something that all of us must continue to discover together, by God's gracious leading.

## Sociopolitical Matters

So far we have seen that evangelizing missions continue across generations—even as Christians keep a special focus on the unreached peoples of the world. So do missions aimed at growing and maturing churches. Perhaps we can call those efforts "iron-sharpening" missions,

---

12. This point arose earlier, but helping American theology students to wake up to the need to pursue what is now fairly accessible non-Western theological literature is a tremendous way, over the next few generations, of benefiting, in a form of multidirectional missions, from belonging together to the worldwide church.

particularly through give and take between culturally different churches. Finally we come to what may be both the most sensitive and the most excruciating area of all, namely, that of participating with God—in multiple cultural situations—in realizing his kingdom of justice and *shalom.*

We noted in chapter 2 the comprehensive scope of God's mission as restoration and re-creation of his world. Earlier in this chapter we used the phrase "foretastes of the heavenly city." The biblical story line, in its account of God saving an international people, moves from a garden to a city, from Eden to the New Jerusalem. Many missiologists, particularly urban missiologists,[13] see the accelerating urbanization throughout today's world as reflecting how God is pulling the world toward its final essentially urban state. Hence, urban centers today, with their international makeup, structural injustices, shocking areas of poverty, yet loaded potential for beautiful human creativity, present wonderful opportunities and challenges for holistic Christian service.

## Clarifications

Here in this chapter we are discussing the comprehensive scope of missions, as connected to their ongoing character. What I mean by saying that Christian missions are to be comprehensive in scope is that they are to address the three general areas of evangelization, church maturity, and wider areas of public concern. This last area is part of what we described earlier (in chapter 6) as the corporate discipling of the respective nations into which God has placed us as his international people.

Evangelicals increasingly want to be holistic in missions approaches, which is often put into a framework of "word and deed" ministry. Many evangelicals insist on prioritizing evangelism and church-planting over holistic ministries, or "word" over "deed."[14] Other evangelicals point to the compartmentalized, Enlightenment-based thinking underlying

13. Just a few of those widely known and respected people are Ray Bakke, Harvie Conn, Roger Greenway, Tim Keller, Robert Linthicum, John Perkins, and Manuel Ortiz.

14. The American missionary statesman David J. Hesselgrave has been at the forefront of standing for a "traditional prioritism" of evangelism and spiritual transformation. Cf. David J. Hesselgrave, *Paradigms in Conflict: 10 Key Questions in Christian Missions Today* (Grand Rapids: Kregel Publications, 2005), 117–39.

the "word-deed" distinction, calling for a focus on the whole of God's *new order* rather than on its parts.[15] As a rule, non-Western evangelicals have consistently responded to the discussion with an assumed seamless outlook that senses little compulsion, biblical or otherwise, to distinguish between allegedly different aspects of gospel ministry.[16] In any case, most agree that wider ministries have their place in missions. We can all concur that God's restorative mission is comprehensive. We can perhaps all concur as well that urban missions in particular, if they are to be relevant at all, must be holistic and multidimensional in scope. We can then start listing off other areas, such as medical missions, street-children care, micro-enterprise and other economic development, and disaster relief. In fact, evangelicals are often at the forefront of these types of ministries, compelled by the love of Christ for people's total needs.

This whole topic of "mercy ministry" or "holistic ministry" is too broad to address adequately here, but allow me to make four brief further clarifications before moving ahead to the area I want to address more specifically.

With respect to the whole matter of the world's poor and global poverty, for some Christians such issues can constitute the most basic framework for guiding missions activities in the world today. Some readers may have been scolding me all along for not more explicitly bringing poverty to the forefront. I do not mean to slight this area in the least by not giving it more attention. As explained in chapter 1, I am choosing to focus the book's discussion on what it means for Americans to suffer the loss of assumed control, rights, and privileges. Let me reaffirm my belief that how American Christians respond to the world's poor—including the poor in our own neighborhoods and cities—is as central an issue as any other. Careful thought and risky action are needed with respect to, for example, the amount of money put toward the American missionary enterprise, Christians' lifestyles, and our ignorance of global economic

---

15. Cf. Wilbert R. Shenk, *Changing Frontiers of Mission*, American Society of Missiology Series, no. 28 (Maryknoll, NY: Orbis Books, 1999), 28–29.

16. Examples are legion. Two are Samuel Escobar and John Driver, *Christian Mission and Social Justice*, Institute of Mennonite Studies, no. 5 (Scottsdale, PA: Herald Press, 1978), and C. René Padilla, *Mission between the Times: Essays on the Kingdom* (Grand Rapids: Eerdmans, 1985), especially the chapter entitled "The Fullness of Mission," pages 129–41.

structures that greatly affect the daily lives of so many of those who are desperately poor throughout the world.[17]

Second, how could such a book as this not address the AIDS pandemic? The only conceivable excuse is that this book is not meant to cover everything, even including such a vital matter as worldwide HIV/AIDS. Again, I in no way want to denigrate the importance of explicit, intentional American-Christian involvement in this absolutely crucial area.

Third, yes, I do believe that ecological concerns are missions concerns. All people, especially including those of us who have been reconciled to our Creator, are stewards of the world into which God has sent us. How our missions efforts might coalesce with particular environmentalist political initiatives is problematic. Even so, that should not deter us as Jesus' worldwide followers, especially including those of us who consider ourselves "Reformed," from interacting with wider issues (and more glocal ones) dealing with the environment, however they arise.

Finally, for organized missionaries it is not always clear, especially to Americans with our instincts about church-state and word-deed separations, how to act with regard to specifically sociopolitical matters in the foreign countries where we serve. The default rule of thumb has been to steer clear of such matters and behave as a proper guest of the government that has given one visa permission to work there. Certain situations may be so compelling as to demand some type of protest action: South Africa under apartheid might be as clear an example as any. Missionaries serving under the authority of their own governments (including colonial governments) have been more willing to offer political critique. For example, the Rev. Samuel Worcester, an American Board missionary from New England serving among the Cherokee Indians in Georgia in the early 1830s, disobeyed Georgia state legal initiatives to remove the Cherokees from their ancestral lands, even serving time in jail as a result

17. There are numerous helpful works in this area. One that provocatively addresses lifestyle disparities between Western missionaries and those among whom they often serve is Bonk's *Missions and Money*, cited earlier. Another fine work that speaks to how Christians can understand and help with economic development is Bryant L. Myers, *Walking with the Poor: Principles and Practices of Transformational Development* (Maryknoll, NY: Orbis Books, 1999).

It is also imperative that Christians—at least some of us—make the extra effort to be informed about such widely influential world economic organizations as the World Bank, International Monetary Fund, and the World Trade Organization.

(see Appendix B for more on this series of events). In general, however, we evangelical missionaries have most often stayed away from social and political involvement.

## Living Prophetically in America

The same could have been said a few decades ago about evangelicals in America. Social and political involvements were for "liberal" Christians, whereas evangelicals were to stay focused on evangelism and church growth. My, how things have changed since the 1970s advent of the Moral Majority[18] and the so-called Christian Right in general, as well as more "progressive" groups such as Sojourners![19] Through organized efforts and personal interest, U.S. evangelicals are as influential as ever in the national political arena over such issues as sexuality, taxes, the traditional family, education, and the United States' foreign-policy initiatives.

Now let us recall the five themes of this book, and see how they might steer us at this juncture of considering American evangelicals' input into sociopolitical life:

- God is the Superpower in Christian mission.
- The church is inherently (and today more than ever, in fact) international.
- God has sent all of us who make up the church into our respective life contexts.
- Christian missions efforts should be bi- if not multidirectional.
- Christian missions are to be ongoing in all settings (including the United States).

The main (admittedly complex) angle I take from these themes for American Christians is this: Recognizing God's sovereignty over all his world and the various entities therein (including the United States of

18. As of 2004, the "Moral Majority Coalition." See its Web site at http://www.moral majority.org/.

19. Sojourners' stated mission is "to proclaim and practice the biblical call to integrate spiritual renewal and social justice." See its Web site at http://www.sojo.net/index.cfm?action=about_us.mission.

America), we as God's fundamentally international people, the living networks among whom we must keep active, have been sent into the United States as his ambassadors for truth, justice, and Christian ways. A central component of cultivating an engaged, constructive, and prophetic stance toward this American setting into which we have been sent is to listen to, discuss with, and form our judgments in collaboration with the insights of our worldwide brothers and sisters in Christ.

Christians outside the United States generally see America differently from those of us who are Americans. They are not necessarily right, nor are they uniform in what they think. Nevertheless, being corporately identified with the rest of Jesus' international following enables those of us in the United States to carry out our missions activities of addressing sociopolitical issues—of helping to "disciple our nation"—when and where appropriate.

That is, our worldwide identity in Christ must meaningfully inform how we view this country. The multiple cultural elements entering that picture put us in a missions framework. They also help to keep in check, and ideally even reform, our ever-looming racist and nationalistic instincts. In general, a Christian internationalist viewpoint can bring to light facets of situations that might otherwise remain out of sight.

Take, for example, the volatile domestic moral-political issue of legalized abortion. Viewing this matter from a global Christian standpoint does not bring easy solutions. Yet it can shed light on peculiarly American features of the current debate (e.g., the pro-choice emphasis on women's *rights*). One will also see that this matter is *not* a major political issue in many other countries, particularly where the Christian church lives in a significant minority status. One will then quite naturally ask why, by contrast, it *is* such a major political issue in the United States: is part of the reason, for example, pro-lifers' desire to "reclaim" America? In any case, a Christian internationalist viewpoint can help Christians to sift through peculiarly American factors and focus our efforts on what is most central and important: advocating the sanctity of *life* and *shalom* for everyone concerned—particularly the defenseless unborn—whatever political or legal tactics we might choose to employ.

To take a more explicitly international example, what does our worldwide Christian identity mean regarding how we should think about

U.S. foreign policy toward the Middle East and central Asia? The word *how* is key. Christians can, will, and should disagree about particular political strategies. No single political party or tactic converges with the kingdom of God: to think otherwise would be blind nationalistic idolatry. It's crucial to take seriously what the rest of Jesus' worldwide followers think.

American evangelicals were generally, although not unanimously, behind the Bush administration's decision to go to war in Iraq, as the next step following its immediate post-9/11 operations in Afghanistan. Most other Christian communities in the United States—Roman Catholic and mainline Protestant, for example—were opposed to the war. What was interesting to note during all the domestic Christian discussions leading up to the war was that rarely, if ever, were there references to what the wider body of Christ was thinking.[20] For Christians seeking to speak constructively into such a grave situation, in my judgment that was a serious omission. It also revealed how negligible an international self-identity American Christians tend to have, particularly when it comes to dealing with the United States of America per se.[21]

20. The United States Conference of Catholic Bishops, of course, referred to the pope's opposition to the war. Cf. the USCCB March 19, 2003, "Statement on War with Iraq," given by President Wilton D. Gregory, available online at http://www.usccb.org/sdwp/peace/stm31903.shtml.

21. I have attempted the impossible and tried very hard not to express my own political views during our discussion to this point—although some of those views have unavoidably come through. My main goal has been to offer some constructive suggestions for U.S. Christians to be able, in a missions manner, to speak prophetically as internationally connected believers. I would hate for my limited and perhaps unpalatable political opinions to prevent you from interacting with that main objective. Even so, because I think it would be unfair not to disclose more of what I have thought specifically about U.S. foreign policy since 9/11, but so as to keep my explicit political thinking on such matters out of the main body of the text, I will share some of my thoughts in this note, as well as the final one further below.

In a nutshell, after 9/11 I would have favored the Bush administration's leading Americans along the path of learning more of what people throughout the Middle East and central Asia were thinking, rather than simply gearing up to retaliate and trying to communicate, in a one-way fashion, what America's intentions were. Moreover, in its search for a just response to the 9/11 attacks (including in coming to understand what had actually happened), I was wishing the United States had proceeded more multilaterally, or internationally, than forging the unilateral course it so quickly assumed. There was plenty of international political capital after 9/11 to seek a broad consensus of how most effectively to proceed.

To state things more negatively, I was opposed to how the Bush administration framed, in an oversimplified, reductionist, and inherently militaristic manner, the overall post-9/11 situation. Quickly casting people into categories of "good" and "evil" or "freedom-lovers" and "freedom-

One of the ongoing missions responsibilities that we Christians have is to speak prophetically into our respective settings, using the vantage point of our international identity in Christ. This does not mean that we should avoid working for justice in other settings around the world: after all, as we have already argued, we have a collective solidarity as the human race, and as the wider body of Christ we are obliged to help each other. Hence, an evangelical Christian organization such as the International Justice Mission, based in Washington, D.C., but working for justice issues around the world, is entirely appropriate and necessary.[22] Even so, one must always speak first to one's own context, as exemplified by the biblical prophets, including Jesus himself ("You hypocrite, first take the log out of your own eye, and then you will see clearly to take the speck out of your brother's eye" [Matt. 7:5]). And using the wider view of the worldwide body of Christ sharpens the focus of our insight into what is happening in our own settings.

As Americans, we can be tremendously helped by that vantage point as we sort through the intricacies of foreign-policy issues, as well as our country's global roles in general. We should also thus have a wider angle for evaluating U.S. military spending, which

---

haters" was, I believe, laughably simplistic and geared toward preparing the American public for war. I believe the decision to go to war with Iraq was made no later than the summer of 2002, if not earlier, and the U.S. administration was not genuinely interested in finding a political solution—even though it went through all the right motions relative to its allies and the United Nations. Moreover, to this day the apparent lack of horror and compassion (including in the U.S. media) over Afghani and Iraqi civilian losses is appalling.

I should add a quick note as well about a "backdoor" type of evangelical justification for the United States' going to war, unintended as it might be as such. That kind of view suggests that the toppling of Saddam Hussein has had the effect of opening new doors for expatriate missionary activity. In my judgment, making that connection not only unfairly pushes Christians toward softening any critique of the war effort, but also seeks to bring together two topics—Christian ministry and military operations—that do not have a great deal of compatibility with each other (military chaplaincy excepted). I appreciate on the one hand the honest, sensitive ways in which Patrick Johnstone attempts to find redemptive silver linings in such disasters as wars, epidemics, and natural disasters. At the same time, we must be careful about trivializing the horror and tragedy of such catastrophes in and of themselves. Cf. Patrick Johnstone, "Growth through God's Interventions," in *The Church Is Bigger Than You Think: The Unfinished Work of World Evangelisation* (Pasadena, CA: William Carey Library, 1998), 117–28.

At any rate, with respect to how the overwhelming majority of Christians all around the world were absolutely opposed to the United States' going to war, it behooved American Christians then, and still behooves us now, at least to ask them why.

22. See the International Justice Mission Web site at http://www.ijm.org.

outpaces the rest of the world so much as to be more than the next top twelve countries combined.[23] And while spending figures are not always as straightforward as they may seem, this at least is clear: "So important did military spending and the military-industrial sector become during World War II and the Cold War that—with space exploration as a minor adjunct—they have become fundamental to the U.S. economy, U.S. economic growth and above all U.S. technological development."[24] We who are American Christians need others' insights in sorting through what all of this means for living faithfully as Jesus' followers.

Furthermore, American Christians' international identity in Christ will assist in assessing how the ever-burgeoning U.S.-based missions enterprise connects with the superpower United States' global influence. This is a particularly important concern, given the extreme ambivalence of the rest of the world toward America.[25] In what ways, for example, are U.S. missionaries actually, albeit unwittingly, complicit in spreading American influence as a whole?[26] People among whom U.S. missionar-

23. As of 2002, according to the London-based International Institute for Strategic Studies, U.S. annual defense expenditures were $348.5 billion, compared to a combined total of $347.1 billion for countries two through thirteen. Jeffrey Chamberlin, "Comparisons of U.S. and Foreign Military Spending: Data from Selected Public Sources," CRS Report for Congress (January 28, 2004), CRS-5, "Table 1. U.S. and Foreign Defense Spending (by Rank): Data from the IISS and U.S. Department of State," available online at http://fpc.state.gov/documents/organization/30046.pdf. The U.S. figure (for the Department of Defense alone) now tops $400 billion. Cf. U.S. Budget "Summary Tables" (for example, S-2 and S-3), available online at http://www.gpoaccess.gov/usbudget/fy06/pdf/budget/tables.pdf.

24. Anatol Lieven, *America Right or Wrong: An Anatomy of American Nationalism* (New York: Oxford University Press, 2004), 156.

25. As I have heard other traveling Americans remark as well, most people whom I have met around the world enjoy Americans as people, but they strongly dislike what they perceive to be bullying U.S. foreign policy. As one of many analysts on this subject of world opinion about the United States has put it, "On the one hand, people around the world admire American democracy, respect America's scientific and technological achievements, and regard the United States as a 'land of opportunity'. But on the other hand, the percentage of foreign populations with a 'favorable view' of the United States has plummeted since 1999." This same analysis goes on to note how significantly the rest of the world, according to Pew Center research, believes that U.S. foreign policy does not consider the interest of others (despite the fact that most Americans believe just the opposite). Stephen M. Walt, *Taming American Power: The Global Response to U.S. Primacy* (New York: Norton, 2002), 63–67.

26. I don't believe all American missionaries should be paranoid about this, but I don't think they should mindlessly ignore the connections they have with worldwide American influence,

ies live and serve see America's economic and military strength, factors that enabled the missionaries to come in the first place. Also, the influence of U.S. missionaries on the people they serve almost always leads to further American connections—for example, financial partnerships between the indigenous Christians and related U.S. churches, educational connections when people end up attending schools in the United States (or American schools established for the missionaries' children), more short-term teams coming from the United States, and English-language learning. What are the pros and cons of such *American* influences?

Moreover, we must ask why there are increasing numbers of American missionaries (particularly short-termers), despite the larger growth of Christianity in the Global South. How much of that reality is due to economics and to Americans' desires (legitimate as they may be) to tour and "see the world"? Politically speaking, how do the U.S. government and other countries' governments view American missionaries in particular locales—and how should we Christians interact with those various government policies? (See Appendix B for more on "Christian Missions and Civil Authorities.") Investigating these matters is no small task, but neither is living as international Christians. Analyzing, from the standpoint of an international Christian identity, the multifaceted relationship between U.S. missionaries and U.S. global influence is an important and necessary responsibility.

Taking seriously our *international* Christian identity, as *American* Christians, is integral to suffering after Christ's example. Allowing our international identity to inform and shape how we feel and think as Americans—again, because we are *Christians bound together with others in the worldwide body of Christ*—involves relinquishing, or at least quali-

---

either. As one who lived outside the United States over thirteen years, then returned in the late 1990s only to experience 9/11 and subsequent developments, I was often dumbfounded at what I saw as many American evangelicals' narrow, fervent, and unquestioning nationalism. To me at least—as well as to many others, including such keen analysts as Chalmers Johnson, as seen in his recent book, *The Sorrows of Empire: Militarism, Secrecy, and the End of the Republic* (New York: Holt, 2005)—American imperial unilateralism was unfolding right before the world's eyes, including the unquestioning, adoring gaze of U.S. evangelicalism. While I certainly am not in favor of jumping on any sort of "Missionary, go home" bandwagon, I do believe that the question of how U.S. missionaries—long-term and short-term, plus the accompanying infrastructure—might further, or at least support, America's global power is an issue that must be regularly and carefully addressed.

fying, some of our most basic American rights and privileges, namely, to decide *for ourselves* and *on our own* what *we* think and believe. Suggesting that we walk that path of suffering is not to suggest in any way that we who are American Christians run from our *responsibility* to think, discuss, and decide what we believe and how we will act accordingly. It simply calls us to recognize the full extent of Jesus' rule and influence in our lives. *Christ also suffered*: he expects the same from his followers.

As evidenced within our own American-Christian hearts and lives, God's inherently international mission goes on throughout the world, and so do Christian missions. God's mission is all-encompassing. Jesus continues to orchestrate his massive unorganized missions movement. In complementary fashion to those unorganized missions, Christians' organized missions efforts have their significant places in God's economy as well. May we be found faithful in serving *Kurios* Jesus in our respective settings evangelistically, by helping the body of Christ mature, and prophetically working for justice and *shalom* throughout our societies.

## Reflection Questions

- What does the word *missions* mean?

- What is the relationship between missions and evangelism? Is this an important question?

- How do missions figure in maturing the church?

- What difference does it make whether or not we understand sociopolitical involvement to be missions?

- How might 1 Peter 2:13–25 guide us in approaching socioeconomic political matters?

# Conclusion

The message of 1 Peter is a multisided one. Throughout the letter there is a message of *triumph*: Jesus has risen, he reigns, and he is coming again. Christians thus have an unshakable *hope*: our salvation is sure and will be completed "at the revelation of Jesus Christ" (1:7, 13). The theocentric or *God-centered* character of the letter is also unmistakable: God the Father foreknew "before the foundation of the world" (1:20) what he would do for us his people in Christ; his Spirit has both superintended the good news' coming to people and set believers apart for service; and it is in God's might and faithfulness that Christians therefore trust. Peter's letter thus exhibits as well a strong *historical* and *eschatological* sense: prophets and even angels had longed to understand the full impact of "the sufferings of Christ and the subsequent glories" (1:11), which we who live after Jesus' life, death, and resurrection see more clearly but will fully see only when Jesus returns.

This multisided message of 1 Peter was particularly appropriate for its first recipients. As a religious minority group, they lived in a sociopolitical situation marked by struggle and suffering. But no matter how severe their suffering seemed, those first-century Christians could have a sure hope in God's, and their, ultimate triumph in the historical, soon-to-be-completed work of Jesus Christ. That message gave great encouragement. On top of that, being the effective communicator that he was, and under the guidance and inspiration of the Holy Spirit, the apostle Peter focused his message on that to which his readers could easily relate: *the sufferings of Christ.*

Many Christians throughout the world today can also easily relate to Christ's sufferings. They live in situations in which they are tiny minorities, and some of them are oppressively monitored by their governing authorities. While inextricably linked to this "brotherhood throughout the world," we American Christians might not face the same sociopolitical severity as Christian minority groups have in the past and still do today. Nevertheless, Christ's sufferings are central to the faith of all of *Kurios* Jesus' followers, wherever and whenever we live. Those sufferings have removed our sin, and Jesus' example of suffering is ours to follow.

In this book we have been considering the place of American Christians within the worldwide movement of Christian missions. The framework we have articulated asserts first that God's *mission* is his commitment to complete the salvation of his world. Accordingly, Christian *missions* are our efforts to cooperate with God as he uses multiple cultural environments in his mission. As U.S. Christians, here at this juncture in world history and for the foreseeable future, we still have our parts to play within the providential outworking of God's world mission. One peculiar part we have to play, deeply related to following the example of Christ's sufferings, is that of suffering the loss of whatever unique control, rights, and privileges we might imagine ourselves to possess within that mission. *Christ also suffered*, and so should all of us who are his followers.

To use a long-standing image from the history of American Christianity, this same Jesus, the One who suffered and then rose again in triumph, is the One driving his worldwide gospel mission train, just as he always has. American Christians have been on board for the past several generations, making important contributions along the way. Now, more than ever before, the train is full of significant numbers of all kinds of Christians from around the world. We are positioned to continue our ride together, with Jesus as the Conductor, across our respective countries, cultures, and contexts throughout the world.

To say that Jesus will in one way or another take the train to its final destination, or that he will unquestionably fulfill his mission of world restoration, should not breed complacency. It should inspire awe and wonder at his grace and power. And even as we his passengers, Jesus' followers, marvel at how he works in his own unique ways (and usually quite apart from our organized missions efforts), we have the privilege and responsibility to follow and serve him. Part of that privilege and responsibility is to "rejoice insofar as you share Christ's sufferings, that you may also rejoice and be glad when his glory is revealed" (1 Peter 4:13). Even as we anticipate Jesus' ultimate public display of his greatness, for now we have the privilege of suffering after Christ's example.

In Acts 1:8 terms, you and your church can marvel at how Jesus has been fulfilling his own prediction that his people would be his witnesses, starting from first-century Jerusalem and spreading outward in all directions from there. Now in this generation, you and others spread throughout the farthest reaches of the earth have the privilege of cooperating with our CEO and King in the cause of his comprehensive gospel. He alone has the right and privilege of controlling his mission. One particular privilege that we have been given as American Christians is to suffer by relinquishing any assumptions—subconsciously present because of our heritage or because of global U.S. socio-economic-political-military power—that we possess unique control, rights, and privileges in relation to God and to others in carrying out missions activities. We may have unique responsibilities because of U.S. power and influence, but such responsibilities are not the same as rights and privileges in relation to others. Other Christian brothers and sisters are equal partners in the gospel and its worldwide ministry. Humble international partnerships, all forged in humble dependence on God's Spirit, are therefore the constructive way forward in missions.

Such partnerships, wherever their focus of ministry might be, are important because God's love compels us to be and live as his worldwide, international people. We must not be confined solely to the geopolitical interests of our respective countries; neither may we sink into advocating, even unintentionally, the racial interests of our "own kind of people." Rather, we are to encourage and stimulate each other to serve the cause of Jesus' universal gospel humbly and prophetically, wherever he has placed us and wherever else he might take us. We need each other's particular God-given resources and perspectives. People all around the world need to know Jesus; Jesus' church needs ongoing maturity in all of our glocal expressions; all of the world's public, structural, and real-life settings need continual gospel input. God is the One uniquely faithful, capable, and determined enough to see that our missions efforts continue on "to the end of the age" (Matt. 28:20).

Such, I believe, is the Bible's message, including that of 1 Peter. I hope you and your church have heard that message afresh through the stimulus and encouragement I have intended to provide in this book.

The book's focus has been to direct American Christians, along with those around the world who are inextricably linked with us, to consider Christ's sufferings as we follow him in our missions efforts. In particular, as noted in chapter 1, 1 Peter has been our guide in developing really only one aspect of an American "missiology of suffering." Our focus has been on suffering the loss of assumed control, rights, and privileges in world missions. That particular form of suffering pushes us who are Americans away from the relatively strong position of dispensing to others what we have to offer them, and toward the weaker position of receiving God's mission through them. Of course, ministry flowing in both directions, indeed in multiple directions, is needed as we "serve one another." Multidirectional cooperation is needed as well to see that peoples who live apart from access to Christ's gospel are reached by that essential, life-giving message. My prayer is that God's Spirit will continue to come to your aid as you work through, in collaboration with others in Christ's international church, how best to flesh out your and your church's particular involvements with God's mission to his world here in the early twenty-first century and beyond.

May our Master and Hero, Jesus—the only true mission Superpower—continue to bless and use all his people, including those of us who are Americans, for his glory and honor throughout the world and across all generations. As he blesses and uses us, may he do so through enabling us to suffer however he sees fit, even as we always remember that *Christ also suffered*.

# Appendix A

# The Twentieth-Century Development of *Mission* and *Missions*

One of the major discussions that has taken place over the past half-century has dealt with the terms *mission* and *missions*.[1] This "living history" is essential for understanding many important dynamics in our own day.

We must first consider how the international missionary movement took on fresh organizational shape at the 1910 Edinburgh World Missionary Conference. (*International* at that time meant Europeans' and North Americans' cooperating to work elsewhere in the world.) This monumental gathering led to a number of succeeding initiatives, including the eventual creation in 1921—in the devastating wake of World War I—of the International Missionary Council (IMC). Over the next forty years, until its integration into the World Council of Churches (WCC), the IMC organized occasional worldwide conferences to discuss developing missions-related issues.[2]

1. Although dated, one of the clearest descriptions of these historical developments is Rodger C. Bassham's *Mission Theology: 1948–1975 Years of Worldwide Creative Tension—Ecumenical, Evangelical, and Roman Catholic* (Pasadena, CA: William Carey Library, 1979). Two other excellent and more up-to-date summary articles are John A. McIntosh, "Missio Dei," in *Evangelical Dictionary of World Missions*, ed. A. Scott Moreau, Baker Reference Library Series (Grand Rapids: Baker, 2000), 631–33, and A. Scott Moreau, "Mission and Missions," ibid., 636–38.

2. Accounts of the IMC Assemblies abound, including the brief but helpful summary

World War II further contributed to the raising of many challenging questions, particularly from non-Westerners, about the Western missionary movement. At their root, those questions stemmed from a twin reality. On the one hand, there had been the undeniable horror of Western countries, understood to be "Christian nations," literally killing each other. On the other hand, Westerners had an increased awareness of long-standing and even resurgent non-Western religious traditions and their often morally exemplary practitioners. With these two stark realities, how could Western missionaries pretend to tell others about religious truth?

Moreover, there were Christian leaders who were inclined to interpret events as the hand of God moving beyond the narrow confines of the organized church. For example, the expulsion from China—long the crown jewel of many Western missionary efforts—of missionaries in 1949 further pressed the issue of what God was doing in the world. If God truly was providentially in control of all things, was he not orchestrating events in China, and the developing Cold War, and other world events? And since that was the case, if God was somehow behind missionaries' having to leave China, what roles were Western missions, missionaries, and churches to play in God's world?

As church and mission leaders consulted with one another internationally and wrestled with such searching questions, what began to crystallize in many minds was articulated in the increasingly touted phrase *missio Dei*, the "mission of God." The virtues of Western Christian civilization had become tainted. World events—most pointedly two major wars combined with a devastating economic recession and resulting in teetering European empires—had gone in unexpected directions. And while it was impossible to see the expulsion of missionaries from China as anything but negative, some were open to the possibility that the establishment of a new socialist order there might be something positive, or at least a providential act of God. After all, God worked not just through the church and explicitly Christian structures, but through wider sociopolitical realities as well. Furthermore, the church of Jesus Christ

---

on the WCC's Web site, http://www.wcc-coe.org/wcc/what/mission/hist-e.html. It is interesting to note what might be called the site's revisionist historical description of the IMC (I.Missionary.C) conferences as "mission" conferences.

was becoming worldwide, with the "younger" churches in the non-West now serving Christ along with the "older" Western churches.

These Christian leaders were grappling with how to understand this new post–World War II world of the 1950s. For them, a traditional "West-to-the-rest" program of *missions* would no longer do. That approach was too church-centered, and it was too based in the West as well. The more God-centered *missio Dei* was becoming for many a more satisfactory concept to use for understanding Christian mission. It would, in fact, become the single most influential concept in wider (ecumenical) twentieth-century Christian mission theology. Many Christian leaders had moved in their understanding "from missions to mission."[3] Figure 4 summarizes what this shift meant.

To spell things out a little more, the mind-set expressed by *missio Dei* fundamentally rests in the primacy of the triune God in carrying out Christian mission. Thus, *missio Dei* involves three interrelated themes.

First, whereas Christian *missions* had focused—perhaps unwittingly but nevertheless in actuality—on Christians' activities to spread the Christian faith, by contrast *missio Dei* focused on the triune God's initiative and activity. There was the feeling that the Western church had often slipped

FIG. 4

**The shift from "missions" to "mission."**

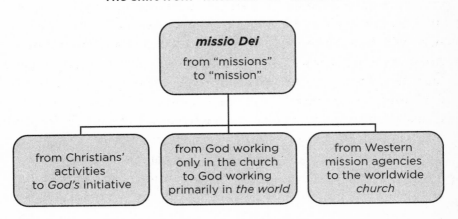

3. This is actually the title of a 1960s book by an influential U.S.-American mission leader: R. Pierce Beaver, *From Missions to Mission: Protestant World Mission Today and Tomorrow* (New York: Association Press, 1964).

into its own planning, initiatives, and programs in carrying out its missionary task. The necessary corrective was to recognize that the Father, Son, and Holy Spirit have been taking the initiative, and continue to do so, in executing the divine mission of bringing salvation to the world.

Second, Western Christianity had been encased within a church-centered understanding of Christian missions that saw the church as God's exclusive instrument in bringing salvation to the world; that is, the view had been that God worked through the church alone to save the world. *Missio Dei* recognized that God also works (some leaders asserted, *primarily* works) directly in world events—that is, nonecclesiastical social, political, and economic realities.

Third, "missions to mission" meant that because of the presence of the Christian church in all regions of the world, Western missions organizations should no longer be the initiators of Christian outreach. The worldwide church, present now throughout the world in its various national and local expressions, was primarily responsible for carrying out the evangelistic task within its respective national and local contexts. Instead of expatriate missions pressing in from the outside, the church in its one mission under God had to find "new ways of outreach—cooperative action, reconciliation, interfaith encounter."[4] Insofar as *missio Dei* meant God's using his church in his worldwide mission, "this concept [of missions to mission] essentially legislated against mission sending organizations in general, replacing them in favor of the normal evangelistic activity of the various existing national churches."[5]

In these three senses, God's mission was thought to have trumped Christian missions.

## Evangelicals Separate and Consolidated

That all sounds fine and good—to a point. And that point (actually a group of points) was the one at which many leaders in international Christian mission(s) circles balked at what was happening within the "ecumenical"

4. This phrase is on the cover of Beaver's *From Missions to Mission*.
5. Ralph W. Winter, "The Significance of One 'S,'" sidebar comments in his "The Rise and Fall of the IMC," *Mission Frontiers* (October 1999), available online at www.missionfrontiers.org/1999/10/imc.htm.

movement. That movement took concrete shape in the 1948 formation of the WCC, and particularly in its emphases that developed through the 1950s and 1960s. We will next look briefly at what happened with these dissenting leaders—evangelicals—in the 1960s and 1970s.

In reaction to the focus on the *missio Dei* and going "from missions to mission," evangelicals became a separate and identifiable movement on a worldwide scale. Evangelicals did not, of course, object to an emphasis on missions' being fundamentally God's mission. Rather, they saw a shift away from a traditional, theologically orthodox emphasis on world evangelization. That had been the spirit of Edinburgh 1910, the evangelicals asserted in the late 1980s, and thus that monumental "conference can rightly be considered the predecessor of the [evangelical] 'Lausanne movement' of our time." By assembling together starting in the 1960s, evangelicals were thus simply getting "back in touch with their historical roots."[6] The underlying issue for evangelicals was whether or not people believed the Bible. They concluded that those in the ecumenical movement had become persuaded by liberal theology (which had emerged out of nineteenth-century Germany) that the Bible's teachings were not literally true.

Organizationally speaking, the initial evangelical gathering was a 1966 World Congress on Evangelism in Berlin convened by Billy Graham. He and others wanted to focus on world evangelization and the Bible's message of salvation for individuals who would believe in Jesus and his death on the cross. That 1966 meeting led to the 1974 Lausanne Congress on World Evangelization (LCOWE), a movement continuing to the present.

Figure 5 presents a brief timeline of the modern missions movement.

## How Evangelicals Defined Themselves

The stated purpose of the LCOWE is *"to further the evangelization of the world by building bridges of understanding and cooperation among Christian leaders everywhere to mobilize the whole church to proclaim the*

---

6. Lausanne Committee for World Evangelization, *The Lausanne Story: The Whole Church Taking the Whole Gospel to the Whole World* (Charlotte, NC: Lausanne Committee for World Evangelization, 1987), 12.

## Fig. 5

### Twentieth-century unification and fragmentation of the modern missions movement.

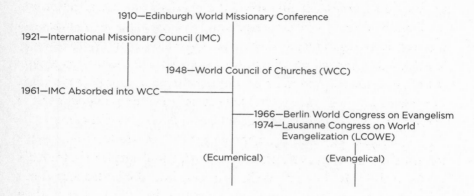

1910—Edinburgh World Missionary Conference

1921—International Missionary Council (IMC)

1948—World Council of Churches (WCC)

1961—IMC Absorbed into WCC

1966—Berlin World Congress on Evangelism
1974—Lausanne Congress on World
Evangelization (LCOWE)

(Ecumenical)                    (Evangelical)

*whole gospel to the whole world.*"[7] This statement clearly has some key and carefully crafted terminology. The wording sheds light on the conscious distinctives of the evangelical, Lausanne movement in distinction from the ecumenical WCC. It also shows how evangelicals were seeking to incorporate positive elements of certain emphases of the *missio Dei* concept outlined above.

These twin objectives of distinguishing and incorporating can be sifted out under three points. First, the purpose is for "the evangelization of the world by ... proclaim[ing] the whole gospel." The term *evangelization* is intended to be more holistic—including both word and deed—than the term *evangelism*, which is "proclamation": "World evangelization requires the whole Church to take the whole gospel to the whole world."[8] This assertion focuses on the distinguishing evangelical characteristic of word proclamation and the need for people to believe verbally expressible content. It also acknowledges that limiting Christian ministry to word proclamation is a truncated view of "the whole gospel." Whereas this is not the same as a *missio Dei* understanding that stresses God's activity in the world outside the church, it does appreciate the stress on the gospel importance of the totality of life beyond what is directly spiritual and church-related.

7. Ibid., 16 (emphasis mine).
8. Ibid., 28–29.

Second is the stated purpose of "building bridges of understanding and cooperation among Christian leaders everywhere to mobilize the whole church." Evangelicals recognized and rejoiced in the church's growth outside the West. To carry out the task of world evangelization, "cooperative action" between Western and non-Western Christian leaders was seen as strategic and even necessary. At the same time, evangelicals (at least Western evangelicals) did not concur with such "new ways of outreach" as the type of "interfaith encounter" that ecumenicals in the WCC were advocating. Christians were to be mobilized not to dialogue but to "proclaim . . . to the whole world" salvation in Jesus Christ alone.

The stress on proclaiming the gospel to "the whole world" points to a third distinctively evangelical emphasis. The absorption in the early 1960s of the IMC into the WCC was based on the belief that God's mission involved the servant church around the world more so than Western-based missions agencies. What concerned evangelicals about this aspect of the ecumenical movement from "missions to mission" was the inevitable focus by newly established churches on ministry within their own countries at the expense of other, still-unreached areas of the world. The separate integrity of missions agencies needed to be cultivated along with that of churches in order to keep Christians' eyes looking ever outward to reaching the unreached with the gospel.[9] Insofar, then, as *missions* centered on preaching Jesus Christ to the world's unevangelized, with the more all-encompassing *mission* of the church possibly losing that cutting edge, the vitality of Christian missions needed to be protected and emphasized in its own right.

## So What's the Big Deal?

By the mid-1970s, then, the ecumenicals and evangelicals had separate parallel organizations, namely, the WCC and the Lausanne movement. The former embraced the *missio Dei* with its divine-initiative, broader-than-the-organized-church, and global-cooperative emphases. The latter emphasized world evangelization, that is, gospel proclamation in word and deed to all the world's peoples, most especially the unreached.

9. Winter, "The Rise and Fall of the IMC."

With the Lausanne movement, missions-to-mission had boomeranged back to a sharpened emphasis on missions.

But were the two movements really so different? Yes. You may be scratching your head at this point and wondering how, because in many ways their respective emphases sound quite similar. After all, ecumenicals and evangelicals both wanted Christianity to minister to people all around the world, right?

Right, there is overlap between the two movements. But there are profound differences as well. (See fig. 6 for a comparison of the movements.) Here is the clearest way I know to describe those differences: from an ecumenical perspective, the evangelicals were (and still are) too narrow- and closed-minded. Evangelicals restricted God to working only in and through the organized church—but didn't God also work in and through social, economic, and political movements as well? Also, evangelicals hung on to old ideas of everybody in the world having to believe in Jesus Christ in the same way that Western Christians had been insisting for centuries—but wasn't that arrogant proselytizing, as well as unfair to a loving God and to other sincere religious people from centuries-old traditions? From an evangelical perspective, ecumenicals had left (and still have not returned to) the basic Christian faith of belief in the Bible as God's perfect Word and in Jesus as the unique Savior of all people. Missions is all about people hearing about Jesus so that they can believe in him and "not perish but have eternal life" (John 3:16).

Ecumenical missionaries and church leaders, therefore, became inclined to focus on such issues as peace, justice, and interreligious dialogue. What happened with apartheid in South Africa, for example, was a major concern of the WCC. Evangelicals, on the other hand, have channeled their energies toward identifying the world's unreached peoples and mobilizing churches to send missionaries to those peoples for evangelization and church-planting.

For ecumenicals, *missio Dei* emphasizes God's initiative throughout the world. How God works is something that we as people must humbly discover as we lovingly serve and learn from others. For evangelicals, *missions* emphasizes God's command and guidance for Christians to work and strategize so that all people can hear about

FIG. 6

**Ecumenical vs. evangelical mission(s) distinctives.**

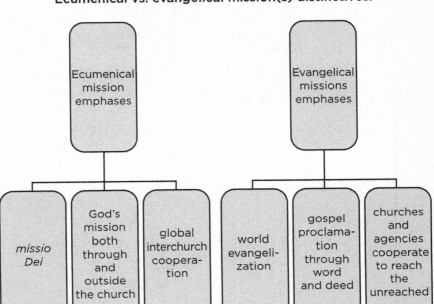

Jesus. If people do not hear, they cannot be saved and are doomed to an eternity in hell.

The difference between those emphases is a big deal. And on top of that, ecumenicals and evangelicals must believe that it's a big enough deal to stay as organizationally separate—as churches, schools, and missions organizations—to date as they have ever been.

225

# Appendix B

## Christian Missions and Civil Authorities: Missionary Civil Disobedience among the Cherokee Indians

Using 1 Peter's message of suffering as a guide, this book's focus is on American Christians' relinquishing our control, rights, and privileges before God and others, particularly in relation to five key themes connected with missions. The understanding of missions here is a three-pronged one: people converting to faith in Jesus Christ, the church maturing, and God's kingdom being manifest in socio-economic-political ways. In wrestling with what this third area of missions involves, we have touched on living prophetically as U.S. Christians in light of America's international superpower status. As we have done that, such theological issues as proper political authority, Christians' responsibilities and obligations to their government, and war and peace have arisen along the way.

The book's limited focus does not permit our delving into these issues as deeply as their importance and complexity deserve. In order to touch on them at least somewhat explicitly and directly, here in this appendix we will consider a series of events that occurred in the 1830s. During that period, various American missionaries took different

227

positions relative to the welfare of Cherokee Indians and the westward expansion of the United States. Examining why those missionaries believed and acted as they did will help us consider how Christian missions intersect with the important matter of Christians' relationships to political authorities.

## The Unstoppable "Trail of Tears"[1]

Most Americans have at least heard of the infamous "Trail of Tears," or "The Trail Where They Cried" (as literally translated from the Cherokee *Nunna daul Tsuny*).[2] Some are familiar with such historical details as when it occurred and who was involved. Yet few are beyond the need of a review of what happened, particularly in relation to the issues we want to consider here.

### The Wider Historical Context

In the broadest of terms, the forced removal by Anglo-Americans of Cherokee Indians from their native lands in northern Georgia all the way to present-day Oklahoma in 1838–39 was the result of the immigration of the Anglos into the Indians' territory. This type of displacement of aboriginals has occurred throughout worldwide human history, including in modern times. Elimination of the aboriginals through warfare, decimation through disease, and assimilation into the new culture have normally taken place as well, and that was certainly true of what happened to the Cherokees and other Native American tribes.

Georgia was one of the original British North American colonies, of course, and by the time of the final approval of the new Constitution by

1. While sources of information about the series of events that transpired are numerous, I have heavily relied on two careful analyses by William G. McLoughlin: "Civil Disobedience and Evangelism among the Missionaries to the Cherokees, 1829–1839," *Journal of Presbyterian History* 51, no. 2 (Summer 1973): 116–39; and *Cherokees and Missionaries, 1789–1839* (New Haven: Yale University Press, 1984). I have also used a helpful collection of documents from the time: Louis Filler and Allen Guttmann, eds., *The Removal of the Cherokee Nation: Manifest Destiny or National Dishonor?* Problems in American Civilization Series (Boston: D. C. Heath, 1962).

2. Golden Ink, "The Trail of Tears" (1997), available online at http://ngeorgia.com/history/nghisttt.html.

all thirteen states in 1789, Georgia had become part of the newly formed United States of America. Even so, "between 1783, when the Cherokee and Creek first ceded land in North Georgia to the whites, and 1828, much of North Georgia remained under Native American control."[3] This continuing Indian land control was protected by treaties they had signed—as independent nations—with the U.S. federal government; the Indians had also signed treaties with individual states along the way. In 1802, however, President Thomas Jefferson made a conflicting agreement with the state of Georgia, namely, to remove at the earliest opportune time the Indians from Georgia in exchange for the state's claim of western lands. The Louisiana Purchase of 1803—with its vast open lands to which Indians could be moved, as could easily be imagined, for a perpetual existence far removed from the United States—and an increasing Anglo-American population in northern Georgia raised the stakes of the inherent conflict between the resident natives and the ever-arriving citizens of an expanding new nation.

Although there was gradual Anglo encroachment, fighting, and ceding of Indian lands, the Cherokees' and Georgia's respective territories were able to coexist through most of the 1820s. In 1827 the Cherokees even adopted their own national constitution, based on that of the United States.[4] But two events in 1828 forced the issue whether the remaining Cherokees would be able to retain their lands independently from both U.S.-federal and Georgia-state control. One was the discovery of gold in northern Georgia, instigating a rush of new Anglo settlers. The second was the election of U.S. President Andrew Jackson and his policy of Indian removal to the west of the Mississippi River. Jackson's 1832 reelection only furthered the implementation of that policy.

## The Jackson Presidency and the State of Georgia

Jackson's first message to Congress as president, given in December 1829, included his stated intention to remove all Indians from lands east

---

3. Golden Ink, "North Georgia, 1783–1828" (2006), available online at http://ngeorgia. com/history/earlyga.html.

4. R. Pierce Beaver, *Church, State, and the American Indians: Two and a Half Centuries of Partnership in Missions between Protestant Churches and Government* (St. Louis: Concordia, 1966), 106.

of the Mississippi. Encouraged by the federal government's long-awaited implementation of Jefferson's earlier agreement with them, the Georgia legislators by the end of the year passed legislation declaring that all Cherokee lands were under the sovereignty of the people of Georgia. In March 1832, however, the U.S. Supreme Court and Chief Justice John Marshall declared Georgia's law unconstitutional because treaties were still in force between the Cherokees and the federal government. Andrew Jackson, for his part, simply refused to enforce the Court's decision, allowing Georgia to continue on its course of assuming control of all territory within its boundaries. Besides furthering his own policy of Indian removal, politically Jackson was further endearing himself to the state of Georgia so as to keep it on the federal side in his battle against South Carolina in the crisis over that state's desire to nullify protective federal tariffs.

In December 1835, Jackson exploited a small faction among the Cherokees to conclude a removal treaty with them. The principal chief and vast majority of the Cherokees objected, but the U.S. Senate ratified the treaty and the U.S. Army moved to implement it. Finally, in the fall of 1838, the Cherokees were forced at bayonet point to march the arduous 800 miles of the "Trail of Tears" to present-day Oklahoma.

## Missionaries' Various Reactions

Integral to the sociopolitical account just given were the presence and actions of missionaries who served among the Cherokees. There had been various itinerant missionary forays into Cherokee territory up through the 1700s, but it was only in 1799 that Moravians became the first to be granted permission to settle there, for the purpose of educating Cherokee children. The Cherokees saw education as the key to becoming equipped to live next to their new neighbors. The U.S. government in turn saw education—along with training in agriculture and such "household arts" as spinning and weaving—as the means to civilize and assimilate the Indians. Missionaries were happy to oblige in helping to provide education, and in return the federal government allocated funds from its "Civilization Fund" to help support the missionaries in their work.[5] Presbyterians, New England missionaries under the American Board of Commissioners for Foreign Missions, Methodists, and Baptists soon followed the Moravians in taking up residence among the Cherokees of northern Georgia and adjacent areas.

## The Mounting Dilemma

Missionaries' sociopolitical postures began to fracture when the removal issue grew more intense in the late 1820s. Up to that point the missionaries among the Cherokees had supported the prevailing U.S. policy of civilizing and Christianizing the Indians. Now that such a policy was dramatically changing course, the missionaries had to "rise above politics" and determine afresh what was "right or wrong."[6] Such a determination, however, was not patently obvious:

> To decide whether Jackson's removal policy was right or wrong required delicate judgments about the rights and wrongs inherent in the very nature of the American political and social system. Did the power of Caesar rest in the federal (or General) government, the state governments, the validity of treaties, the supremacy of the Constitution over states' rights, the sovereignty of Indian nations? How did one define the word *nation* and the term *civil rights*, especially when applied to Indians? Those who turned to Scripture found texts which said that Christians must "obey the powers that be" and must support those ordained of God as rulers. But within the conflicting jurisdiction of the American system, who or what was the ruling power?

Clearly, these moral questions concerning sociopolitical matters were not at all straightforward.

Moreover, for the individual missionaries there were further complicating issues:

5. Francis Paul Prucha, *American Indian Policy in the Formative Years: The Indian Trade and Intercourse Acts, 1790–1834* (Lincoln: University of Nebraska Press, 1962), 213–24.

6. These and the following block quotations are from McLoughlin, *Cherokees and Missionaries*, 242–43.

Was he really free to decide for himself or was he only the employee of his mission board? Should he remain silent until his board spoke and then accept its will or should he follow his own conscience and either support or oppose the government for himself? If he chose to "obey the powers that be", was he free to select among those claiming power or should he simply obey the first authorized civil force that confronted him (be that tribal authority, state authority, or officials of the War Department)? Solomon himself could not have answered these questions with any assurance of righteousness.

This insightful analysis goes on to remark:

> In the end the missionaries could not make the neat separation between Church and State, God and Caesar, which they desperately wanted to make.... The missionaries, like the Cherokees, were caught in the flux of events surrounding America's transition in its national identity. It did not mean the same thing to be an American in 1830 as it had in 1800.

One can make a similar claim about contrasting American identities between today and anytime prior to 9/11.

Privately, among the twenty or so missionaries (plus their wives and daughters) serving the Cherokees in 1829–30 was a virtually unanimous sympathy for the Cherokees as well as opposition to Georgia's and Jackson's removal initiatives. The missionaries' public responses varied, however, largely along the lines of their mission boards' positions. Those positions on the removal issue took shape according to the boards' denominational affiliations, structures, regional locations, and leaders' political inclinations. Thus, for example, the Moravians were neutralized because of their conflicting duties to evangelize and to obey governing powers, whereas the Baptists suffered internal strife because of their board's national membership.[7]

For our purposes here (given my own evangelically Reformed persuasion), studying more closely the positions taken by two missionaries of the American Board is particularly instructive. The American Board's

7. Ibid., 248–50.

Puritan heritage gave it an activist posture, and its missionaries were inclined the same way—even if their actions significantly diverged.

## Daniel Butrick and Samuel Worcester

The first American Board missionaries among the Cherokees of north Georgia arrived in 1817. Daniel Butrick of Massachusetts came in 1818, Samuel Worcester of Vermont in 1825. Both excelled in the Cherokee language; Butrick had even completed a translation of the New Testament by the year Worcester arrived. Both men served out of missions stations in north Georgia.

Matters over the removal issue started to come to a head for these missionaries in late 1830. Because of missionary opposition to Georgia's initiatives to assume full control over Cherokee territory, in December the state legislature passed a law requiring all missionaries (in fact, all white residents) among the Cherokees to recognize Georgia's sovereignty over the Indians' land and obtain a license to preach, or leave the state by March. Worcester had already called a concurrent meeting of twelve other missionaries representing all four denominations in the area. Butrick and Worcester were among the nine American Board missionaries (along with one Baptist and two Moravians; the Methodist who attended abstained) who signed a resulting manifesto with eight resolutions against removal of the Cherokees and protesting the legislature's various actions (although the missionaries did not learn of the new "Oath Law" until January).[8]

After consulting their board and receiving its full permission to do so, the American Board missionaries decided to remain at their posts and challenge the new law. Being native citizens of states other than Georgia buttressed their defiant stances. Three of the missionaries (including Worcester) were arrested, but a judge soon released them because they were federal "agents" (since they were receiving federal funding for their teaching; Worcester was also a postmaster) and therefore were not subject to state law. The irate Georgia governor wrote to both the U.S. postmaster general (who promptly dismissed Worcester from his postmaster position) and secretary of war (who replied that the government did not consider the missionaries to be its agents). These latest developments

8. Ibid., 255–57.

were reported to the missionaries on June 1, at which time they were given ten days either to sign the oath or to leave Georgia.[9]

It is here that Butrick and Worcester diverged. Butrick, along with the two missionaries who had been arrested with Worcester, decided—in opposition to the American Board's majority opinion but in exercise of the board-granted permission to act as they individually saw fit—that they should leave Georgia (for nearby Tennessee) and thereafter conduct only itinerant ministry among the Georgian Cherokees. Butrick and the others reasoned that they had been serving among the Cherokees in Georgia under the U.S. president's permission and that the federal government's decision to transfer its authority in the matter to the state meant that Georgia was now the authoritative power to be obeyed—and to resist in this case would be more for worldly political reasons than out of Christian meekness. Worcester, however, stayed the same course of resistance and, along with the remaining American Board missionary residing in Georgia (Dr. Butler, a missionary doctor), was arrested and jailed in July 1831. They and nine other whites were convicted in September. While the nine others took the presiding judge's offer to release any who would either sign the oath of allegiance to Georgia or leave, Worcester and Butler stood firm and began to serve a four-year prison term of hard labor.[10]

Butrick's and Worcester's contrasting roles in the ongoing story were not yet complete. With respect to Worcester, national public opinion was decidedly sympathetic to the imprisoned missionaries. (One of countless particular examples was the "outrage" that Princeton Seminary students felt over the missionaries' imprisonment, in line with the running disapproval by them and by Archibald Alexander—the seminary principal at the time—of any Indian removal policy.[11]) There was therefore widespread concurrence with the U.S. Supreme Court's decision in March 1832 (noted earlier) in the missionaries' appeal case: John Marshall and the majority upheld the validity of the ongoing U.S.-Cherokee treaties over the Georgia legislation regarding the Cherokee lands, and they

9. Ibid., 258–60.
10. Ibid., 260–62.
11. David B. Calhoun, "The Last Command: Princeton Theological Seminary and Missions (1812–1862)" (Ph.D. diss., Princeton Theological Seminary, 1983), 384.

ordered Worcester's and Butler's immediate release. But the two missionaries' dilemma only shifted at this point. They remained in prison when the Georgia Superior Court and U.S. President Jackson—who was easily reelected in November—simply did not implement the U.S. Supreme Court's decision. The missionaries' final legal recourse would have been to force Georgia's and Jackson's hands by having their lack of compliance reported to the Supreme Court when its next session opened in January 1833. The grave possible implication of such a legal step, however, was a split in the federal union and possible civil war, since Jackson's dispute with South Carolina over the tariff-nullification process was still raging. An accompanying rift between the federal executive and the state of Georgia could prove disastrous. Georgia did not welcome such a scenario, so in November 1832, the legislature repealed the law under which the missionaries had been convicted and offered them a pardon if they would not go through with reporting to the U.S. Supreme Court in January. "Somehow, what had started out as a simple act of Christian duty and morality had placed Worcester and Butler at the center of a major national crisis, perhaps the most momentous crisis since the founding of the nation."[12]

Despite urgings from Cherokees and others to stay the course, and after much wrestling of conscience, Worcester and Butler decided to withdraw their motion to the Supreme Court and accept their pardons. It was not long, however, before their missions buildings had been taken over by the state of Georgia and occupied by its citizens. Acquiescing to what had become inevitable, Worcester moved to Cherokee Nation West (present-day northeastern Oklahoma) in April 1835.

Butrick had all the while remained among the eastern Cherokees, even returning to Georgia (from next-door Tennessee) in 1833 after the repeal of the state law that had compelled him to leave two years earlier. He was later the last American Board missionary to give up his station in Georgia, in December 1835, at which time he moved to the nearby Brainerd missions station (in present-day Chattanooga, Tennessee).[13] At that same time, Butrick began vehemently denouncing

12. McLoughlin, *Cherokees and Missionaries*, 265.
13. Ibid., 311.

the land-removal treaty signed in late 1835 by a schismatic group of Cherokees (noted earlier) through the agency of one Rev. John F. Schermerhorn. Butrick justified this political involvement—seemingly contrary to his withdrawal from such confrontation four years earlier—by explaining that the treaty faction had disobeyed the proper powers that be, namely, tribal law and the Cherokee Nation's leadership. He also criticized the American Board for accepting funds out of the Cherokees' received land payment for improvements they had made during their years in the Cherokee Nation East.[14]

Butrick (and Butler, Worcester's former fellow prison inmate) remained among the 14,000 eastern Cherokees until the end, marching with them at bayonet point along the long and bitter "Trail of Tears."

## Theologizing about Political Authority

Given their common American Board affiliation, how could Daniel Butrick's and Samuel Worcester's religiously motivated political postures diverge at such a critical point in 1831, and then seemingly flip-flop just a few years later? Exploring the two men's relative degrees of sincerity and devotion as missionaries would not help us here: besides the fact that such qualities are next to impossible to evaluate from the outside, both men evidenced the fullest commitment to, and willingness to sacrifice for the sake of, the Cherokees and the progress of the Christian gospel among them. Key for them and for us is their relative theological understandings of political authority and of how Christians should act accordingly.

### Embedded Activism and Strategic Obedience

Roughly speaking, Worcester exemplified an activist bent shaped by personal involvement within particular sociopolitical situations. Butrick, for his part, strategically obeyed the relevant political authority he found to be most compatible with his moral instincts. These two profiles are neither mutually exclusive nor necessarily opposed to each other. Indeed,

14. McLoughlin, "Civil Disobedience and Evangelism," 134–36.

they overlap considerably. As we have seen, Worcester's and Butrick's (and others') sociopolitical actions were identical up through 1830 and the signing of Worcester's eight-point manifesto. Even after the events of 1831, both men maintained a posture morally sympathetic to the Cherokees. At the same time, other factors were at work that caused Worcester and Butrick to act differently, and their respective "embedded activist" and "strategic obedient" postures gave shape to the two men's diverging reactions to their complex situations.

Worcester was not afraid to *do something* in the midst of the crisis over the removal issue in which he and his fellow missionaries found themselves. He called missionaries together for that December 1830 meeting that issued a manifesto, a draft of which Worcester himself had prepared. He resisted the Georgia law to the point of arrest and imprisonment. He filed a legal suit against the state of Georgia, resulting in a U.S. Supreme Court decision in his favor. Despite the compulsion to continue his resistance against the state of Georgia and the removal of the Cherokees, Worcester accepted a pardon in order to help avert a national civil war. When he concluded that the remaining Cherokees were in fact going to be moved westward, Worcester picked up and moved west to live and minister among them and their fellow Cherokees who were already there. Religious, moral conviction drove an acute, realistic sensibility to act for righteousness before God and on behalf of others.

Butrick's actions accent more of a selected deference to authority than Worcester's morally driven actions demanded by pressing issues—although, again, these two postures significantly overlap. Whereas Worcester carried through with his intention to challenge the Georgia state law because he believed it to be unrighteous, Butrick obeyed the same law (by choosing the alternative to leave the state) because it represented God-given authority. Butrick's commitment to the Cherokees and to moral righteousness was proved by his return to Georgia in 1833—when it was legally permissible to do so. Furthermore, Butrick's identification with the Cherokees, cultivated over many years through linguistic and cultural assimilation among them, so shaped his moral instincts as to compel him to combat the 1835 removal treaty to which only a small fraction of the Cherokees had agreed. Butrick's central argument was that the proper, God-given authority—that of the Cherokee

Nation—had been flouted. Butrick's identification with the Cherokees, and his respect for their own authority structure (as well as that of the United States), carried him through the long, forced march westward.

## Ever-Changing Historical Contexts

As is the case with all other people, Worcester and Butrick were men of their day and were shaped by their own experiences. For example, both grew in their admiration of Cherokee language and culture, such that Butrick even remarked, "In many respects their language is far superior to ours."[15] At the same time, "both saw themselves as divinely commissioned to Christianize, civilize and Americanize the 'wild savages of the forest.'"[16] Hence, "despite their loyalty to the Cherokees as a suffering people, the New Englanders could not help expressing their ethnocentric and racial prejudice."[17] Particularly noteworthy as well is how both Worcester and Butrick, throughout the turmoil of the 1830s, continued to embrace what was practically an ultimate devotion to their country, the United States of America. Even if they opposed Jacksonian policy on the removal issue, their political ire was directed toward the state of Georgia and not the United States per se. In the end it was his love of country that persuaded Worcester to make the painfully difficult choice of accepting pardon, and Butrick's patriotism also figured into his ongoing compliance with U.S. interests in relation to national expansion and the Indians' relationship to that unstoppable reality.

One understandable way of characterizing Worcester's and Butrick's respective political postures is that of "liberal-activist" and "conservative-compliant."[18] Within such a framework, one can see how "Worcester was ready and willing to look behind the law to its motivation and purpose. Butrick preferred to avoid these subtleties. . . . Butrick merely took

---

15. McLoughlin, *Cherokees and Missionaries*, 137.
16. McLoughlin, "Civil Disobedience and Evangelism," 121.
17. McLoughlin, *Cherokees and Missionaries*, 259.
18. McLoughlin does not use these exact phrases, but he comes close to applying the related characterizations to Worcester and Butrick by noting, for example, "Butrick's conservative theological position" in contrast to advocating "the duty of Christian conscience to apply to the best of one's ability the absolute judgments of Scripture truth to pressing social issues. Otherwise how is God's kingdom to come on earth?" McLoughlin, "Civil Disobedience and Evangelism," 126.

the law as it was and tried to find a way to do the Lord's work despite it."[19] While this kind of "liberal-conservative" categorization is in some ways accurate and helpful, its problem is threefold. First, distinguishing the two men by placing them in such oppositional categories could overshadow how similar they were—for example, in what they both wanted for the Indians whom they served. Second, labeling Worcester as a socio-political-theological liberal and Butrick as a contrasting conservative would oversimplify both the two men and the complex and fluctuating time within which they lived. Third, it is too easy to make a "liberal-conservative" framework—speaking sociopolitically or even theologically—universal and normative in ways that obscure the particularity of people and their situations. Worcester was not simply a social-liberal-activist, nor was Butrick merely a conservative advocate of the "spirituality of the church." We must be careful to understand Worcester and Butrick, as well as their context, on their own terms instead of quickly attaching labels that are familiar to us.

Perhaps the most telling of all the descriptive banners over the situation of Worcester, Butrick, and their contemporaries was the growth of the recently formed United States of America that was occurring. The "Trail of Tears" that the U.S. Army forced the Cherokees to take may not have been inevitable, but it certainly became unstoppable. The Cherokees were set to remain on their ancestral lands based on their own traditions and assumptions, as well as on U.S. treaties and policies until Jackson's presidency, a limited Anglo-American frontier population, and most missionaries' sympathies. The nineteenth-century westward expansion of the United States, however, forced the Cherokees either to assimilate or to leave.

Within that changing situation, the New England missionaries serving in faraway Georgia had varied authorities to obey and responsibilities to fulfill. How best to serve faithfully was not always clear and sometimes demanded that difficult decisions be made. As noted earlier, wise King Solomon himself would have struggled with knowing what to do. At the heart of the missionaries' struggle was their theological understanding of political authority and of how they should act accordingly.

19. Ibid., 130–31.

In reflecting on the multifaceted situation within which various Americans and Cherokees worked out the Indian removal issue during the decade leading up to 1838, we can learn first that it helps for Christians—including organized missionaries—to have organizational, ecclesiastical, and theological connections upon which to draw. Worcester, Butrick, and other missionaries, as well as Cherokee Christians, were in regular consultation with others about what they should do. As American Board missionaries, Worcester and Butrick had a Puritan heritage that served them well in striving for moral righteousness, love for others, and respect for political authority—even when it was difficult to reach all those goals collectively. It is almost inconceivable that, apart from the support and input of their various connections, any missionary or other Christian could have acted responsibly and constructively within such a trying situation.

As a balance to this first lesson, we can also learn that all organizational, ecclesiastical, and theological connections are limited. All such connections have developed within particular historical contexts. None of them is perfectly suited to meet all situations. Within God's providence, the complexity, particularity, and fluctuations of the settings within which Christians have to work out their theological understanding of political authority and of how they should act accordingly demand fresh analysis and courageous decision-making. Worcester and Butrick had guidance for their actions, but they had no foolproof, specifically designed blueprints to follow.

## Implications for U.S. Christians Today

Post-9/11 American Christians have various organizational, ecclesiastical, and theological connections to guide us in our theological understanding of political authority and how we should act accordingly. Theologically we have the European Reformers—preeminently John Calvin for those of us who are evangelically Reformed—to guide us within an Augustinian tradition of understanding the "City of God and City of Man." Twentieth-century resources include such profound thinkers as Helmut Thielicke, who as a member of the Confessing Church in

Germany criticized the Nazi Regime and wrote extensively about political ethics and state power.[20] Abraham Kuyper and Herman Dooyeweerd are among recent Dutch Reformed, Neo-Calvinist theologians who have given us a multifaceted framework of "Calvinism as a life system"[21] and "sphere sovereignty" for understanding political authority both on its own terms and in relation to God's overarching rule.

Contemporary examples of political theology are extensive. Paul Marshall's introductory *God and Constitution: Christianity and American Politics* draws on both modern Catholic and modern Calvinist political thought and relates them "to American constitutional thought and the principles which underlie the founding of America." Marshall writes of "the form of power properly called authority," how the apostle Paul "described authority as an aspect of the authority of Jesus Christ," and that "he told the Roman Christians [in Romans 13] to . . . submit to that authority," but that government—for example, the Roman emperor—was limited and "*under* God." In a way similar to how I have merged political and religious language in this book, Marshall notes how the early Christian church applied Roman imperial "titles and symbols to Jesus, . . . necessarily denied them to Caesar and, so, challenged his claim to ultimate authority."[22] In other words, Jesus alone is the ultimate *sovereign*, not any other specifically political ruler or entity.

What that means concretely for U.S. Christians is not as simple as we might wish to think. Politically speaking, medieval European sovereigns saw their personal authority morph into modern sovereign nation-states. The nineteenth-century colonial empires that then developed were followed by twentieth-century superpower hegemony.[23] Over the course of those several centuries, the meaning of political sovereignty underwent

20. Cf. Helmut Thielicke, *Politics*, vol. 2 of *Theological Ethics*, ed. William H. Lazareth (Philadelphia: Fortress Press, 1969).

21. Cf. Abraham Kuyper's Stone Lectures of 1898, delivered at Princeton Seminary and entitled "Lectures on Calvinism."

22. Paul Marshall, *God and Constitution: Christianity and American Politics* (Lanham, MD: Rowman & Littlefield Publishers, 2002), x, 44, 50–52 (emphasis in original). This work was also referenced in chapter 3.

23. Cf. the helpful historical summary section, "A Brief History of Sovereignty," in Robin W. Lovin, "The Future of Sovereignty: A Christian Realist Perspective," in *The Sacred and the Sovereign: Religion and International Politics*, ed. John D. Carlson and Erik C. Owens (Washington, DC: Georgetown University Press, 2003), 156–61.

a dramatic shift from divine law governing a ruler to (in the West) the ultimacy of the popular will, such that " 'sovereignty' became a corporate personality, or source of will, which gave the body politic its identity."[24] Post–Cold War American Christians now face the challenge of dealing with our proper religious allegiance and the political sovereignty of our uniquely powerful superpower "body politic."

One analysis suggests that there are three familiar (and ultimately unacceptable) strategies for meeting this challenge. The first is to "transmute the state into God and make of it a proper object of unsurpassable and comprehensive allegiance," as happened in Hitler's Germany or the Holy Roman Empire. The second is more mainstream:

> A second strategy is to develop an understanding of the state such that its claims to sovereignty are properly religious, even though it is not itself God and its claims are not (or may not be) exhaustive of the demands of religious allegiance. This typically means that allegiance to the core interests of the state, however exactly these interests are construed, is understood as a proper part of the demands of religious sovereignty but not as co-extensive with it. Some readers might argue that the forms and procedures of a democratic state (perhaps of the kind that citizens of the United States inhabit) are just what God wants for us in the spheres of social and communal life and that, for precisely that reason, our allegiance to them in those spheres ought to be unsurpassable for us. Such moves make allegiance to the state's sovereignty an aspect or element of properly religious allegiance.
>
> In a constitutional democracy such as that of the United States, a sign or mark of this move having been made is treatment of the claims of the Constitution as having sacred significance.

This second strategy "transmutes the state's claims into sentences spoken by God and the state into God's political presence here below." In practice in the United States, what "almost inevitably and certainly" happens is "the transmutation of God into a servant of the democratic state and of God's word into the constitution of that state." The third strategy is to "recognize the irreconcilable tension" between

24. Oliver O'Donovan, *The Desire of the Nations: Rediscovering the Roots of Political Theology* (Cambridge: Cambridge University Press, 1996), 240–41.

one's religious allegiance and the United States' political sovereignty, whereby one "understands the state's claims as the trivial or pernicious mutterings of idolaters and the state's sovereignty as a matter of no deep interest or abiding concern."[25] The Old Amish Order is one example of this last response; privatized religion is the most common manifestation.

We should note as well how a previously mentioned new study of four recent, prominent evangelical political thinkers (Carl F. H. Henry, Abraham Kuyper, Francis Schaeffer, John Howard Yoder) finds them lacking and indeed full of "serious problems."[26] As was the case with the ambiguous socio-political-theological situation facing Samuel Worcester, Daniel Butrick, and their contemporaries, the challenge of faithfully fulfilling our Christian responsibilities as U.S. citizens today would have vexed even King Solomon.

## European Christendom

As noted elsewhere in this book, one of the historical legacies contributing to our present challenge is that of a medieval European Christendom. On the one hand, that era is over: helpful starting and ending points are the Edict of Milan in A.D. 313 (when Rome gave political legitimacy to Christianity) and the approval of the First Amendment to the U.S. Constitution in 1791. But even with the development of the citizenry's political sovereignty and individual rights, Christendom's "idea of a confessionally Christian government, at once 'secular' (in the proper sense of that word, confined to the present age) and obedient to Christ," persists.[27]

In terms of negotiating the relationship between religious allegiance and political sovereignty, the persistence of the idea of Christendom presents at least two challenges. First, our familiar solutions,

25. Paul J. Griffiths, "Religious Allegiance and Political Sovereignty: An Irreconcilable Tension?" in *The Sacred and the Sovereign: Religion and International Politics*, ed. John D. Carlson and Erik C. Owens (Washington, DC: Georgetown University Press, 2003), 249–53.

26. J. Budziskewski, *Evangelicals in the Public Square: Four Formative Voices on Political Thought and Action* (Grand Rapids: Baker Academic, 2006), 119–20.

27. O'Donovan, *The Desire of the Nations*, 195.

even if they are self-consciously post-Christian and postmodern, have been drawn up within Christendom's wake. They thus operate largely within its two main Augustinian categories of the present order and a normative standard. As Andrew Walls put it at the end of the twentieth century, "Our existing theologies of Church and State were carved out of the experience of Western Christendom, and were never meant to deal with anything as complicated as the networks of political and economic structures which will characterize the 21st century." That means that Christians today will need to take "a theology of the State to further and deeper reaches than it has seen before," including, for example, how to deal with principalities and powers in ways similar to how the New Testament treats them.[28] This is yet another example of how U.S. Christians can learn from believers in other sectors of the worldwide church, in this case those who are more aware of spiritual forces than are we.

A second, problematic challenge is that *mission* and *missions* are difficult to understand within an assumed Christendom context:

> Once the two societies [spiritual and secular] came be to seen as a single society, it was more difficult to frame the church-state partnership in terms of the eschatological Kingdom. It could seem, by a kind of optical illusion, that there was no more mission to be done. The peril of the Christendom idea—precisely the same peril that attends upon the post-Christendom idea of the religiously neutral state—was that of negative collusion: the pretence that there was now no further challenge to be issued to the rulers in the name of the ruling Christ.[29]

Thus, while the American Board missionaries could readily see the need for missions among the pagan Cherokees, they could not see the same need among their Anglo countrymen's culture and sociopolitical context. Similarly, we American Christians today must develop the sensibilities to be sent on Christ's mission into, and to conduct missions in, our own culture and sociopolitical context.

28. Andrew F. Walls, "Africa in Christian History," *Journal of African Christian Thought* 1, no. 1 (June 1998): 13.

29. O'Donovan, *The Desire of the Nations*, 212–13.

## Expansion and Imperialism

Worcester, Butrick, and most of their missionary contemporaries opposed their own federal government's removal policy as it accelerated under Jackson. They also lamented the adverse effects that the increasing population of Anglo-American frontiersmen had, through avarice and licentiousness, on the Cherokees. Even so, they did not conclude that their government and countrymen were therefore in need of missions efforts. Having been internationalized through their deep interaction with Cherokee culture, the missionaries were in an ideal personal position to take prophetic missions initiatives toward their own countrymen. Yet the prevailing Christendom sense that their country and people had been Christianized prevented them from developing the operative, intellectual category that the United States and Anglo-Americans were, in an ongoing way, to be recipients of God's mission and of Christians' missions efforts. They could see that political and evangelistic efforts were needed, but not *missions*, since missions were only from "us" to "others."

U.S. Christians today face challenges remarkably similar to those faced by Worcester and Butrick. U.S. missionaries serving outside the United States must relate to various political entities: the host country, the host local authorities, the United States government, one's own state. Where do one's loyalties lie if a conflict arises between them, for example, regarding tax laws or, worse yet, war? All U.S. Christians, organized or unorganized, living within or outside the United States, are citizens of an immensely powerful socio-economic-political-military superpower. What does it mean to be sent into this ever-changing country—seen by many as an expanding empire—as prophetic missionaries who are part of the international church of Jesus Christ, the entirety of which has been sent into this ever-changing world?

## War

Some of the greatest tests that Christians undergo relate to war. Many wartime struggles are common to people irrespective of religious affiliation: all types of combatants have to kill and are killed, and all types of civilians suffer loss of life and property. In particular, Christians (and certain other religions' affiliates) struggle with matters of conscience in relation to their patriotic duties, or how to reconcile their religious allegiance and the political sovereignty to which they owe obedience as citizens.

Pacifists and historic peace churches—Brethren, Mennonite, Quaker—have already taken their stances before wartime situations arise. Most U.S. Christians fall outside these boundaries, however, and thus face the dilemmas that war inevitably foists upon soldiers and civilians alike. What types of guidelines and examples are there to help?

One guide for how to respond to U.S. declarations of war is the distinction between Worcester and Butrick described earlier: "Worcester was ready and willing to look behind the law to its motivation and purpose. Butrick preferred to avoid these subtleties. . . . Butrick merely took the law as it was and tried to find a way to do the Lord's work despite it."[30] More than simply urging compliance based on an appeal to Romans 13, we can see whether our sanctified bent is more toward Worcester's type of "embedded activism" or Butrick's "strategic obedience." Having this self-awareness will help in determining, before God and his Word, how constructively to incorporate others' input and what course of action to take.

Another guideline is to distinguish between fighting in and otherwise supporting a U.S. war effort based on patriotic loyalty and falling into a frenzied demonizing of the enemy to help drum up support for the war. During the days of World War II, pulling the trigger to shoot at a German soldier was one thing; changing the names of German streets in St. Louis was quite another. Fighting against the Japanese Navy was a legitimate military necessity for the United States; rounding up Japanese Americans and placing them in detention camps went beyond what was necessary to wage war. With respect to the recent U.S. invasion of Iraq, fulfilling one's professed duty as part of the U.S. military carries a legitimacy that simplistic name-calling of the enemy as insane or "freedom-haters" does not. A certain level of reason must guide decisions about war, rather than jingoistic hysteria.

Finally, demonstrations of the wider and more fundamental unity of Christians across warring national boundaries are a powerful witness

30. McLoughlin, "Civil Disobedience and Evangelism," 130–31.

to Christ's gospel. One of the most poignant of such examples was Russian Bishop Nicolai's service in Japan a century ago. During the 1904–5 Russo-Japanese War, Nicolai remained in Japan according to the wishes of his Japanese church members. This action brought a certain measure of personal risk, and after the war there was reduced financial support from Russia. Even so, that act of devotion to the church and Christ's gospel spoke louder and had a wider effect than any single sermon that Nicolai could have preached.

# Index of Scripture

249

# Index of Subjects and Names

Nelson Jennings and his wife, Kathy, currently live in St. Louis, Missouri, where Nelson teaches the subject of world mission at Covenant Theological Seminary. Earlier they served in Japan, starting in 1986, with Mission to the World of the Presbyterian Church in America. Nelson received his Ph.D. from the Centre for the Study of Christianity in the Non-Western World (Edinburgh University) in 1995, after which he taught international Christian studies at Tokyo Christian University until 1999. The Jenningses' three daughters are in various parts of the world, pursuing avenues of service in music education, dance, and international relations.